NATIONAL GEOGRAPHIC

TRAVELER
Venice

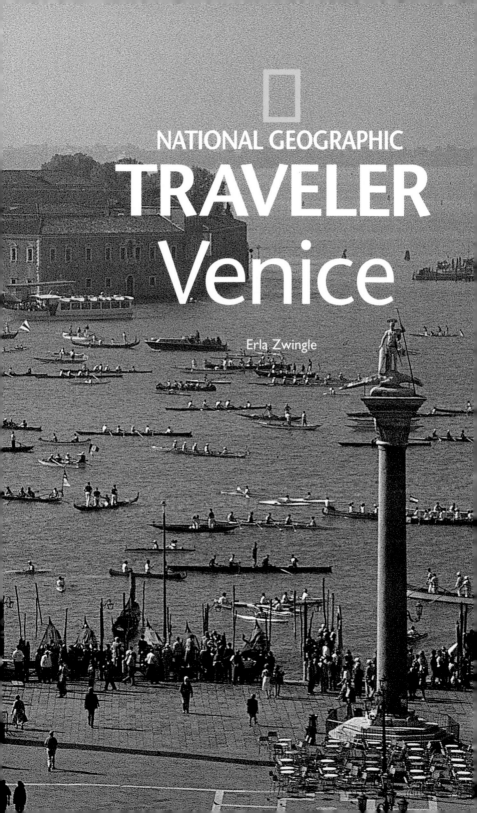

NATIONAL GEOGRAPHIC

TRAVELER
Venice

Erla Zwingle

Contents

How to use this guide 6–7   About the author 8
Venice area 47–234   Travelwise 235–64
Index 265–69   Credits 270–71

Page 1: Gondolas parked near San Marco
Pages 2–3: The start of the "Vogalonga," an
event in May open to anyone who uses an oar
Left: Caffè Florian, a landmark of Piazza San
Marco since 1720

How to use this guide

See back flap for keys to text and map symbols.

The *National Geographic Traveler* brings you the best of Venice in text, pictures, and maps. Divided into three main sections, the guide begins with an overview of history and culture. Following are seven area chapters with featured sites chosen by the author for their particular interest and treated in depth. A final chapter suggests possible excursions from Venice. Each chapter opens with its own contents list for easy reference.

A map introduces each area of the city, highlighting the featured sites and locating other places of interest. Walks, plotted on their own maps, suggest routes for discovering the most about an area. Features and sidebars offer intriguing detail on history, culture, or contemporary life.

The final section, Travelwise, lists essential information for the traveler—pre-trip planning, getting around, practical advice, and emergencies—plus a selection of hotels and restaurants arranged by area, shops, and entertainment possibilities.

To the best of our knowledge, all information is accurate as of the press date. However, it's always advisable to call ahead when possible.

78

Color coding
Each area of the city is color coded for easy reference. Find the area you want on the map on the front flap, and look for the color flash at the top of the pages of the relevant chapter. Hotel and restaurant listings in **Travelwise** are also color coded to each area.

Palazzo Venier dei Leoni (Collezione Peggy Guggenheim)
🅰 Map p. 67
✉ Calle San Cristoforo
☎ 041 520 6288
🕐 Closed Tues.
💲 $$
🚤 1, 82 to Accademia; 1 to Salute

Visitor information
Practical information for most sites is given in the side column (see key to symbols on back flap). The map reference gives the page number where the site is shown on a map. Other details include the site's address, telephone number, days closed, entrance fee in a range from $ (under $4) to $$$$$ (over $25), and nearest vaporetto stop. Visitor information for smaller sites is listed in italics and parentheses in the text.

TRAVELWISE

| Color-coded region name |
| **SAN MARCO** |

🏨 **GRITTI PALACE** — Hotel name & price range
$$$$$ ★★★★★

SAN MARCO 2357, CAMPO SANTA MARIA DEL GIGLIO, 30124 — Address, telephone & fax numbers
TEL 041 794 611
FAX 041 520 0942

Once a palace belonging to one of Venice's greatest families and still one of Venice's greatest hotels. — Brief description of hotel

🛏 93 🚤 Giglio 🔄 ♿ — Hotel facilities & credit card details
💳 All major cards

🍴 **HARRY'S BAR** — Restaurant name & price range
$$$$

SAN MARCO 1323, CALLE VALLARESSO, 30124 — Address & telephone number
TEL 041 528 5777

A crowded bar but the dining room has an intelligent menu and flawless service. — Brief description of restaurant

🍽 80 🚤 Vallaresso ♿ — Restaurant closures & credit card details
💳 All major cards

Hotel & restaurant prices
An explanation of the price bands used in entries is given in the Hotels & restaurants section (beginning on p. 244).

AREA MAPS

Important featured sites

Point of interest

Vaporetto stops

- A locator map accompanies each area map and shows the location of that area in the city.

WALKING TOURS

Walk route

Direction of walk route

Red numbered bullets link site on map to descriptions in the text.

Featured site (in bold) on walk route

Building outline

Point of interest not on walk route

Start point

- An information box gives the starting and ending points, time and length of walk, and places not to be missed along the route.
- Where two walks are marked on the map, the second route is shown in orange.

EXCURSION MAPS

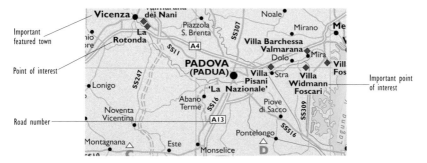

Important featured town

Point of interest

Road number

Important point of interest

- Towns and sites described in the Excursions chapter (pp. 211–234) are highlighted in yellow on the map. Other suggested places to visit are shown with a red diamond symbol.

☐

NATIONAL GEOGRAPHIC

TRAVELER

Venice

About the author

Erla Zwingle was born in Kansas City, Missouri. After graduating from the State University of New York at Albany with a B.A. in Art History, she worked in New York City as managing editor at *American Photographer* magazine and as senior editor at *Vis-A-Vis* magazine (former inflight magazine for United Airlines), before moving on to Washington, D.C., to work on the NATIONAL GEOGRAPHIC magazine as assistant editor. Since 1994 Erla has lived in Venice, working as a freelancer and contributing to countless magazines, including the NATIONAL GEOGRAPHIC magazine and various National Geographic books, as well as to *American Photographer, Ultrasport, Outdoor Photographer, Horizon, Esquire, Travel & Leisure,* and *The Yacht* magazines. Erla has also written a biography of photographer William Albert Allard.

History & culture

One of the four horses atop the Basilica di San Marco

Venice today

VENICE CAN SEEM LIKE THE MOST UNREAL CITY ON EARTH. IT IS OFTEN called the most beautiful. However it may strike you—moody and mysterious, confusing, even claustrophobic—it is unquestionably one of the most fascinating, improbable, and ingenious creations of the hand of man.

Built on some 100 small, marshy islands, connected by nearly 400 bridges that span some 177 canals, Venice covers a mere 3 square miles (8 sq km). Yet once you're within the city, it seems to go on forever. Odd corners, dead ends, secret courtyards, Venice twists and turns upon itself, as intricate as its 1,500-year history. There is very little here that operates according to the rules that most visitors are probably accustomed to—or any apparent rules at all—and that suits the Venetians just fine. "Just keep going straight," anyone will tell you when you finally admit you're lost. The funny thing is, there is no "straight" in Venice.

Venice is one of the world's greatest cities of art, with 95 churches and 20 museums, all full to overflowing with paintings and sculpture. Yet the city itself is as much a work of art as anything it contains. Millions of tourists visit every year, yet Venetians are as much in love with their city as any art historian or honeymoon couple. Beyond the city's scenic delights, every corner contains some personal connection, the memory of a friend, a fight, a kiss.

Venetians are aware of their city's astonishing beauty—they admit to being frequently surprised to discover something they've never noticed before. But their sense of Venice's fascination is deepened by elements that elude the visitor who arrives too fast, stays too brief a time, and clings too firmly to a map and guidebook: the atmosphere, the turn of the tide, the life of the surrounding Lagoon, the spring arrival of the cuttlefish called *seppie,* the autumn arrival of the little ducks called *fisole.* Venetians also savor the rhythm and texture of life, the sudden street-corner encounters, the leisurely pace, the intimacy of a town in which you are always face to face. And they are surrounded by proof of their magnificent past. It gives them the pride, even that sense of superiority, that distinguishes natives of all great cities, a pride that far belies what their city has gradually become: part open-air museum, part theme park, a struggling small town, and one of the world's most public places.

CITY AREAS & POPULATION

The map reveals six *sestieri,* or districts, which were already defined in the 12th century. These are subdivided again into some 30 parishes. Although you could walk from one end of the city to the other in an hour, the reality for most Venetians until World War II was to stick to their own immediate neighborhoods. Small shops abounded everywhere, and there was little reason to range farther afield to the Rialto or San Marco. Venetians could instantly tell by the way a person spoke which *sestiere* he came from, and it meant something. Though this is now fading, you may still hear an exasperated mother in Dorsoduro scold her unruly little boy with the words: "Quit shouting! You sound just like somebody from Castello!"

You should also be aware, if only dimly, that there's more to Venice than meets the eye: namely, the city of Mestre. With a population of 175,000, it lies just on the other side of the causeway and has technically been part of the Municipality of Venice since 1926. While there are many Venetians who have moved there, people from Mestre almost always tell outsiders they're "from Venice." This is unimportant to the lover of art and history, but a crucial factor in the city's future, as both halves struggle for funding and attention from City Hall (on the Grand Canal). Dredging canals isn't a pressing concern to someone in Mestre, nor is truck pollution a big worry to those in Venice.

The gondolier, like Venice itself, works hard to maintain ancient traditions while keeping abreast of modern technology.

The world wonders whether Venice is sinking; in fact, Venice is shrinking, by some 1,500 people a year who move out (a rate that only slowed in 2000). The population at the time of writing is about 65,000, down from 138,000 just 30 years ago. There are several reasons for this: The costs of living, housing, and doing business (Venice is Italy's most expensive city) and a very limited job market. And ultimately there is also the fact that the city doesn't offer most of the things that younger people want,

from cars and nightlife to air-conditioning and elevators. Recent surveys revealed that Venice has the highest median age population of all Italian cities—ironic, in a place that demands so much physical effort.

VENICE & ITS ECONOMY

After Rome, Venice is the most-visited city in Italy: Some 12 million tourists came to Venice in 1999, and the number has been increasing each year. There is no debating the fact that

tourism has become the central element in its economic survival. Marco Polo Airport is the third busiest airport in Italy, with some thousand flights a week; many European capitals are a mere hour and a half away by air, so a large number of Europeans come here on long holiday weekends.

Many tourists arrive in organized groups, and most stay only a day or two—some, in fact, stay no longer than a few hours. The Venetians call it "bite and run" tourism, and it

Seen from atop the campanile of San Marco, Venice appears as the island universe it is, dense and compact.

has created a series of logistical and aesthetic problems that are far more stressful to the city's fragile fabric than the famous but erratic high tides could ever be.

Yet within living memory, in fact the last 40 years of the 20th century, Venice was still an economic force, a city that worked. The

February's Carnival brings revelers from around the world, many of whom pose for photographers in front of the Bridge of Sighs.

Molino Stucky, a pasta factory on the Giudecca, was one of scores of thriving enterprises; not only was the Arsenale still active, there were factories that produced cigarettes, cotton thread, fireworks, pianos, watches, and beer. There were slaughterhouses and even dairies. Going slightly farther back, a simple reading of the street signs (with the help of a Venetian dictionary) reveals an entire universe of activity: wool weaving, cloth dyeing (Venetian scarlet was a jealously guarded secret), baking, gold-leafing, spice-selling, buckle-making; the production of candles, coins, gondola-cabins, oars. In the 18th century there were no less than 71 workshops that did nothing but emboss gold onto leather, a luxury product much in demand for covering books, chairs, and even palace walls. There were 90 pharmacies that specialized in concocting *therica,* an all-purpose medicine found throughout Europe, of which the Venetian variety was especially prized.

Today the enterprises and employers not related to tourism are few. There are two universities, the Università Ca' Foscari di Venezia (generally abbreviated to just Ca' Foscari) and

the University of Architecture, which total some 20,000 students between them, and account for a small but lively youth scene in a town that has little to offer at night. There are also two prisons, one for women on the Giudecca, and a severely outdated and overcrowded maximum-security facility near Piazzale Roma. The beleaguered glassmaking businesses on Murano are not so much supported by the necklace or set of glasses you buy, but by unglamorous industrial glass.

The Port of Venice is currently enjoying a resurgence. The increases in air, rail, and road transportation have affected all ports to some extent, but Venice has had to make a big effort to attract traffic, and is vulnerable to disruptions such as the wars in the Balkans, most recently in Kosovo, which make shipping companies reluctant to come so close to the danger zones. Yet it has managed to become fifth among all Italian ports, and second (after Trieste) among Adriatic ports. A boom in cruise ships has helped, with 759,000 passengers brought in during the peak year of 1998.

Venice is still the administrative center of the Comune, or municipality, of Venice, which

In Dorsoduro, Vitale Rossi and his wife, Anna, represent two other Venetian traditions: the small neighborhood shopkeeper, and last *luganegher*, or prosciutto maker, in Venice.

means that City Hall and its assorted government agencies are located here, as well as offices for the government of the Veneto region, courts, and police. There is also a thick stratum of professionals common in every city, such as lawyers, doctors, accountants, dentists, the occasional psychiatrist, and so forth. But largish companies, private or state owned, have almost all left the city center for more spacious, more modern, and less expensive facilities on the mainland. Private business people who remain in the city tend to be hotel, restaurant, or store owners, or independent artisans, whose major preoccupations are the never ending issues of rent, building maintenance, the cost of gas and electricity, and taxes which can come to a punishing 60 percent of their gross income.

Perhaps surprisingly, Venice earns the greatest income each year from its *casinò*; some 80 miliardi lire (1 miliardo = one billion lire) in 1999. A second casino, which has opened on the mainland at Ca' Noghera not far from the airport, may divert a good deal of these gamblers and the revenues they contribute.

MOTO ONDOSO

This city was built by people who rowed—virtually every palace and church was constructed in the epoch when the only forms of power to propel boats were oars and arms. Sand, bricks, marble, and wooden beams all arrived on boats that were rowed. The tide rose and fell, and the city had nothing to fear from the water that surrounded it.

Today, except for gondoliers, professional racers, and a sturdy but shrinking cadre of sportsmen and traditionalists, nobody rows. Since the sixties the motorboat has gradually come to dominate every movement on the water, from families out for a summer Sunday afternoon to taxis, barges, 100-passenger launches, vaporettos, motoscafos, and so on. Although speed limits have been established, they are rarely observed, and the resulting waves and their damage have become the city's first, perhaps only, real environmental danger. Venetians refer to it as *moto* (motor) *ondoso* (from *onde*, meaning "waves").

In the past ten years, the problem has reached crisis levels. Monitors in the Grand Canal have registered that a wave strikes a

building every second and a half and there is no canal in the city that doesn't reveal some damage to its buildings; many structures have gaping holes in their foundations. And along both sides of the Giudecca canal, large cracks have opened up between buildings and the embankment as the entire sidewalk continues to crumble from beneath, devoured by the incessant waves.

The city's first protective measures were the installation of defensive cofferdams to bear the brunt of the waves and prevent further damage. Then began an expensive program that entailed the complete rebuilding of the embankments, an enterprise which the authorities have claimed as a victory of city management while postponing yet again any serious attention to the causes of the damage. It appears certain that until the types and quantity of motorized traffic return to reasonable levels, no amount of rebuilding will keep Venice on its feet forever.

VENETIAN LIFE

Now more than 1,500 years old, Venice has always been important: first as one of the maritime, political, and commercial fulcrums of the entire eastern Mediterranean; then as political pawn in European power struggles; and today as tourist mecca beyond compare and almost beyond supporting.

Superlatives are Venice's due, yet not all are positive, and the resident population has specific problems. Housing is a prime

At Caffè Quadri on the Piazza San Marco, the seats are arranged like theater rows so you can watch the panoply of passersby.

example: Many houses remain shut because the owners have moved to the mainland, or because the owner has died and the heirs don't want to live here; rental space is scarce and expensive, because complex laws that favor the tenant make owners reluctant to rent; if you buy, the price will be high and the costs of

maintenance and utilities even higher. Employment? Jobs are hard to find everywhere in Italy, and in Venice it's even harder. Between finding the jobs and the houses they want, Venetians are almost fated to be commuters: some 20,000 people a day travel to jobs on the mainland, while almost the same number come into the city to work.

Summing it up, living in Venice is something like a vocation. It's not for everybody. It is an arduous city to live in, requiring sturdy shoes and sturdier feet to confront the constant walking and strong lungs to deal with the summer humidity, the winter fog, the dust, pollen, mold and mildew, and the wind. Emotionally, it can be an extremely isolating place; Venetians are really more interested in their city than anywhere or anything else, and conversations about the world at large often return, rather quickly, to Venetian subjects. One French woman described her first married years here as resembling a "spiritual

retreat." Yet if you stay the course, the city and her people will slowly take you in. As a Venetian once said, "Everyone who loves Venice is part of Venice."

The Venetians *(veneziani)* are quick to distinguish themselves from other natives of the Veneto region *(veneti)*. They do not accept that residents of Mestre *(mestrini)* could be justified in calling themselves Venetians (which often happens), even though both places belong to the same municipal entity.

An artist beneath the Rialto Bridge seems oblivious to wedding guests gathered outside Ca' Farsetti (City Hall).

They are proud of being Venetian in the same way that native New Yorkers are proud: It's so obvious it doesn't even bear comment. They are island people, with the island outlook. And yet, living so close together for much of their lives, they've also learned to tolerate each other's flaws and foibles, and one of the worst

Venetians and visitors alike love to take time to chat—a pastime that often involves coffee at one of the city's myriad cafés.

things they can say of someone is that he or she is a gossip. They're sociable, with a dry sense of humor often expressed in jokes or quips at their own expense (or even better, at the expense of neighboring non-Venetians). Venetians can be gregarious, curious, and extremely generous, with money or time. Although they have a reputation earned over centuries for being shrewd in business, in a bit of old-fashioned doggerel describing the main trait of each of the Veneto towns, the Venetians are called *grand signori*, or great lords—not literally a great lord, but someone who acts like one, quick to pick up the tab, master of the spontaneous and very handsome gesture.

VENETIANS AT LEISURE

Venetians are not much different from their mainland counterparts when it comes to how they spend their free time. It's true that there are still neighborhood joints where old men gather to smoke and play cards as in days of yore, and there are even a few *bocce* clubs.

Somewhat younger Venetians, though, often join sports clubs (many of which are on the Lido) to enjoy horseback riding, tennis, golf, archery, rowing (both crew and Venetian style), and fishing from the Adriatic-facing seawalls. There are also a number of health clubs in the city. On weekends, the streets of the Lido are full of people pedaling along on bicycles, and it's not unusual to see joggers, especially in the morning or evening, along the Zattere or the Fondamente Nuove.

In the winter, it can be somewhat startling to encounter people walking down Venice's narrow streets toting skis; they will be off to the winter-sports resorts on the mainland. Schools close for the "white week" holiday in winter, when groups of students and teachers head off to the slopes.

Boating means rowing, fishing, or sailing (or all three in one afternoon). A small but passionate number of Venetians—more of them older than younger, it must be admitted—belong to some 42 private rowing clubs,

Tourists and birds all flock to the Piazza San Marco, where vendors sell bags of corn for Venice's nearly 200,000 pigeons.

and many of those only row in the Venetian way, like gondoliers: standing up, facing forward. It's not poling, but a long stroke with the oar, occasionally followed by a shorter one on the return. Kayaking and sculling are popular among the young but these sports are increasingly difficult and even dangerous in the high seas of the city's surrounding waters.

There are several small harbors for conventional sailboats, which sail in the Adriatic. However, the Lagoon can be dotted with the colorful gaff-rigged sails *(vela a terzo)* hoisted on traditional flat-bottomed wooden boats such as the *sampierotta* which can skim over the shallows in the light breezes typical of Venetian summer afternoons.

Amateur fishermen pay a modest fee for a license to fish in the Lagoon, and the older Venetian men, who just love to talk about fish, have a keen eye for the seasons and the conditions. They are the ones who still really understand the Lagoon in a deep and intimate way. One older Venetian man was heard to scoff at a young man with a fishing pole trying his luck from the dock at the Lido—it was obvious, the older man said, that the fisherman had virtually no chance of catching anything there because the tide was going out, and also because the type of fish he was hoping for would never have been so close to shore. On spring evenings you can still see men standing on the embankments fishing for the newly arriving seppie (look at the stones and you'll see plenty of black ink splotches). Boats float around at night in the Bacino of San Marco, with men hoping to snag *branzini* or *passarini*. And whole families, armed with beach umbrellas and dogs and kids, still head out to certain sandbanks to spend the entire summer day digging for the tiny clams called *capparossoli*. Though progress has in many ways come between the Venetians and their Lagoon, altering their appreciation and even their experience of this complex environment, there's no question that most Venetians would still rather be outdoors than in. ∎

Food & drink

VENETIANS ARE INTENSELY PROUD OF THEIR CULINARY TRADITION. HAVING flourished for centuries as one of Europe's primary ports, Venice had first crack at many foods (coffee, sugar, and rice first arrived in Europe through Venice), and they appreciate any interest on the part of the visitor. While it's easy to eat well at home in the city, it can be a little more challenging to find a memorable meal for a reasonable price in a restaurant. Discovering that mythical little unknown spot with great food at low prices...it just won't happen here.

The Venetian kitchen draws on a wealth of delectable seasonal ingredients, from fresh Lagoon fish to local fruits and vegetables from the nearby island of Sant' Erasmo, the "garden island": artichokes, fresh peas, cardoons, fava beans, and the tiny, short-lived spring plants known as *carletti* and *bruscandoli,* which are great in risotto. Summer is awash in luscious fruit: cherries, apricots, melons, peaches, and tiny wild strawberries.

The Lagoon (see pp. 218–19) teems with some 30 varieties of fish. These are either caught in nets or "farmed" in various areas: plaice, gobies, giltheads, bass, shrimp, eels, and *seppie,* or cuttlefish, which are delectable roasted or cooked in their own ink and served over spaghetti or in a risotto. (This is the only fish that the Venetians top with grated parmesan cheese.) And there are crabs, mussels, and clams.

EATING OUT

In spite of the relatively high prices, restaurants sometimes take culinary shortcuts: Fresh seppie are in season in April and May, then July through October, and that's it. If a dish with the ink of the seppie is listed in other months, the sauce will inevitably have been reconstituted from powder.

Any chance you have to eat typical Venetian dishes rather than the standard tourist fare will be rewarding. Look for *bigoli in salsa* (salted anchovies and onions over whole wheat spaghetti); *sarde in saor* (Adriatic sardines in a sweet-sour onion sauce, once the sailor's standard fare because it doesn't spoil); spaghetti with *capparossoli* (local clams); seppie with polenta; *risi e bisi* (risotto with fresh peas, the May favorite). *Cichetti* are little snacks available in most bars, especially in the *bacari,* which are the typically Venetian wine

bars. There will be scores of tidbits lined up in the glass case by the bar: tiny sandwiches with fresh prosciutto or mortadella, chunks of cheese, deep-fried *polpette* (meatballs), tiny new artichokes with garlic and olive oil, little roasted seppie, wooden skewers of roasted potato or Greek olives, and so on. You order them by the piece, and could probably make a satisfying light meal of them—just point, and the barman will fix a plate for you. This is the real Venetian "fast food," and it's usual to eat these standing at the bar, though there may be a place to perch.

WINE & LIQUOR

Wine, either from the Veneto or imported, has always been one of Venice's major trade commodities, as reflected in many street names. The wines of the Veneto are light, between sweet and dry, with a fairly low alcoholic content (11 percent). The whites are Tocai, Soave, Sauvignon, and Chardonnay. *Bianco di Custoza,* a wine from Verona, is also very popular. Prosecco, the Venetian sparkling white wine, is light and refreshing, but its slightly sweet character and effervescence are a better complement to dessert, rather than an accompaniment to an appetizer or entrée. The most common reds are Raboso di Piave, Cabernet, Merlot, and Valpolicella.

If you are in Venice around November, the bars will briefly be selling the season's unbottled first pressings, by the glass. The cloudy white is called *torbolino,* and the red is *fragolino.* Some bacari may also have the somewhat oddly named Clinton, which has nothing to do with the former American

At the Rialto Pescheria, a fishmonger sells his fresh catch, taken from as near as the Lagoon and as far as the North Sea.

President; this dark red wine is now almost exclusively made in private homes.

The classic Venetian refreshers are the *ombra* and the *spritz*. The ombra, which literally means "shadow," is a small glass of white wine that is typically drunk in the late morning as lunchtime begins to loom. The name is said to come from the earliest days, when the Piazza San Marco was a market area. There was a wine stall next to the Campanile, which was regularly repositioned throughout the day in order to remain in the cool of the tower's shadow. From saying "Let's go have a drink in the shadow," it was an easy step to "Let's drink a shadow."

The spritz (or *spritzetto* if it's small) is made of white wine, a dash of bitter liquor such as Campari, Aperol, Select, or Cynar (you specify your preference), and topped with sparkling water. It can be made with Prosecco.

Wine has inspired many expressive Venetian proverbs that are still in use today,

including "It comes and goes, like wine from Cyprus," meaning something (or someone) that varies unpredictably, and "big vineyard, but pretty puny grapes" to describe a person who is all show, but little substance.

Grappa is the region's most noted *digestivo*, or after-dinner drink. It is colorless, but may have things inside the bottle for flavoring: twigs of licorice root, fronds of rue, juniper berries, or mixed mountain herbs. Its terrifyingly weird flavor—bitter, sharp, merciless—is

Many Venetian houses are crowned by an *altana*, roof terrace, though this one on the Grand Canal is more elaborate than most.

almost immediately mitigated by its powerful alcoholic punch (90 proof, or even more). There will be many other *digestivos* behind the bar: Fernet, Ramazzotti, or Elisir, the bitterer the better. Restaurants sometimes bring a *sgroppino* after your main course; white and frothy, its main ingredient is vodka. ∎

History of Venice

VENICE, DRIFTING LIKE A MIRAGE OF SINUOUS GOTHIC CURVES shimmering in watery reflections, has always fascinated visitors. But beyond its beauty, there was power. For more than a millennium, Venice inspired as much fear as admiration, an independent nation dominating politics and trade throughout the eastern Mediterranean. How a few merchants and fishermen contrived to reach the pinnacles of power and then lose it all is a tale even more amazing than the fact that they built an entire city in the middle of the sea.

"For you live like sea birds," wrote the Roman prefect Cassiodorus to the early Venetians in A.D 537. "It seems as if you glide over the fields, because from afar one can't distinguish the canals between the wetlands…and while others tie their animals at the door of their houses, at your houses of wicker and reeds you tie your boats."

Very brief histories of Venice sometimes give the impression that the mainland Romans and indigenous people, the Veneti, suddenly buckled in the fourth century under the onslaughts of barbarians and fled en masse into the Lagoon. A closer look reveals that island settlement was a more gradual process, one that had already begun as life under the crumbling Roman Empire became increasingly insecure. The Lagoon's shore dwellers had long been accustomed to coming and going in the tidal estuary, fishing, hunting, or harvesting salt, sometimes staying for brief periods that eventually grew longer and longer.

However, when Attila the Hun destroyed the coastal city of Aquileia in 452, many people fled into the Lagoon. Others followed during the turbulent two centuries that ensued, as regional control shifted from the Ostrogoths to the Byzantine Greeks based in Constantinople. In 568 the Lombards invaded Italy, an event that led decisively to the founding of new Lagoon villages, notably Torcello, and Malamocco. In 639 the bishop of Altinum transferred his seat to the island of Torcello, acknowledging what had already become the reality.

THE CITY COALESCES

Venice didn't yet exist as a city, but the Lagoon was in continual development, and its island communities were often at odds with each other. The Byzantine emperor Leo III, in order

to stabilize this western outpost of his empire as a bulwark against further barbarian incursions, sought to unite the islands under a duke (*doge* in the Venetian dialect). Legend holds that a certain Paoluccio Anafesto (a character impossible to document with certainty) was elected in 697, the first of what would come to 120 doges over the next (precisely) 1,100 years. In 742 its seat of government shifted

from Eraclea, on the mainland coast, to Malamocco, on the barrier island separating the Adriatic from the Lagoon.

In 810 came the next great turning point—the attempted invasion of the Lagoon by Pepin the Short, the father of Charlemagne. His forces had already conquered Grado, Eraclea, and Jesolo, but when the Frankish fleet entered the Lagoon, the island dwellers showed the shrewdness that would become their hallmark over the years. Realizing that they couldn't win by force, they pulled up the flimsy stakes that marked the deeper canals wending among the many tidal sandbanks. When the advancing enemy ships ran aground, the Venetians came out and slaughtered them all. The canal running from San Servolo toward Malamocco is still called the Canale del Orfano, because so many orphans were made that day. As a result, the Franks gave up any claim to the Lagoon territory, and the islanders decided to move the bishop's seat from the more vulnerable Malamocco to the safer Rivoaltum, the central agglomeration of islets that, four centuries later, would take the name of Venice. In 811, under the Pax Nicephori between Charlemagne and the Byzantine emperor, Venice became a semi-independent province of Byzantium.

RISE TO POWER

The Venetians scarcely had enough terrain for their houses, much less for agriculture, so instead they cultivated their skills as sailors and merchants. Venetian ships went farther and farther afield, and their cargoes made the

The *Serenissima*, the modern equivalent of the doge's ceremonial barge, always leads important boat processions.

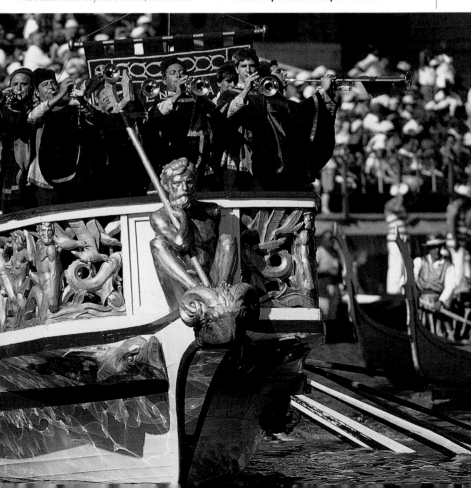

Tintoretto's son Domenico painted "The Conquest of Constantinople" for the Palazzo Ducale, evoking Venetian pride in the sack of the world's richest city in 1204.

fortunes of individual families as well as the city as a whole, bringing back ivory, amber, gold, silk, and above all, spices. Rice, coffee, and sugar all reached Europe for the first time through the port of Venice, and the ships would sail up the Grand Canal to unload directly into the first-floor warehouses of their owners' palaces. The city became one of the greatest banking centers in Europe, and it was here that the concept of insuring ships and their cargoes first developed. The canny Venetians knew how to profit by political maneuvering, trading their support to other governments in exchange for commercial privileges.

But marauding Adriatic pirates, called *narentani*, put everything at risk. As fierce as the barbarian hordes, they harried shipping and towns along the Dalmatian coast even as far as Grado. Finally Doge Pietro Orseolo II made a pact with the coastal cities and led a joint fleet to vanquish these outlaws. His

decisive victory on Ascension Day, 1000, gained for Venice long tracts of the Yugoslavian coast (vital for stone and timber), and was the first step in making the Adriatic "the gulf of Venice" and the creation of the Venetian empire. Though Venice later had to quell occasional raiding, the victory on La Sensa was a critical moment. Every year thereafter until 1797, Ascension Day witnessed one of the city's greatest ceremonies, the "marriage of the sea." When the doge flung the golden ring into the Lagoon and intoned the words, "I wed thee, O Sea, in sign of perpetual dominion," he was reminding kings, princes, and patriarchs that Venice intended to continue to dominate the Mediterranean.

MEDIEVAL GLORY

During the next two centuries Venice consolidated its power. By agreeing to aid the Byzantine emperor in defeating the Normans, it not only gained new territories but also its independence (though the *gonfalone*, the distinctive Venetian banner, still bears the red and gold hues of Byzantium). The explosion of Adriatic trade that followed was led by the merchants of Venice—merchants who, for the most part, were also the political leaders of the city. Each victory, each new trading pact, enriched and strengthened the city and reinforced the fierce pride each Venetian, however humble, felt for his city-state.

The Crusades crowned Venice's ascent; its location, ships, and riches all made its collaboration crucial to the crusading armies. The two contending Christian factions finally made peace when Doge Sebastiano Ziani, in 1177, convinced Pope Alexander III and the Holy Roman Emperor, Frederick Barbarossa to meet in the Basilica di San Marco (a stone in the entrance marks the place of their greeting). Then, when the Byzantine emperor incited the jealous Greeks in Constantinople to undertake a horrendous pogrom against the Venetians living there, Venice threw in its lot with the Western crusaders, not only to help regain the Holy Land, but to take its revenge by conquering Constantinople as well.

The Fourth Crusade departed from Venice on October 8, 1202, the Venetian contingent led by the blind Doge Enrico Dandolo. More than 300 ships filled the Bacino di San Marco, all flying their banners and full of soldiers in glinting armor. Trumpets sounded and priests and warriors alike sang the *"Veni, Creator spiritus"* as this unprecedented convoy sailed past San Nicolò on the Lido, where the shore teemed with cheering crowds.

The struggle for Constantinople was ferocious, with the fate of the richest city in the known world shifting between two contending emperors and the forces of the Orthodox and the Latin, or Roman, Christians. When the city finally fell on April 12, 1204, the pillage was tremendous—Venice sailed away with riches that included money, jewels, religious relics, sculptures of marble and ivory, paintings, manuscripts, and the famous four bronze horses of the Basilica di San Marco; it also had won new territories that extended strategic Venetian dominion from Dalmatia to the Black Sea. Now, directly or indirectly, Venice had a monopoly on all the great commercial routes between the Levant and the Occident.

In 1297 came the Serrata, or closing, of the ranks of the Venetian nobility, a fact that determined the social and political shape of the city for centuries to come. With their names inscribed in the official *Libro d'Oro* ("book of gold"), this closing meant that the government of the city would now be limited to a finite number of families. Not all citizens agreed, and unrest and plotting simmered.

Two coups were attempted. In 1310 three Venetian nobles, Baiamonte Tiepolo, Marco Querini, and Badoero Badoer, claiming to represent the desire of the restive Venetians (though in fact pursuing their own interests) launched an attack on the Palazzo Ducale, but were overcome by the doge's forces. Tiepolo was banished, Querini died in the fighting, and Badoer was executed. Then, in 1355, the doge himself, Martino Faliero, was discovered to be plotting to take absolute power. He was beheaded, and his body displayed on the balcony of the Palazzo Ducale facing the campanile—the two pinkish columns were placed there to indicate forever the infamous spot, and every portrait of him was expunged. The Council of Ten (actually 18) was then formed to protect the state "by any means necessary," with everything that phrase implies: spies, interrogations, and its own prison. Its meeting room was crowned by a painting by Paolo Veronese depicting the not very subtle theme, "Jove Hurling Thunderbolts on the Vices."

Genoa, Venice's ancient rival, battled on to overcome Venetian preeminence, but in 1380, after years of conflict, Venice definitively defeated the Genoese forces at Chioggia. The Venetians now called their realm the Stato da mar—the Sea-State. Other rulers referred to her simply as the Dominante.

THE VENETIAN GOVERNMENT

Venice was essentially an oligarchy, governed by a closed number of noble families. But stability was their guiding principle, almost a mania, and over time they developed a complex structure that was virtually guaranteed to prevent power from falling into the hands of any individual. It was essentially a system of checks and balances (though it had certain aspects of a police state), and for centuries was highly respected by political philosophers. When the American Founding Fathers were considering possible models for the United States Constitution, they also studied the Venetian arrangement.

There were no political parties; every aspect of civic life served to glorify the Venetian state rather than the individual, and

Sebastiano Venier, victor of the Battle of Lepanto, was doge only in 1577–78. He was a difficult doge, much better suited to commanding than to governing.

to strengthen each citizen's identification with it. Venice liked to see itself represented as "Justice," like the impartial statue crowning the Palazzo Ducale with her blindfold, scales, and sword, and not subject, like so many other Italian city-states, to debilitating civil wars. The sobriquet La Serenissima (most serene) arose from this fact. It is certainly true that there were periods of tension, and very occasionally a doge was liable to be deposed, imprisoned, mutilated, blinded, or assassinated, but the arc of history shows Venice to have been extraordinarily stable.

The doge was elected for life, and there are tales of utterly senile dukes, such as the 90-year-old Nicolò da Ponte, who would sleep so soundly in council meetings that they eventually built a special chair to keep him from falling over. However, as the doge was mainly a figurehead, this kind of situation did not present insuperable problems.

In order to prevent skulduggery, the election of the doge went like this: An urn was set up in the Great Council Hall containing a ball for every member, all painted silver except for 30 that were gold. Those who drew the 30 golden balls met and voted to select nine of their group. These 9 met and voted on an additional 40 to join them. These 49 voted for 12; these elected an additional 25; these chose another 9, and these voted for another 45, who then selected 11 from the group, who elected 41 councillors. It was these final 41 who voted on the doge. Like papal conclaves, the process could drag on for months. On his election, the doge was presented to the people with the ritual phrase, "This is the doge, if it pleases you." By that point, it should have.

THE EMPIRE & THE TURKISH THREAT

Venice was aware that its dominance of the seas would always be in danger if the mainland at its back were undefended. And so the Venetians began a campaign of expansion to the west, which in the year 1404 netted them a series of rich tributary cities: Padua, Vicenza, Verona, and Brescia, among others. When the Peace of Lodi was signed in 1454 the Republic of San Marco was at its zenith. Venetian territory stretched from the Greek islands of the Aegean westward through Dalmatia and Friuli all the way to Bergamo, and northward from the River Po to the Alps, including much of the Trentino region. Lord Byron eulogized Venice's apogee by referring, in *Childe Harold's Pilgrimage,* to the era when "many a subject land/Looked to the wing'd Lion's marble piles." Most of these subject lands contained their own winged lions, the insignias of domination still visible today crowning everything from columns in main squares to the portal of the fortress guarding the harbor in Heraklion, on the island of Crete.

But the wars of expansion had cost Venice a great deal, and despite its grandeur, its navy had been seriously neglected. In 1453 the Ottoman Turks conquered Constantinople, the "Rome of the East," and were advancing into Europe. Venice spent some 300 years in intermittent warfare with Turkey, sometimes savage, often deeply damaging, a constant drain on resources and diversion from other matters of empire. Treaties were signed, treaties were broken, trade suffered, atrocities were inflicted. And Venice couldn't always count on Christian allies, many of whom were ancient rivals who would much rather have seen the city hurt than helped. Between the cost of war and the lost trade, the ongoing conflicts with the Turks between 1453 and 1718 did much, despite many dazzling victories, to bring the Venetian empire to an end.

THE LEAGUE OF CAMBRAI

Venice, like any other sovereign state, was constantly seeking profit and advantage, but with hindsight it is clear that while it sometimes exercised farseeing shrewdness, it was more often distracted by short-term gain. Venice's mainland enemies—France, Spain, Hungary, Austria—from whom it had earlier torn prized possessions, kept reappearing. The political scene throughout Europe was not unlike a kaleidoscope, in which myriad different patterns are made with the same pieces over and over again. In 1504, anyone who had a quarrel with Venice or could possibly benefit by its defeat formed the League of Cambrai. In 1508 they declared war. They were aided, so they thought, by the fact that the pope had threatened excommunication of anyone who maintained commercial relations with La Serenissima.

Battles were joined, battles were lost. But Venice's mainland territories resisted the advancing armies and the Senate held firm, convinced that the alliance was vulnerable. Exercising the same cunning with which they had defeated Pepin the Short (by pulling up the canal markers), their spies and emissaries worked in secret to aggravate the jealousies and egotism of the league's members. Allying itself with the papacy and Spain—who, of course, until recently had counted among its enemies—Venice managed to overcome the weakened and demoralized league, and the peace signed at Bologna in 1529 left its territories virtually intact. Venetian prestige had hardly been greater, having shown itself capable of resisting the major forces of Europe. But the effort had exhausted its treasury, left its cities devastated, and the countryside desolate.

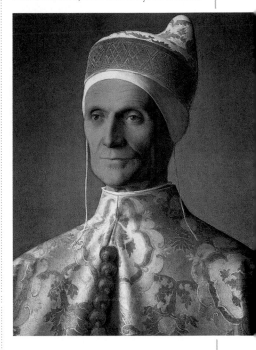

Doge Leonardo Loredan, painted by Bellini in 1501, shrewdly defended Venice against the attacks of the League of Cambrai.

THE RENAISSANCE

The key to Venetian influence was always trade. By the 15th century, sea routes had long since been established to facilitate the pursuit of business. Twice a year its ships, organized into *mude,* or small fleets, departed on specific routes with definite schedules and ports, accompanied by warships. There was the muda of Syria, Egypt, Romania (which stopped at Constantinople), Flanders (which stopped in Tripoli, Tangier, and Spain, even reaching London), as well as the muda of the Tana, which went deep into the Black Sea region to trade with Tartars and Russians. In

1423, Venice's merchant fleet amounted to 3,900 ships, with some 17,000 sailors, many of them Dalmatian and Istrian. Many of these vessels could rapidly be converted to warships.

Venice itself was a city of 150,000, renowned for its artists and artisans. Ninety pharmacies produced *therica*, an all-purpose medicine of uncertain composition of which the Venetian version was the most prized. Dyeing and all manner of work on wool, silk, and brocades went on apace (though dyers, among other specified trades, were forbidden to use the public water supply and had to find alternative sources, either from wells or from tankers). The street names list an endless litany of trades—mirror-makers, iron forgers, hoopers, fletchers—and products, such as spices, vinegar, and varnish.

Sharing as well as creating this prosperity were scores of ethnic communities, whose people filled the streets with different languages, costumes, and the aromas of their

cooking: Armenians, Turks, Arabs, Germans, Flemings, and Jews. As many as 5,000 Greeks lived here after the Muslim Turks conquered Constantinople in 1453.

Visiting royalty were entertained with a splendor inconceivable today, with fireworks, balls, mock battles and bullfights, and regattas in the Grand Canal attended by the patrician families in their sumptuously decorated gondolas and *peatas*. The nobles themselves organized endless diversions, from weddings to

Despite some differences in proportion, this 17th-century aerial view of Venice by J. Heintz is still remarkably accurate today.

hunting parties in the Lagoon to evening serenades in their illuminated gondolas.

Processions, religious or civil, were brilliant pieces of state theater. When Marino Grimani was elected doge, for instance, his patrician wife, Morosina Morosini, was escorted to the Palazzo Ducale in this manner: At 6 p.m. on

May 4, 1597, the doge's state galley, the *Bucintoro*, came to her palace, along with the state barges of the councillors, the Grand Chancellor, and other nobles. To the sound of trumpets and artillery fire, they all mounted the stairs and entered the hall where she greeted them by giving each of them a bag that contained a golden medal with her name, face, and the date, struck for the occasion.

Then the dogaressa went aboard the *Bucintoro*, which sailed down the Grand Canal accompanied by a huge number of boats, some of them richly decorated. At the Piazzetta of San Marco they all debarked and walked in procession around the Piazza San Marco, with bombardiers, representatives of each of the guilds, and musicians leading the way, followed by various ranks of noblewomen. Finally, preceded by six damsels dressed in green and "two beautiful dwarfs, a male and a female," came the dogaressa herself, wearing a pleated golden dress and white mantle, on her head the ducal *corno*. Seated on the throne in the Great Council Hall, she then presided over a magnificent celebration, complete with intricately shaped sweets, which had first been carried around the Piazza San Marco, illuminated by the light of 60 torches.

A city this wealthy and this devoted to luxury naturally required artists, and Venice lavished commissions, private and public, on the greatest artists of its day: Tintoretto, Titian, Giorgione, Veronese, the three Bellinis, and the two Negrettis, father (Palma the Old) and his great newphew (Palma the Young). The greatest architects of Italy made, and remade, the city's face, with churches and palaces that rivaled each other in magnificence.

Proud of its tolerance, the city established the Biblioteca Marciana, the first public library in Europe, and fostered the development of typography and paper production, as well as printing and bookbinding. Aldus Manutius and his Aldine Press took the lead in publishing works that were forbidden elsewhere. A book, after all, was just another lucrative form of merchandise. Not everyone shared this view.

CONFRONTING THE VATICAN

The popes, being princes and rulers themselves, had periodically tried to influence policy in Venice as they had elsewhere. But Venice, pious yet proud, had always resisted. In fact, the bishop's cathedral, San Pietro, had been located out in the remote reaches of Castello as far from the seat of government as possible. As early as 1284 the Vatican placed the city under the first of what became a series of papal interdicts. When the Church issued an "Index of Forbidden Books" in 1559, Venetian printers paid absolutely no attention.

Then, in 1605, came Pope Paul V, who dreamed of restoring the Church's omnipotence on Earth. A year later, when two Venetian priests were found guilty of civil crimes, Doge Leonardo Donà refused to accept the pope's claim of ecclesiastical immunity for them, stating that he "didn't intend to account to anyone in temporal matters, recognizing the Lord God Almighty as his only superior." The pope retaliated by threatening to excommunicate the entire Venetian Senate, and forbade the celebration of any religious rite within Venetian territory. The Senate promptly prohibited the publication of the ban, and ordered the clergy to continue their work on pain of imprisonment. Only the Jesuits obeyed the pope, and were expelled from the city.

All Europe watched the "war of the scriptures," till a Venetian friar, Paolo Sarpi, came up with the solution. His doctrine stated that "God has instituted two governments in the world, one spiritual and the other temporal, each of them supreme and independent of the other." This appeared to settle the matter, but the theologians who agreed with this found themselves persecuted by the papacy, not least of them Sarpi himself, who suffered an assassination attempt. But the crisis of state was over.

THE BATTLE OF LEPANTO

One of the great naval battles, and one of the epic confrontations between Christian and infidel in European history, the Battle of Lepanto had both political and commercial advantage at stake. Since the Turkish conquest of Constantinople in 1453, a series of battles had forced the Venetians' gradual retreat from their lucrative Greek territories. The peace treaty of 1540 not only cost La Serenissima 300,000 ducats, but all of its Aegean colonies.

By the late 16th century, the Ottoman Empire had reached its maximum power and territory, and Venice found itself caught

The Venetian victory at the Battle of Lepanto in 1571 was attributed, as seen in this painting by Andrea Vicentino, to direct divine intervention.

between the threat of the Spaniards, who dominated Milan and Genoa, and the encroaching Muslims, who controlled the area from Budapest to the Balkans to Greece, and across North Africa as far as Algeria. When Turkey besieged Cyprus—a crucial military base as well as a source of wine and other goods—Venice finally retaliated. Organizing a fleet with the collaboration of Pope Pius V (who was alert to the Crusading possibilities), and the aid of Naples, Austria, Sicily, and Genoa, the Venetians set sail.

On October 7, 1571, a total of 450 ships and 120,000 men met in the Gulf of Corinth near the small port of Lepanto, now called Nafpaktos. Battle commenced at noon, and was fought on three fronts simultaneously. The Ottomans had a slight advantage in numbers, but the Christians had more artillery, and when the smoke cleared, it was said that the waters of the Gulf were red with blood: 30,000 Turks were dead, to only 8,000 Christians.

News of this victory was greeted with incredible jubilation in Venice, where the bells of the more than one hundred churches all rang. Shops were shut for a week of celebration, many of them bearing the sign "Closed due to the death of the Turks."

But the happy ending was not to last. The Christian alliance unraveled, and the Muslim fleet reappeared, even stronger, a year later. Venice again had to pay tribute to the Turks, and never regained Cyprus. "Between your loss and ours," the Turkish ambassador to Venice commented dryly, "there's a profound difference. By taking Cyprus away from you, we cut off your arm; defeating our fleet, you merely shaved our beard. The amputated arm never grows back, but the shaved beard grows back even thicker than before." The victory of Lepanto, from which Venice never completely recovered economically or in terms of naval power, was a major step toward her inexorable decline.

Technically illegal, private gambling houses flourished during Carnival. The convenience of masks made these establishments fertile ground for a variety of vices.

THE LONG TWILIGHT

Now came years of slow retreat. Venetian commerce had been based on ties with the Levant, Asia Minor, and even distant China, trading with ports along the eastern Mediterranean coast. Not only Marco Polo, but other adventurers—Marin Sanudo, Giovanni and Sebastiano Caboto, and Alvise da Mosto—had voyaged afar. But their discoveries probably inadvertently aided their competitors, for Da Mosto got as far as the Cape Verde Islands on Africa's west coast, then accepted a captain's commission from the Portuguese. Ironically, the Portuguese Vasco da Gama almost certainly benefited from Da Mosto's discoveries when he finally reached Calcutta by sailing around the Cape of Good Hope, a feat which dealt a crippling blow to the entire Venetian economy.

The Venetians had once studied the possibility of cutting a canal through the Isthmus of Suez, but the difficulties were too great. Now Indian spices brought in by ship cost less than those in Egyptian and Syrian markets, and the Venetians could neither meet the cost of similar long voyages nor convince foreign governments to lower their customs duties. Similarly, impoverished foreign markets could no longer afford to buy Venetian goods. Merchants who once bought spices in Venice now went to Lisbon, and in 1514 came the

that in consequence he inadvertently caused the tragic explosion of the Turkish powder magazine atop the Acropolis that virtually destroyed the Parthenon. By the time the Treaty of Passarowitz was signed in 1718, which confirmed the Turkish conquests, both sides were utterly exhausted and only tiny shreds of the Venetian empire remained.

Daniele Manin was head of the short-lived Republic of Venice, established after the temporary overthrow of the Austrians in 1848.

bitter day when a Portuguese ship laden with spices sailed into the Bacino di San Marco.

In 1575, and then again in 1630, devastating plagues decimated Venice, carrying off a third of the population. Incessant conflict with Turkey drained every Venetian resource, from men to money. From 1644 to 1669 the Turks besieged Candia (Crete); when the island finally fell after more than 25 years, the war had not only cost Venice the last jewel in its colonial crown, but also some 150 million ducats, an inconceivable fortune. Even today the Venetians have an expression to convey extreme desperation or ruin: *esser incandio,* to be as they were in Candia.

The brilliant victories of Francesco Morosini in recapturing the Peloponnese bore little fruit in the end—not to mention the fact

"Once she did hold the gorgeous East in fee/and was the safeguard of the West," English poet William Wordsworth eulogized the once proud La Serenissima. Now the winged lion returned to its lair, still noble and majestic, but no longer willing or able to fight.

With its power gone, all that remained was its splendor, and the 18th century was filled with a magnificence that belied the inner decay. Families were ruined, and rich families from elsewhere bought them out. To replenish the treasury, the Senate began to sell membership in the *Libro d'Oro*. The glorious festivals and entertainments continued for another 80 years, immortalized in the paintings of Tiepolo, Canaletto, and Veronese, but economic distress led inevitably to political decadence. The Venice of Carnival was also a Venice that no longer had the means to

Venice in the 19th century was no longer rich; here, fishermen's families in the Campo della Sponza on the Giudecca.

enforce its own will. Its navy had deteriorated, its mainland provinces were discontented. To be beautiful had become its only reason for being. And yet there were those who still desired the city. Austria was one.

THE 19TH CENTURY: SURRENDER

In 1797 Napoleon entered Italy intending to seize Venice to use as a pawn in negotiations with Austria. The French advanced through the Veneto, conquering each of Venice's provinces: Verona, Vicenza, Padova (Padua). The Great Council vacillated. On May 12, the council met and Doge Ludovico Manin declared himself ready to resign; only one councillor rose to protest. Then, panic-stricken by a volley of rifle-fire outside (not the French, as it turned out), the council voted to accept Napoleon's proposed "reforms." With 512 votes in favor, and only 20 opposed, the Republic of San Marco ceased to exist. Manin

removed his ducal corno, saying, "I won't be needing this any more."

Napoleon proceeded to sack the city: Every lion of San Marco, every ducal insignia, was torn away. The *Bucintoro,* the doge's ceremonial galley, was stripped of its gold. The four bronze horses were taken from the Basilica di San Marco and sent to Paris, passing through the city streets in a mournful cortege. The treasury of the basilica was pillaged. Churches and monasteries were suppressed, and many demolished. And then he gave Venice to Austria. "Men are we," wrote William Wordsworth in his poem, *On the Extinction of the Venetian Republic,* "and must grieve when even the Shade/of that which once was great is pass'd away."

On January 18, 1798, the Austrians entered Venice. For the first time in more than a thousand years, Venice was a mere province of a distant capital. But her masters also accomplished useful works: The streets were paved, gaslights were installed, sea defenses strengthened, and in 1846 a railroad bridge connected Venice to the mainland for the first time in history.

In 1848 Daniele Manin, a Venetian (not related to the last doge) led a valiant uprising against the Austrian domination. This was the year in which all Europe was in revolutionary ferment, and for a time Manin's Republic of Venice appeared to have some hope. Only by means of a drastic siege did Austria prevail, essentially starving the city into submission.

In 1866 Venice was ceded back to France, who gave her to the new Kingdom of Italy.

THE LAST HUNDRED YEARS

Venice at the turn of the 20th century was in economic difficulties, and the situation worsened during World War I as the city suffered Austrian bombing. Immediately thereafter the plan to develop Porto Marghera on the mainland shore was launched. The result wasn't quite what its proponents had hoped; the industrial plants that they had expected would give employment to Venetians instead drew lower cost labor from the surrounding area, and the resulting pollution seriously disturbed the Lagoon ecosystem. In 1926 the town of Mestre was added to the Municipality of Venice.

The notorious "high water" comes first to the Piazza San Marco, the lowest point in the city, but lasts only a few hours.

World War II brought privation, though the city again escaped serious damage from Allied bombs, which were aimed instead at the industrial and shipping installations at nearby Mestre and Porto Marghera.

In the second half of the 20th century, the economy came to focus almost exclusively on tourism. In the 1980s, the relaunching of Carnival gave the winter season a needed boost, though many Venetians now feel that its crowds have become as much a problem as a solution. A falling birth rate, rising costs, and emigration out of the city center have not only shrunk the population but changed its character—Venice now has the highest median age in all Italy. Native Venetians have come to regard themselves as an endangered species, and prize their traditions all the more. The future of Venice as a city rather than a tourist attraction depends on its managers addressing the problems of scarce employment and expensive housing. ■

The arts

WHERE ART IS CONCERNED, VENICE'S CUP RUNNETH OVER. MUSEUMS, churches, monasteries and convents, private palaces, public offices—the city contains one of the richest and densest concentrations of art anywhere, even in art-saturated Italy. Add to this the fact that the city itself is a work of art, and you'll understand why even Venetians keep discovering things they never noticed before.

In its great days, Venice was one of the most important centers of art in Europe, and this made sense, since art was a business. Between their incessant involvement in both trade and war, and being perfectly situated between East and West, Venetians were the ideal buyers, sellers, and consumers of a seemingly endless stream of styles and fashions in art. Artisans as well as artists, Venetian craftsmen were among the best in Europe, admired for their skill in printing and binding books, dyeing silk (Venetian scarlet was a jealously guarded recipe), and of course producing hand-blown glass. Venetian nobles and merchants, many of whom were inconceivably rich, also had an unabashed love of novelty and luxury, and this all created the perfect environment for a flourishing of art in almost all its forms.

ARCHITECTURE

It is not only the water that gives Venice its particular fascination. It also has a fantastic variety of architecture, and you don't need to be an expert to savor the rich and eccentric variations, the faded pastel walls, the intricate carving of windows, balconies, and doorways. The fact that many buildings are a mishmash of styles only adds to their appeal.

The earliest buildings were made of wood, but as the city prospered, houses naturally became more substantial and more impressive. The first important style was Byzantine— from the 7th to the 10th century, Venice was still a colony of the Byzantine Empire, so churches such as the Basilica di San Marco and the churches on Murano and Torcello (the oldest intact building in the Lagoon) reflect the basic design. This consisted of a Greek cross layout, embellished with heavy mosaic decoration. San Giacometto at the Rialto, Santa Eufemia on the Giudecca, and San Nicolò dei Mendicoli in Dorsoduro are the few surviving parish churches of the Byzantine

era (note that their bell towers are not attached), though it is difficult, as well as pointless, to try to establish now which is precisely the oldest. The few palaces surviving from that era, such as Ca' Farsetti, show the small, round-arched windows with heavy carving called the Veneto-Byzantine style.

The Gothic period (13th to 14th centuries) was one of Venice's best, and has left us palaces with fretted windows that are framed with curved ogee arches, made more sinuous by the Levantine and Moorish influences brought back from the Middle East by traders and crusaders. Having many windows made the building lighter in both illumination and weight. The Ca' d'Oro is probably the best example of the peak of the Venetian Gothic.

The Renaissance style of architecture (15th century) came slightly later to Venice than it did elsewhere. Along with introducing classical elements harking back to ancient Greece and Rome, it also introduced some of the first names that we associate with Venetian monuments, foremost being Mauro Coducci, or Codussi (the church of San Michele in Isola, Santa Maria Formosa, Palazzo Vendramin-Calergi). Pietro Lombardo, from Tuscany, was also influential, noted for his use of colored marble (Santa Maria dei Miracoli, Ca' Dario).

The Venetian High Renaissance (16th century) rejoices in the name of Jacopo Tatti, called Il Sansovino, born in Tuscany, whose handiwork (San Francesco della Vigna, Biblioteca Marciana, Procuratorie Nuove) gave Venice a muscular, marble new look reflecting his years in Rome. Like a number of architects, he was also a sculptor, and when King Henry III of France was being

The Basilica di Santa Maria della Salute, designed by Baldassare Longhena in 1631, is a Renaissance masterpiece.

entertained, Sansovino was called upon by the Foscari family—they of the fabulous parties—to design the plates, silverware, and table decorations (which were made out of sugar). His lesser but equally busy colleagues included Vincenzo Scamozzi (1552–1616).

The baroque architecture of the 17th century tends to overwhelm its more refined neighbors, but Baldassare Longhena's masterpiece, the church of Santa Maria della Salute, led one critic to call it the "greatest baroque edifice outside of Rome." His artistic heirs carried on with this ponderous style at Santa Maria del Giglio, the church of the Scalzi, and San Moisè. After this, the baroque in Venice had basically topped out.

The Venetian 18th century may be the one we most easily recognize, thanks to its two primary painters, Giambattista Tiepolo and Antonio Canal, known as Canaletto. Tiepolo, along with his son, Giandomenico, captured the effervescence of the city that now seemed

to live only for pleasure, painting scenes of luminous color and carefree delight even when the subject was sacred. Canaletto was Venice's master documentarian, who depicted cityscapes not only filled with monuments, but also boats and stonecutters, with scrupulous attention and obvious pride. Francesco Guardi, Bernardo Bellotto, Sebastiano Ricci and Giambattista Piazzetta also contributed numerous paintings worthy of Venice's last great moment of artistic and political glory.

"The Crucifixion," one of the few works signed and dated by Jacopo Tintoretto (1565), is the pride of Scuola di San Rocco.

The 19th and 20th centuries did not contributed anything as memorable to Venice's architecture. The Molino Stucky, a former pasta factory on the Giudecca, is now part of the family despite its terribly Teutonic turrets; Venetians (many of whom worked there until it was closed in the 1950s) resisted the

The Volta de Canal, between palazzos Balbi and Foscari, still looks remarkably as Canaletto painted it here in the 18th century, full of preparations for a regatta.

suggestion that it should be demolished, though ideas for its future have so far come to naught. Dorsoduro's former cotton-thread factory is now the University of Architecture. But Carlo Scarpa (1906–1978) is the only modern Venetian architect to have achieved some international note.

PAINTING

Aside from its architecture, painting is Venice's glory—the hundreds, possibly even thousands, of pictures either by, for or of Venetians form a peerless trove of art on canvas, wood, mosaic, and even fresco. And in Venice you can experience the surprising pleasure of seeing a painting of a local scene and realizing you walked by that very spot only half an hour ago. Not every work is a masterpiece, but many paintings gain their real beauty from the fact that they still rest in the place for which they were created.

The early Renaissance (15th century) Venetian painters were led by the Bellini family (Jacopo and his sons, Gentile and Giovanni) whose work is mostly immediately identifiable by its gleaming, jewel-like colors. The altarpiece of the Madonna and Child in the sacristy of the Frari is unforgettable. Close rivals in this period bridging the Gothic and more naturalistic Renaissance were the Vivarinis (the brothers Antonio and Bartolomeo). Notable but somewhat less remarkable was Sebastiano Luciani, called "del Piombo."

In the High Renaissance (16th century), Venice boasted some of the greatest names in the history of Western art. Tintoretto and Titian head the list, but Giorgione, Lorenzo Lotto, Giovanni Licinio (Il Pordenone), and Jacopo Bassano all deserve admiration. Though not Venetian, Paolo Veronese painted some of his greatest works here.

The baroque and rococo eras (17th and 18th centuries) are noted for names that are better known to experts: Luca Giordano, Sebastiano Ricci, Francesco Guardi, and

The Coro Serenissima often adds Venetian songs to public ceremonies.

Giovanni Battista Piazzetta. The one who stands out above them all, especially for his meticulous scenes of Venice in all its splendor, was Giovanni Antonio Canal, called Canaletto (1697–1768). The master of rococo fantasies, especially in ceiling frescoes, was his contemporary, Giambattista Tiepolo (1696–1770). His heroes and cherubs floating among frothy Venetian clouds give a marvelous indication of Venice's sense of itself in its last days of glory. The less grandiose but equally detailed genre scenes of Venetian daily life by Pietro Longhi (1702–1785) bring us quickly back to Earth.

Many of the palaces along the Grand Canal once glowed with frescoes; time and the elements have mostly taken care of that, but you can glimpse frescoes in many surprising spots, usually under a portico or covered arch.

MUSIC

In the 16th century Venice set itself to music in some of the most melodious and haunting pieces ever written in the Renaissance and baroque styles. As an important center of both musical training and the printing of music, the city could attract the most famous names of the era. It was in Venice that the idea of giving public concerts was first advanced. Before that, concerts had been for the private enjoyment of wealthy families in their homes.

Baldassare Galuppi (1706–1785) was the only famous son of the island of Burano, and he made up in quantity what may have been slightly lacking in quality in his music. He composed 112 pieces for theater, some of them settings of texts by his contemporary, Carlo Goldoni (see p. 46). Robert Browning (1812–1889) took him as the theme of his poem, "A Toccata of Galuppi's."

The name everyone knows and loves is Antonio Vivaldi (1677–1741), the "red priest" (for the color of his hair) who composed countless works for the renowned musicians of the Ospedale della Pietà. This was only one of several hospices that taught music, as well as a trade, to its poor but worthy charges.

Other important composers were Benedetto Marcello (1686–1739), for whom the still active music conservatory is named, and the Gabrielis—Andrea (1510–1586) and Giovanni (1557–1612)—whose sacred music in polyphonic style made the most of the echoing acoustics of the Basilica di San Marco.

Venetian songs are not nearly as well known as they should be, though if you ask your tenor nicely during a gondola ride he will switch from the inevitable "Santa Lucia" and "Ò Sole Mio" (which are Neapolitan songs and have absolutely no place in Venice) and give you a taste of the lilting songs Venetians love and sing when they're out boating: "La Biondina in Gondoleta," ("The Little Blonde in the Gondola," who was probably Marina Querini Benzon), "La Gondoliera," "Nina Nana Veneziana," (Venetian Lullaby) or "Ciaro de Luna" (Moonlight). Their irresistible tunes are set to the gentle rhythm of a boat being rowed, and

Antonio Vivaldi wrote some of his best known pieces for his younger students at the Ospedale della Pietà.

almost all of them are love songs, not merely to a woman, but to the Lagoon itself.

Opera in Venice is the province of La Fenice, for which Giuseppe Verdi composed *La Traviata* and *Rigoletto* (it's said that he kept the aria "La donna è mobile" a secret till the last moment; otherwise, he commented,

"Every gondolier in the city will be singing it."). The quality of the musicians is still high, but since the fire of 1996 the performances are given in a large tent at Tronchetto.

The Biennale (see box below) sponsors more demanding musical events such as modern chamber music. Visiting school choirs from the United States and Britain often give free concerts, and there are even Venetian choirs that specialize in American gospel music.

THEATER & LITERATURE

Venice prides itself on one world-class dramatist: Carlo Goldoni (1707–1793), whose comedies in Venetian dialect have been compared to Molière and Shakespeare. His affectionate but accurate portraits of Venetian people and life were a major step from the *Commedia dell' Arte* to more human, naturalistic comedies.

An interesting variety of plays are offered throughout the year (more in winter than summer); a few amateur companies perform modern minor classics, or Goldoni's simpler comedies, while the Teatro Goldoni presents everything from its namesake's greatest works on up to Greek tragedies and Shakespearean classics. However, these are always either in Italian or in the Venetian dialect.

Venetian writers are not that many, and not that well-known abroad. Among them, Riccardo Selvatico (1849–1901), who was mayor as well as author of poems and comedies in dialect, is well regarded. Otherwise it's probably fair to say that the apparently inexhaustible flood of prose and poetry devoted to Venice has come from foreign writers, from 17th-century travelers to Joseph Brodsky, the Russian poet who won the Nobel Prize in 1987 and who is buried here. ■

The Venice Biennale

In 1895 the mayor of Venice, poet Riccardo Selvatico, launched the idea of a national art festival in Venice, which soon became a biannual international exhibition implicitly dedicated to modern art. Some very famous artists have been invited to participate (Monet, Sargent, Rodin). Today the Biennale also includes concerts, dance, theater, and other events, many of an avant-garde nature. ■

One of the world's great-est "streets," Canalazzo, the "big canal," is a natural waterway—the extension of the Brenta River. It flows past the superb palaces lining its banks, magically defining the reality and the fantasy that are Venice.

Canal Grande

The gondola's bowpiece, the *ferro*, serves as a counter-weight to the boat.

Canal Grande

THE CANAL GRANDE, OR GRAND CANAL, FASCINATES EVEN THE VENETIANS, who regard it with both reverence and affection: reverence for what it represents of the city's greatness, and the affection you feel for your hometown's Main Street. It is one of only two of Venice's interior waterways that is actually called "canal" (the other is the Canale di Cannaregio); all the others are termed *rio*. Historically the unrivaled setting for lavish boat processions and races in honor of visiting royalty, ambassadors, and heads of state, the Grand Canal is also the everyday avenue on which most of Venice gets at least part of its daily work done. With all the hustle of water taxis, vaporettos, and barges, it's not always at its most romantic. But the allure is there, all the same.

One of the first of the early settlements that eventually grew into Venice was established on the Grand Canal along the Rivoaltus, or "high bank" (Rialto). Since this was the market and financial area, wooden houses and storerooms soon sprang up, lining the nearby shores. Ships of the early centuries would sail right up the Grand Canal to unload their cargo directly into the first-floor storerooms of the merchant's residences; you can still notice a few palaces of this design, with the porticoed entrance at water level. There were even a few mills at the canal's edge, which were operated by the power of the tidal flow. Mud was dredged occasionally, and some of it was utilized as landfill elsewhere—on at least one occasion to form an extension to the Riva degli Schiavoni.

To really see the Grand Canal requires more than one journey. The absolute minimum would be to take one trip each way, looking at only one side each time, though certainly it is possible to watch both if you find a good spot toward the bow of the vaporetto. To have truly experienced the grandeur and even mystery of the canal, though, requires many journeys at all times of the day and night—to have seen it at dawn, then at noon, and then at midnight, is to have discovered something vital of Venice's soul.

Your first voyage on the Grand Canal will almost certainly begin at Piazzale Roma, or its neighbor, the train station, and conclude in the Bacino di San Marco, and so that is the direction this chapter follows, describing the sights in order of sequence. ■

For centuries the Rialto Bridge was the only bridge across the Grand Canal. The current span, the most recent of several, was built in 1588–1590.

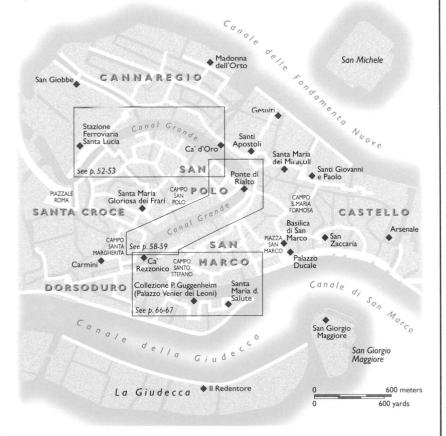

Canale delle Fondamenta Nuove

San Michele

Madonna dell'Orto

San Giobbe

CANNAREGIO

Gesuiti

Stazione Ferroviaria Santa Lucia

Canal Grande

Ca' d'Oro

Santi Apostoli

Santa Maria dei Miracoli

Santi Giovanni e Paolo

See p. 52-53

SAN

Ponte di Rialto

PIAZZALE ROMA

Santa Maria Gloriosa dei Frari

CAMPO SAN POLO

POLO

CAMPO S. MARIA FORMOSA

CASTELLO

SANTA CROCE

Canal Grande

Arsenale

Basilica di San Marco

San Zaccaria

CAMPO SANTA MARGHERITA

See p. 58-59

SAN

PIAZZA SAN MARCO

Carmini

Ca' Rezzonico

CAMPO SANTO STEFANO

MARCO

Palazzo Ducale

DORSODURO

Collezione P. Guggenheim (Palazzo Venier dei Leoni)

Santa Maria d. Salute

Canale di San Marco

See p. 66-67

Canale della Giudecca

San Giorgio Maggiore

San Giorgio Maggiore

La Giudecca

Il Redentore

| 0 | | | 600 meters |
| 0 | | | 600 yards |

Gateway of grandeur

**Fondaco dei Turchi
(Museum of
Natural History)**

- Map p. 53
- Fontego dei Turchi
- 041 524 0885
- Closed for restoration until 2002
- 1 to San Stae

**Palazzo
Vendramin-Calergi**

- Map p. 53
- Calle Larga Vendramin
- 041 529 7111
- 1 to San Marcuola; 41, 42, 51, 52 to Guglie

**Ca' d'Oro (Giorgio
Franchetti
Collection)**

- Map p. 53
- Calle di Ca' d'Oro
- 041 523 8790
- Closed Mon.
- $
- 1 to Ca' d'Oro; 41, 42, 51, 52 to Fondamenta Nuove

**Once lavishly
embellished with
gold leaf, the Ca`
d`Oro, or "house
of gold" (1434), is
one of the gems
of Venetian
Gothic design.**

THE GRAND CANAL FLOWS IN SINUOUS CURVES, NOT IN one grand sweep, revealing Venice in languid stretches. Boarding a vaporetto at the end closest to the mainland—either at Piazzale Roma or the train station—and traveling toward the Bacino di San Marco, you are immediately surrounded by the essence of Venetian splendor: magnificent palaces, soaring domed churches, and what appears to be a hundred bell towers. Within ten minutes, you will have glimpsed one of Venice's most humble houses, and one of its most fantastic.

From the station (Stazione Ferroviaria Santa Lucia), you will pass beneath the Ponte degli Scalzi, then just beyond the Riva di Biasio vaporetto stop, the canal curves to the right. Here, on the right side—not shown on tourist maps, so you need to keep a sharp lookout—is a one-story house with a pointed Gothic doorway as the water entrance. This is **Casa del Boia,** painted a dull brick-red, pretty much the color of dried blood, which is appropriate. This was the house the Venetian government gave to the *boia* (executioner). The daily list of crime and punishment under the Venetian republic makes for heavy reading, but the executioner was nothing more than a paid employee doing a job. Even today, though, "boia" is one of the worst curse words an angry Venetian can use. The casa is now a private residence.

A little farther along on the right is the multiarched **Fondaco dei Turchi.** The Palmieri family built this Veneto-Byzantine palace in the 13th century, and the first-floor arcade was clearly the entrance to the warehouse. In 1381 it became the property of the Venetian government, which used it for centuries as a suitably luxurious residence for visiting royalty. From the 17th century until 1838 it was leased by the Turkish merchant community, who used the space for

meetings and the storage of bales of Chinese silk, ginger, and pepper, and even added baths and a mosque. It fell into almost total degradation, and was substantially rebuilt—some say badly—in 1868. Once again undergoing restoration (*scheduled for completion in 2002),* the building now houses the Museum of Natural History.

Across the little canal that runs down the side of the Fondaco dei Turchi is a sturdy brick structure, the **Deposito del Megio,** formerly one of several municipal grain storehouses (*megio* is Venetian for "millet"). Often at war, and always dependent on imported food, Venice was at special risk of food shortages, not to say famine— there were very serious ones in 1348 and 1559. The majestic stone lion of San Marco on the facade is a 19th-century replacement of the one destroyed by Napoleon in 1797. The building is now used as a school and is not open.

On the opposite side of the Grand Canal is the magnificent **Palazzo Vendramin-Calergi.** It was built for the Loredan family by architect Mauro Codussi (1481–1509), and was admired for its classical facade in an era that still favored the Gothic. The palace was long known as "Non Nobis," for the large plaque on the facade reading *"Non Nobis Domine"* ("Not Unto Us, O Lord"), the motto of the Knights

Palazzo Vendramin-Calergi (1481) was one of the first classical palaces built on the Grand Canal.

Area of map detail also see p. 49

palace now belongs to the city.

Other stately palaces line the banks, but standing out from them all is the sumptuous **Ca' d'Oro,** the "house of gold," on the left bank opposite the fish market.

When Venice was a republic, only the Palazzo Ducale could be called a palace; all the others were termed "houses," the word *casa* being shortened to *ca'*. This High Gothic marvel was built for Marino Contarini in 1434 and he intended it to be what it still is, one of the city's most marvelous buildings. When the team of Venetian and Lombard architects and craftsmen were finished, it was clear that this wasn't going to be called "Ca' Contarini." The facade shimmered with lavish touches of ultramarine, lapis lazuli, and even gold leaf, which immediately earned it the

Templars. Richard Wagner rented 20 rooms here in 1882; his visiting father-in-law, the Hungarian composer Franz Liszt, wrote the opera *The Lugubrious Gondolier* here. Wagner died here on February 13, 1883, and his room can still be seen. The

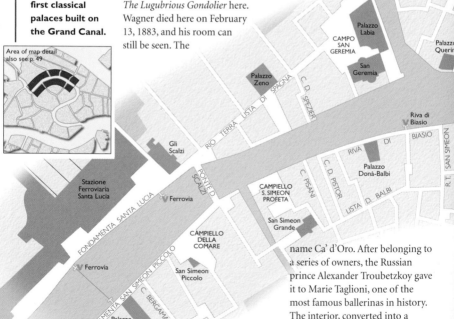

name Ca' d'Oro. After belonging to a series of owners, the Russian prince Alexander Troubetzkoy gave it to Marie Taglioni, one of the most famous ballerinas in history. The interior, converted into a museum in 1984, has been restored, though the gold now survives only in the name.

The entrance retains the original rose-colored Verona-marble wellhead carved by Bartolomeo Bon in 1427, which its most recent owner, Baron Franchetti, retrieved from an art dealer in Paris. This, and the view of the Grand Canal from the second-floor balcony, would make a visit worthwhile, but there are other treasures, too—though not so many that they are overwhelming.

On the second floor is one of the greatest pieces, "St. Sebastian" by Andrea Mantegna (1506), Franchetti's most cherished painting and Mantegna's last. Here also are two superb paintings by Vittore Carpaccio: "The Annunciation" and "The Death of the Virgin" (both 1504)—serene, elegant, with delicate architectural details. "The Annunciation" features an unusual pose, in which the Virgin is only half-turned toward the angel, as if listening calmly more to an inner whisper than to a stunning announcement (in contrast to Tintoretto's shocked peasant girl in the Scuola di San Rocco).

The third floor has a "Venus" by Titian, a subject he always treated with particularly sensual delicacy. Even more interesting are the fragments of frescoes painted by Titian and his student, Giorgione. The sight of Venetian buildings in faded pastels has become familiar, and it's worth recalling that many of them were "illustrated" with frescoes by some of the finest artists.

If you go onto the balcony to admire the view of the Grand Canal, look for the marble relief of an elephant on the right wall. This engaging creature has the oddest feet—more like lion's paws—suggesting that the artist had probably never seen an elephant, and that when he reached that point he came up with the best thing he could think of. ■

Motorboats rather than princes are now the rulers of the Grand Canal.

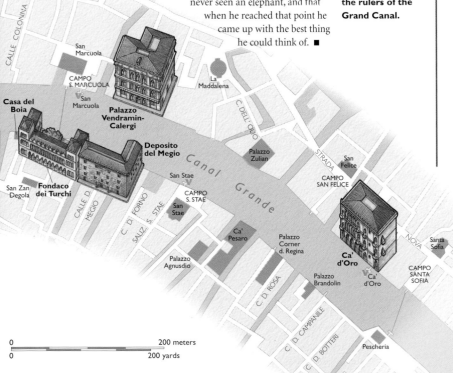

0   200 meters
0   200 yards

Building Venice

Venice may appear to float on the water, but that's exactly what its inhabitants didn't want. The ingenuity with which the city has been constructed is almost more impressive than its charm. Venice is built on about a hundred small muddy islets, threaded with myriad canals, and the greatest challenge to the early settlers was to create a firm foundation that would reliably support the weight of the structures.

Repairing house foundations requires first installing a metal wall and pumping out the canal's water.

There were two methods for preparing the ground, both involving wooden pilings. From the 15th century onward, construction methods utilized pilings that were about 13 feet (4 m) long and rounded, measuring about eight inches (20 cm) in diameter, and were made of oak, bay oak, or larch. In the relatively rare cases where there was a hard clay substratum under the building site, the pilings would be driven down till they rested firmly on it. More commonly a bulkhead or caisson would first be constructed around the area, then the land would be drained, and finally the pilings would be "planted," as they say, working from the outside toward the center, with about nine pilings per square yard. Needless to say, the pilings were pounded by hand (even up until the early years of the 20th century), with

several men at a time holding on to a chunk of wood with which they pounded the piling slowly downward, often chanting as they went to set the rhythm. When the pilings would go no deeper, and they were all level across the top, heavy beams were laid across them, which were in turn covered by two layers of larchwood strips filled in with a reinforced cement aggregate that contained pieces of stone or brick. This is still a common form of Venetian flooring and can be seen in many palaces.

Prior to the 15th century, the Venetians had used basically the same approach, but their results were somewhat less reliable because the pilings were of alder, and were only about 3 feet (1 m) long. The floor was constructed only from a layer of larch or elm.

With all this in mind, it becomes clear that Venetian architects, especially those of the Byzantine and Gothic eras, had many stratagems for minimizing the weight of the building. The use of wood, large windows, slender columns, and brick covered by only slim slabs (rather than blocks) of stone all helped. It also goes some way to explaining why some bell towers have developed a list, or have even collapsed, the most recent being the Campanile of San Marco itself, which fell in 1902.

**Compa
and cla**

Ancient pilings pulled out in the course of restoration have invariably been found to be in perfect condition. Unlike the pilings that mark canals, which are exposed to damaging cycles of wet and dry, the submerged pilings have been completely protected for centuries by the mud that covered them. ■

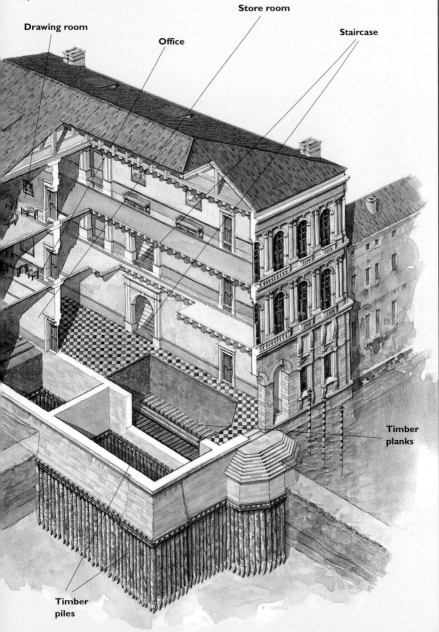

Drawing room

Office

Store room

Staircase

Timber planks

Timber piles

Heart of empire

IF YOU CAN SEE THE PONTE DI RIALTO (RIALTO BRIDGE) from either its upstream or downstream side, you are in the ancient core of Venice. Here was the central market, where every exotic cargo from silk to spices was bought and sold. Gold workers and bankers congregated here, Armenians and Arabs and Germans and Turks, along with the first maritime insurance brokers and anyone with a piece of news to tell. Venice was great because it was rich, and its riches streamed up the Grand Canal to its narrowest point where the shoreline was highest: Rialto.

Fondaco dei Tedeschi
🅜 Map p. 59
✉ Campo San Bartolomeo
🚤 1, 82 to Rialto

Just past the Ca' d'Oro, look to the right for a marvelous view of the Pescheria (fish market), soon followed by the arcades and porticoes of the Fabbriche Vecchie and Fabbriche Nuove—once the trading center of the Venetian Empire. But divert your attention to the opposite bank, where you will easily pick out the **Ca' Da Mosto,** dating originally from the 13th century (the third floor was added in the 17th century and the fourth in the 18th century). The fact that this is the oldest palace on the Grand Canal is immediately apparent, not only because of its somewhat tired appearance, but also because it is covered with the stone coats of arms of many noble families. The Da Mosto family is most noted for its intrepid explorer son, Alvise (born 1432), who discovered the Cape Verde Islands. One could argue that in doing so, he sowed the seed of the fall of the Venetian empire some 300 years later (see p. 36). The family died out in the 16th century, and today the palace contains private apartments.

Rounding a bend in the canal, the Rialto Bridge hoves into view, and to its right we see the forbidding, whitish, rhomboid shape of the **Palazzo dei Camerlenghi.** Built between 1525 and 1528, probably by Guglielmo de' Grigi, as the offices of the *camerlenghi* (financial

Opposite: The Rialto Bridge spans the busy Grand Canal.

magistrates), it is one of the first buildings in Europe to have been built specifically as offices (it also contained a prison). Its walls were once adorned with an astonishing art collection, as each departing magistrate donated a religious painting that also showed either his coat of arms or his portrait—a number of these works can still be seen in the Accademia and Cini galleries. The building is still in use as the seat of the Corte dei Conti (financial court).

On the opposite bank, immediately before the bridge, is the **Fondaco dei Tedeschi.** Like all *fondacos,* this was intended to be an all-purpose building for the use of a specific foreign community, in this case, the Germans, and contained rooms for storage and meetings, as well as bedrooms. After a fire in 1505, the present building was constructed in 1508 by a man the records only name as Girolamo Tedesco (Jerome the German). It is now the main post office.

Just at the curve, at the canal's narrowest point, the two banks are joined by the majestic **Ponte di Rialto,** one of Venice's timeless symbols. This is one of only three bridges that span the Grand Canal (the others are the bridge of the Scalzi at the train station, and the Ponte Accademia). The first Rialto bridge was built on boats in 1180,

then more permanent wooden versions followed in 1264 and 1310 (the latter being the one that is clearly depicted in Carpaccio's paintings of Venice in the Accademia). But in 1444 the bridge collapsed under the weight of onlookers who had gathered to see the wife of the Marquis of

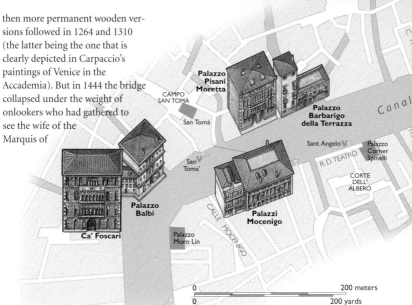

Palazzo Pisani Moretta

CAMPO SAN TOMÀ

San Tomà

Palazzo Barbarigo della Terrazza

Canal

Sant'Angelo

R.D. TEATRO

Palazzo Corner Spinelli

CORTE DELL' ALBERO

San Toma'

Palazzo Balbi

CALLE MOCENIGO

Palazzi Mocenigo

Ca' Foscari

Palazzo Moro Lin

C. TIEPOLO

TRAGHE...

0   200 meters

0   200 yards

Area of map detail also see p. 49

Ferrara pass by, and it was clearly time for stronger measures.

The present bridge was built over three years (1588–1590) though some debate remains as to whether the design was by builder Antonio da Ponte or the nobleman Giovanni Alvise Boldù. Three years

must have seemed a very long time to the inconvenienced merchants of the Rialto area, because rude remarks began to circulate that the bridge wouldn't be finished till the male organ grew fingernails and the female counterpart caught fire. As a retort to these jibes, da Ponte

Left: If not twins, at least very close cousins, these two Veneto-Byzantine palaces serve as the city hall.

[Map labels:] Santa Sofia · STRADA NOVA · CAMPO SANTA SOFIA · Palazzo Michiel d. Colonne · CAMPO DEI SANTI APOSTOLI · Pescheria · Ca' Da Mosto · CAMPO DELLA PESCHERIA · CAMPO BECCARIE · Fabbriche Nuove · CAMPO ERBERIA · San Giovanni Elemosinario · Fabbriche Vecchie · Palazzo dei Camerlenghi · San Giovanni Crisostomo · C. MODENA · San Giacomo di Rialto · Fondaco dei Tedeschi · C. DEI CINQUE · C. D. STORIONE · Ponte di Rialto · CAMPO SAN BARTOLOMEO · C. DOLERA · CAMPO SAN SILVESTRO · San Silvestro · RIVA DEL VIN · Rialto · RIVA DEL FERRO · San Bartolomeo · azzo adopoli · San Silvestro · Palazzo Loredan · Palazzo Bembo · C. L. MAZZINI · CAMPO SAN SALVADOR · Grande · Ca' Farsetti · C. BEMBO · Teatro Goldoni · C. GRIMANI · C. D. CARBON · San eneto · San Luca · CAMPO SAN BENETO · uny

placed two small relief carvings of these very events on the facade of the Palazzo dei Camerlenghi, where you can still see them, albeit with a little difficulty— one is on the right, visible if you stand a few steps up on the outer staircase of the bridge right next to the palazzo, and the other to the left of the main doorway.

There are shops on the Rialto Bridge, like the Ponte Vecchio in Florence, that specialize in cosmetics, gold jewelry, leather, and silk.

Heading southwest now, you will pass several palaces before reaching, on the left, the **Palazzo Loredan** and **Ca' Farsetti**. These two 13th-century Veneto-Byzantine palaces seem to be twins, though the Palazzo Loredan (the white one) may have imitated Ca'

Above right: The 13th-century palace of the Da Mosto family is the oldest on the Grand Canal.

Farsetti after a fire necessitated some rebuilding, and the facade of Palazzo Loredan was repositioned facing the Grand Canal. The two are now joined and serve as City Hall and municipal offices; anyone can enter, but what you can see on the first floor inside is relatively limited and uninteresting.

The series of relief carvings on the facade of Palazzo Loredan show David and Goliath; Justice and Strength; the royal coat of arms of the royal family of Lusignan (which had a semibusiness connection in 1366 with the owner, Federico Corner), and the Corner coat of arms. The palace's greatest fame, though, is due to Elena Lucrezia Cornaro Piscopia (see p. 94).

Some way farther along on the right is the distinctive, apricot-colored **Palazzo Pisani-Moretta,** and this is definitely its best side—the land entrance is not rewarding. What constitutes the present palace is the result of an extensive restoration in the second half of the 1700s, by an architect

The Gothic Palazzo Pisani-Moretta's quatrefoils echo those of the Palazzo Ducale.

Palazzi Mocenigo

 Map p. 58

✉ Calle Mocenigo Casa Vecchia

🚤 82 to San Samuele

named Filippini. To the original 15th-century palazzo (architect unknown), he added the fourth floor and the balcony that you can see from the canal, and other features inside such as a large staircase. This High Gothic palace is available for a fee for private parties and wedding receptions, and even the occasional scene for a movie has been shot here. When parties are under way inside, the balconies are often lined with flaming candles, once a common Venetian festive custom. The two doors reveal that it was once the dwelling of two branches of the Pisani family of bankers, who, in the 14th century, were the first to establish a currency exchange at the Rialto. By the 17th century the Pisanis had become one of the richest families in Venice.

A little farther, on the left, you will see the **Palazzi Mocenigo,** actually three adjoining palaces. They were all built by the Mocenigo family, which gave seven doges and an even larger number of superb military commanders to the republic. On the left is the Casa Vecchia (14th century), on the right the 15th-century Nero, or "black" palace, and in the center the 16th-century Casa Nuova, or new house.

A large plaque on the facade facing the Grand Canal recalls that English poet George Gordon, Lord Byron lived here from 1818–19. He rented an entire floor in the Casa Nuova, arriving with 14 servants, a majordomo, and a gondolier, as well as two monkeys, a bear, two parrots, and a fox, which all wandered the palace at liberty. He

wrote the first two cantos of *Don Juan* here. Today the palaces are private apartments.

You are now approaching the hairpin curve that the Venetians call the Volta de Canal. It is on this bend, just before the Rio di Ca' Foscari angles off to the west, that you will see **Palazzo Balbi** (1682) on the right bank. This has been the finish line for regattas ever since they began to be organized in 1315, and a plaque inside the entrance to the palazzo commemorates the fact that Napoleon witnessed a series of races from the balcony in 1807. In the entrance you can also see the massive wooden coat of arms that was attached to the stern of the galley that Balbi commanded. His victories earned him both the title *capitano da mar* and the right to

put *guglie*, or obelisks, on the corners of the palace's roof. Today, the palace houses offices of the government of the Veneto region.

On the other side of the Rio di Ca' Foscari is the **Ca' Foscari.** Built for the Giustinian family in 1420, this palace was later bought at auction by Francesco Foscari, doge from 1423–1457. It was once the site of legendary festivities for a seemingly endless procession of illustrious guests—including Henry III of France. On his visit, a floating glass-blowing furnace was worked all night in the canal in front of the palace. Ca' Foscari is now the seat of the University of Venice, housing offices and classrooms. The walled courtyard with its wellhead give a glimpse of what the enclosed world of a patrician palace looked like. ∎

Palazzo Mocenigo "il Nero," one of the family's three connecting palaces, was built in the 15th century.

Palazzo Balbi
- Map p. 58
- Calle Balbi
- 041 279 2111
- Closed Sat. & Sun.
- 1, 82 to San Tomà

Ca' Foscari
- Map p. 58
- Calle Foscari
- 041 257 8111
- Closed Aug. 12–20
- 1, 82 to San Tomà

Venetian boats

The Venetian empire became a great power due in large part to its oceangoing merchant ships. It was also a city that was bustling with smaller boats, as evidenced in hundreds of Venetian paintings. There was no land link with the mainland until 1846, so everything that was done here had to be done by boat, and everyone knew how to row. There were even special laws for disputes between boatmen. Today, Venetian boats (and their rowers) represent one of the few remnants of authentic Venetian culture that has remained intact under the pressure of progress, and in their own way these vessels have a good claim to being considered works of art as well as masterpieces of nautical engineering.

At the peak of the city's power, there were some 80 different types of Venetian boats, each adapted to a particular use—the gondola, for instance, only carried people, never cargo—but only about 20 different types still survive. The majority are owned by the 42 rowing clubs, partly because of the shortage of "parking" space for private boats. The heavy, six-oar *caorlina* was the classic transporter, primarily used for such tasks as bringing produce to market, or hay to the dairies. The *gondolino* is the slim, two-oar racing gondola, while the *sandolo* is the all-purpose workhorse, that can be rowed by between one and four people. In more delicate form it becomes the *mascareta*, the boat best suited to women rowers. *Pupparino, s'ciopòn, topetta, sampierotta, battello, musin*—each has its own history and character. Even the gondola-like *traghetto*, with its broader beam and no metal *ferro* on the prow, is technically not called a gondola, but a *barchetta*. At least six different types can be seen as protagonists in Venetian regattas, either the smaller races organized by the clubs, or in the city's official summer calendar of races culminating with the Regata Storica.

The gondola, of course, is the royalty of Venetian craft. Constantly modified and improved over nearly a thousand years, it is made of eight different types of wood, is exactly 36 feet long (14 m), and can take three months to build in one of the four remaining *squeri*, or gondola yards. Its asymmetrical shape is no accident—this helps to keep the boat going straight, resisting the impulse to veer left when rowed by one person. A new gondola can cost L30 million (about $13,000), but can last up to 25 years.

The technique of Venetian rowing is perfectly adapted to its environment: Standing up, facing forward, the rower is able to watch for the shifting sandbanks in the Lagoon, as well as for oncoming traffic in the city. And the physics of oar and *forcola* (the wooden oarlock) demand only the minimum of exertion from the rower, which is good news for the gondoliers who have to keep at it for hours. A recent study revealed that a 170-pound (77 kilos) man rowing a fully loaded gondola (almost 2,000 pounds/900 kilos total weight) expended no more energy than he would by simply walking down the street.

Numerous place-names, on streets, bridges, or courtyards, attest to the activities involving boats that once flourished here. Among them are *felzi* (the wooden cabins once placed on the gondolas); *rasse* (the heavy woolen cloth covering the felzi); *barcaroli* (rowers of gondola traghettos); battello (a barge like a caorlina); *burchielle* (barges for hauling construction garbage); *remorchianti* (rowers who towed other boats); *sabbionera* (a boat that carried sand for ballast to ships); *scoazzera* (a household garbage barge); traghetto (gondola ferry); *vele* (snails); *remer* (oarmaker) and, obviously, squero, or gondola yard. ■

Opposite: Fully furnished and bedecked gondolas are used for special occasions such as weddings.

Pride & power

AFTER ITS SECOND AND FINAL GREAT CURVE, THE GRAND Canal stretches toward the Lagoon. Many of the palaces along its banks are relatively late arrivals, Renaissance and baroque marvels built by families whose uncountable wealth was the only thing that surpassed their ambition. But at the mouth of the canal, a great solemnity reigns: The crownlike cupola of the church of Santa Maria della Salute lofts heavenward, the city's eternal thanksgiving for salvation from a devastating plague. And just beyond, secure and seemingly changeless, the Palazzo Ducale (Doge's Palace) and the Basilica di San Marco stand guard over the thousand years of pride and power that made Venice great.

**Ca' Rezzonico
(Museum of the
Venetian 18th
Century)**
- Map p. 66
- Fondamenta
  Rezzonico
- 041 241 0100
- 1 to Ca' Rezzonico

Rounding the bend in the canal that will eventually lead into the Bacino di San Marco, you will see on your right the **Ca' Rezzonico.** This is another of those Venetian jewels, a museum in a palace, which means you get to see the house as well as the artworks. And it's always a pleasure to see any work of art in its original setting. The museum, which opened in 1934, also occasionally mounts ambitious special exhibitions. It has recently reopened after extensive restorations, with a major gift

(from a so-far unidentified Venetian collector) of 300 additional paintings to display.

English art historian John Ruskin stated that "This is the only building I know in Venice that's as ugly as those we build today." But his contemporary, the American novelist Henry James, called it a "majestic temple of the baroque." It was unquestionably one of Venice's most luxurious palaces. Built in the second half of the 17th century by Baldassare Longhena, it was later bought by the Rezzonico family. Its

main treasures are the marvelous ceiling frescoes by Giambattista Tiepolo, including the joyous "Nuptial Allegory" to celebrate the wedding of Lodovico Rezzonico and Faustina Savorgnan in 1758. There is also a collection of 18th-century genre paintings of Venetian life by Pietro Longhi. The endless sumptuous parties the family gave for visiting popes and kings eventually caused its financial ruin.

In 1888 the house came into the ownership of English poet Robert Browning, who died here in 1889. On a stone plaque on the left flank of the building, just visible inside the adjacent small canal, is his famous remark: "Open my heart and you will see/Graven inside it: Italy."

Continuing around the wide bend in the canal, you will pass under the wooden Ponte dell'Accademia, or Accademia Bridge (for Accademia Gallery see pp. 183–87). Then there are lovely gardens on both banks, leading to the **Palazzo Venier dei Leoni,** which now houses the **Collezione Peggy Guggenheim** (Peggy Guggenheim Collection).

This curious building— strangely truncated, yet still so in harmony with its surroundings— was intended to be a full-fledged palace. It was begun in 1749 by architect Lorenzo Boschetti for the Venier family who, the story goes, made no secret of their intention to build a palace even more magnificent than that of the Corner family just across the Grand Canal. Explanations vary as to why they managed to get only the first floor built. One version holds that the family ran out of money, another that the Corners blocked the project. Both sound plausible. In any case, it is now universally admired as one of those mistakes that turned out for the best, and its contents—one of the most important private collections of 20th-century art outside the United States—could hardly have found a more striking home.

Peggy Guggenheim, American heiress and patron of the arts, bought the palace in 1949. She had already rejected London, New York, and Nice as homes for the art she had amassed in Paris, and although

The terrace of the Hotel Monaco is a good vantage point for admiring the Basilica of the Salute and 16th-century Dogana da Mar (Custom-house), which oversaw cargoes arriving by sea.

Palazzo Venier dei Leoni (Collezione Peggy Guggenheim)

🅰 Map p. 67
✉ Calle San Cristoforo
☎ 041 520 6288
🕐 Closed Tues.
💲 $$
🚤 1, 82 to Accademia; 1 to Salute

she once famously remarked that the Venetians didn't deserve Venice, they seem to have appreciated her eccentric flamboyance and obvious love of the city. She occupied the museum until she died in 1979, and wasn't abashed by visitors occasionally straying into her bedroom.

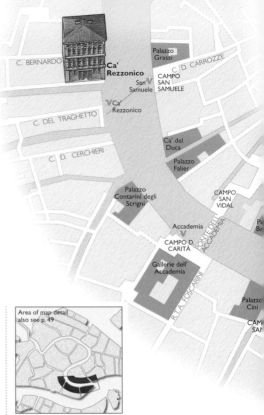

Area of map detail also see p. 49

Her collection contains some of the best art of the 20th century, presented in a state-of-the-art installation. Its great names spring from the Paris of the 1920s and '30s: Picasso ("La Baignade," 1937), Max Ernst ("The Attiring of the Bride," 1940), Marcel Duchamp ("Sad Young Man on a Train," 1911), Giorgio De Chirico ("Red Tower," 1913), René Magritte ("Domain of Lights," 1954), as well as Giacometti, Chagall, and Mondrian. Brancusi's sculpture "Bird in Space" (1929) was once classified by U.S. Customs inspectors as a stair rail. The gallery also contains works by Peggy's own personal discovery, Jackson Pollock.

The smallish rooms can become claustrophobic under the crush of summer crowds, but there is a heavenly garden, punctuated with

sculpture by Arp, Moore, and others (as well as Peggy's grave and that of her poodles). The café and the leafy shade of the trees give you a chance to relax for a moment, and the view of the Grand Canal from the terrace at water's edge is one of the best, comprising the stretch that sweeps from the Accademia Bridge to the Bacino di San Marco. One character who will be sharing your panorama is a bronze of a nude man astride a horse (even better viewed from the water). This is the "Angel of the Citadel" (1949) by Marino Marini, and his outstretched arms are no less rigid than his more intimate part. They say that Peggy would occasionally unscrew this element, but it is now firmly fixed.

The entrance to the garden from the street is decorated by a pair of

Left: Modern art fills the Guggenheim's garden.

Right: The Guggenheim terrace is the ideal spot to view both the Grand Canal and Sansovino's Palazzo Corner, or "Ca' Grande," now the seat of the Prefettura.

large gates of intricate metal wires entwined around huge chunks of Murano glass by the Cenedese workshop (Claire Falkenstein, 1961). Traveling exhibitions are regularly presented, and the expanded gift shop on the Fondamenta Venier dei Leoni is amply stocked with books and gifts.

The distinctive **Palazzo Dario,** or Ca' Dario, next door to the Guggenheim, shows the same type of stonework medallions that ornament the Church of Santa Maria dei Miracoli (1487; see p. 126), typical of the architect Pietro Lombardo. It has lately come to have the reputation of being under

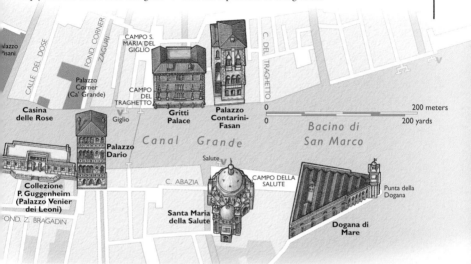

a curse, since a series of owners have come to a tragic end.

The small red palace set back behind a charming flowery garden is the **Casina delle Rose,** once the workshop of the sculptor Antonio Canova (1757–1821). The highly unabashed poet and novelist Gabriele d'Annunzio (1863–1938) stayed here, and set his novel *Il Fuoco (The Fire)* in Venice. It is now a private home.

Just beyond the famous **Gritti Palace** hotel (see pp. 70 and 245) you will see on your right one of the most distinctive features of the Venetian skyline, the church of **Santa Maria della Salute** (St. Mary of Health), a major landmark both for its architectural and emotional significance. In 1630 plague struck the city—claiming a third of

the population—and the Senate made a vow to the Virgin Mary that it would build a splendid church in her honor if she would intercede on the city's behalf. The plague soon passed, and the promise was honored with this incomparable baroque votive temple by Baldassare Longhena. His massive edifice, consciously echoing the domes of the Basilica di San Marco, rests on 100,000 wooden pilings. Space was created by demolishing a medieval church and monastery dedicated to the Holy Trinity, and the new church took some 50 years to build, being consecrated in 1687. The distinctive volutes surrounding the dome are meant to suggest the Virgin's crown.

The church's greatest treasure is the Greco-Byzantine icon over the

high altar, "The Image of the Virgin," brought from Crete in 1672 by Francesco Morosini. Its austere beauty is framed by a baroque marble altarpiece by Giusto Le Corte (1627–1679), surmounted by three figures: the Virgin, the Plague (represented as a fleeing crone), and Venice, an elegant kneeling noblewoman. There are fine paintings by Tintoretto, Titian, and Palma il Vecchio in the sacristy.

Every year on November 21, Venice celebrates the Feast of the Presentation of the Virgin, here simply called Festa della Salute. A votive bridge is built over the Grand Canal, and every Venetian makes a visit at some point during the day to offer a candle.

Opposite the church is the **Palazzo Contarini-Fasan**, which for no historical reason has come to be known as Desdemona's Palace. There was indeed a Venetian general named Otello, though his surname was probably Guoro, and the fate of his wife and that of another nobleman seem to have been mingled and altered by Shakespeare. However, there is no verifiable connection between the doomed wife of the Moor of Venice and this entrancing palace.

The triangular building next to the church of the Salute, pointing toward the Bacino di San Marco like a ship's prow, is the **Dogana di Mar,** or Customhouse. This 17th-century building was where the papers of arriving ships were inspected. The gleaming figure—a weather vane—poised atop the huge golden ball represents Fortune. ■

The Basilica of the Salute and the Customhouse look even more stately by the light of the Redentore fireworks.

Santa Maria della Salute

🅐 Map p. 67

✉ Campo Santa Maria della Salute

☎ 041 522 5558

💲 Sacristy: $

🚤 1 to Salute

More places to visit on the Canal Grande

GRITTI PALACE

The Gothic Gritti Palace, which has long been famous as a luxury hotel, was once the home of the Gritti family. Doge Andrea Gritti (1455–1538) commissioned the palace in 1525, and it later served as the residence of the Vatican ambassadors to Venice. The Gritti family traced its origins to Venetian antiquity: Giovanni Gritti was one of the crusader captains at the Battle of Acre in Palestine in 1104; Andrea presided with the grandeur of a monarch over some of Venice's most sumptuous celebrations and most intricate diplomatic feats, though the social decadence that would prove fatal had already begun to take root.

Gritti's weakness for splendor was matched by an intense personal charm that had served him well in his early years in the grain market at Constantinople; speaking Turkish, among several other languages, he had proved useful

Palazzo Barbarigo at San Vio, on the Grand Canal

to both the sultan and the Venetians.

Casanova has little to brag about compared to this earlier Venetian: While in Turkey, Gritti took a series of Ottoman lovers (when his election as doge was being hotly debated in the Senate, one outraged aristocrat shouted that it was unthinkable that Venice should have a doge who had four bastards in Turkey).

In fact, when he was briefly imprisoned for spying, a troop of Turkish noblewomen came to the prison to personally plead for his freedom. On into his eighties, he continued to find fascinating companions who occasionally became the mothers of his children, including one who was a nun.

Illustrious visitors of every stripe have stayed at the Gritti Palace, from English art historian John Ruskin, who wrote much of *The Stones of Venice* here, to Somerset Maugham and Ernest Hemingway (his room, on the third-floor corner, is still in use). Anyone can enter the public areas on the first floor, and you can take a leisurely look at the small but lavish reception rooms, with their painted beams, Murano mirrors, and sensuous damask silk upholstery woven on antique Venetian looms. A snack, tea, or after-dinner drink in the bar or on the terrace would be the perfect excuse to come inside (see p. 245).
🔼 Map p. 67 ✉ San Marco 2467, Campo Santa Maria del Giglio ☎ 041 794 611 ⛴ 1 to Giglio

PALAZZO BARBARIGO DELLA TERRAZZA

At the corner, literally, of the Grand Canal and the large side canal called the Rio di San Polo, is the Palazzo Barbarigo "della Terrazza," so named because of the distinctive large terrace that appears to have been sliced out of the top two stories. There's no eccentric story to explain this fact: It was designed this way by Bernardino Contin, who built the palace between 1566 and 1570 for Daniele Barbarigo to replace two smaller Barbarigo palaces. The space, now rather sterile and awkward, once boasted a lush garden of trees and climbing plants, the only one of its kind in a Venetian palace. It's also worth noting that, undoubtedly due to this feature, the palace turns its shoulder to the Grand Canal and extends its imposing facade along the Rio di San Polo instead.

Today the palace, beautifully restored but closed to the public, houses the German Center for Venetian Studies.
🔼 Map p. 58 ✉ San Polo 2765, Calle Corner ☎ 041 523 5946 ⛴ San Toma' ∎

The district named for the city's patron saint is the essence of Venice. Monuments, palaces, and countless art works still eloquently attest to the pride and the power of the Most Serene Republic.

San Marco

Christ triumphant on the facade of the Basilica di San Marco

San Marco

TO A VENETIAN, "SAN MARCO" CAN REFER TO ANY NUMBER OF THINGS—THE city's patron saint, the main square, the golden cathedral-basilica, the ancient republic, a parish, a body of water, or even the assault cry of the *lagunari,* the Venetian marines. To the mailman, it means just one thing—the *sestiere* stretching from the Bacino to the Rialto Bridge, the area that is the symbolic as well as geographic heart of Venice.

This district has always been the lowest point of land in the city and subject to flooding, yet it was settled early, probably because of its strategic location between the city's main landmass and the point where the Grand Canal flows into the Lagoon and out to sea. A tiny canal wended through the area that is now the piazza, and two small churches faced each other—one, on the site now occupied by the basilica, was an oratory dedicated to the then patron saint San Teodoro (St. Theodore); the other, at the far end of the piazza where the Correr Museum now stands, was a sanctuary to San Geminiano, demolished in the early 19th century in order to make room for

the long building that now stretches across the far end of the piazza. When St. Mark was chosen as the city's new patron saint, the more modest St. Theodore was deposed and his oratory was razed and replaced by the sumptuous new basilica adjoining the Palazzo Ducale. This virtually sealed the piazza's destiny as the ceremonial as well as political heart of the city.

San Marco offers the essence of Venice: magnificent churches from the Byzantine to the baroque; the ancient as well as current seat of government; and the

Canal Grande

RIVA DEL CARBON
Palazzo Loreda
C. CAVALLI
Ca' Farsetti
San Beneto
San Luca
RAMO D. T.
TEATRO
Sant'Angelo
Palazzo Corner Spinelli
CAMPO SAN BENETO
SALIZ. CHIESA
E TEATRO
CAMPO MANIN
CORTE DELL' ALBERO
Palazzo Fortuny
CALLE D. AVVOCATI
LOCA
Palazzi Mocenigo
CALLE D. VERONA
Palazz Conta del Bov
CALLE MOCENIGO
SALIZ. S. SAMUELE
C. D. PESTRIN
PISCINA S. SAMUELE
Palazzo Moro Lin
CAMPIELLO NUOVO
CAMPO SANT' ANGELO
C. D.
CAFFETTIER
Palazzo Grassi
C. D. CARROZZE
C. D. ORBI
Santo Stefano
CAMPO S. FANTIN
San Samuele
CAMPO SAN SAMUELE
C. D. TEATRO
San Fan
CAMPO SANTO STEFANO
CAMPIELLO CALEGHERI
CALLE D. VESTE
Ca' del Duca
CALLE FRUTTAROL
Palazzo Loredan
C. D. SPEZIER
San Maurizio
Santa Maria del Giglio
La Fenice
Palazzo Falier
Palazzo Morosini
CAMPO SAN MAURIZIO
CALLE LARGA X
CAMPO SAN VIDAL
Palazzo Pisani
Rio del Santissimo
CALLE DEL DOSE
FOND CORNER ZAGURI
CAMPO S. MARIA DEL GIGLIO
Rio del
C. D. PESTRIN
CALLE DEL
PONTE DELL' ACCADEMIA
Palazzo Barbaro
Palazzo Corner (Ca' Grande)
CAMPO DEL TRAGHETTO
Gritti Palace
Palazzo Contarini-Fasan
Casina delle Rose
Giglio
Canal Grande

0 ____ 200 meters
0 ____ 200 yards

city's two most important theaters—the Teatro Goldoni and the opera house, La Fenice. Here, too, are the unforgettable, defining places—the Basilica di San Marco, the Palazzo Ducale (Doge's Palace), the towering Campanile (the Venetians call it *el paròn de casa*—the head of the household), as well as the prisons and the justly famed Marciana

Library. But there are also secret places tucked away along the back streets, and unsung palaces containing surprising treasures: the Palazzo Contarini del Bovolo, with its spiral "snailshell" staircase; the Palazzo Fortuny, now a museum dedicated to the artist Mariano Fortuny. And there are smaller but no less wonderful treasures, led by the two red porphyry lions, irresistibly gruff, that guard the basilica's left flank. Certainly there is more to Venice than San Marco, but if there were no San Marco, Venice would have lost its soul. ■

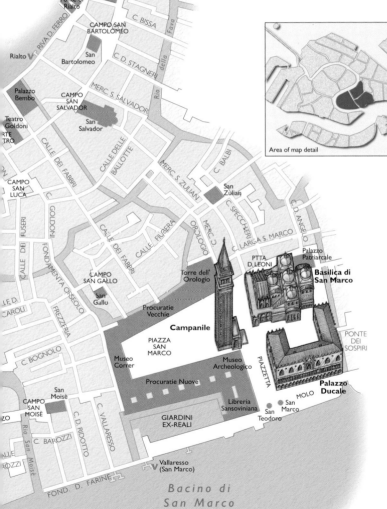

Area of map detail

Piazza San Marco

NAPOLEON FAMOUSLY REMARKED THAT THIS SQUARE IS "the most beautiful drawing room in Europe," and even Venetians are forced to agree. The Piazza San Marco embodies an ineffable combination of elements—variety, proportion, astonishing history—that no other city square can match. Venetians call it simply "The Piazza," as if there could be no other.

Opposite: Doges and princes once debarked before the two columns and crossed the Piazzetta to enter the basilica.

Over the centuries it has served as everything from occasional garden and market area to the setting for Venice's most magnificent religious and civil processions—fantastic revels including tournaments and bullfights—and her saddest and bitterest moments. There are hundreds of paintings that show the piazza in all its aspects; it's a place that has never failed to fascinate artist and visitor alike. Although the cathedral was way out in Castello and the market was up at Rialto, San Marco has always been, and remains the core of the city.

The piazza started small, as a rustic little island dotted with trees; a canal ran between it and the Palazzo Ducale, and the Lagoon covered much of what is now the Molo. Later there was a *broglio* (garden) outside the Palazzo Ducale that was the scene of hectic vote-seeking by prospective senators, hence the word *imbroglio*, meaning "cheating."

In 1174 the canal was filled in, and in 1267 the ground was paved with bricks laid in herringbone pattern (replaced by stones 1722–1735). The distinctive lines of white marble (designed by Andrea Tirali, same period) are no random decoration—they were laid out to indicate the assigned positions of the temporary stands that occupied the square during special fairs. (Merchants came from all over the eastern Mediterranean for the two-week Ascension Day fair in May, offering a vast assortment of

perfumes and cosmetics of every kind, inlaid mirrors, embroidered velvets, and so on.) Look closely: You can still discern a few of the inscriptions on these marble strips; the one in front of the Caffè Quadri reads *calegheri,* Venetian for "shoemaker."

The best approach to the piazza is to take the vaporetto to Vallaresso and enter the square from the bocca de Piazza; it hits you all at once— piazza, basilica, and campanile.

If you do this, you will be standing under the **Museo Correr.** This is the museum of Venetian history—not as famous as some other museums, perhaps, but it has some paintings and exhibits on Venetian society that are well worth the visit. The early Renaissance paintings of Venice are especially appealing. Napoleon's stepson, Eugene Beauharnais, Viceroy of Italy, ordered the destruction of Sansovino's church of San Geminiano to make room for this unremarkable edifice, which he used as an annex to his residence in the Procuratorie. It is called the Ala Napoleonica, or Napoleonic Wing. On the facade there is an empty space in the center of the row of Roman kings. Napoleon intended to place a statue of himself there in order, he is reputed to have said, that he could "look down on San Marco." Venetians are immensely gratified that he died before he could see it through.

The two rows of buildings of the Procuratorie form the "walls" of

projected reopening to the public is not even guessed at.

While you are in this corner of the piazza, go into the adjoining **Piazzetta dei Leoni** and take a look at the two 18th-century crouching red porphyry lions that are unquestionably the masters and main attraction of this little square. You would swear that when Giovanni Bonazza received this commission from Doge Alvise III Mocenigo in 1722, he made a conscious decision to make them utterly irresistible to small children. The lions' heavy gruff faces are mere bluff: Their shiny smooth backs attest to the fact that, even to this very day, children (and not a few adults) of every nation have never hesitated for an instant to climb aboard. Also in the piazzetta is the **Palazzo Patriarcale,** or Palace of the Patriarch of Venice *(not open to the public).*

Crossing in front of the basilica (see pp. 78–85) and the Palazzo Ducale (see pp. 88–91), head toward the water and you will come to the Molo, where everything from flour to doges once came ashore. The two columns of **San Marco** and **San Teodoro** marked the spot of public executions.

Facing the Palazzo Ducale is the **Libreria Sansoviniana.** The entire enterprise and building are officially known as the Biblioteca Nazionale Marciana (National Library of Mark); the Libreria Sansoviniana denotes the oldest part of the building, which occasionally hosts smallish exhibitions. This full-fledged baroque building was designed by Jacopo Sansovino, who came to Venice from Florence in 1527. To use the library itself requires a phone call to arrange permission, but anyone can enter to admire the interior. The magnificent staircase and painted ceilings are worth seeing (the trompe l'oeil,

Though more often it is photographers who seek to capture Venetian vignettes, painters are a common sight.

Campanile

🅐 Map p. 73

✉ Piazza San Marco

☎ 041 522 4064

💲 $$

🚤 1, 51, 52 to San Zaccaria; 1 to Vallaresso; 82 to San Marco

Opposite: The campanile of San Marco was inaugurated in 1515. Each of its eight bells had a name and rang for a specific purpose.

the piazza. They were the offices and also homes for the procurators, who administered San Marco and other property owned by the government. On the right, as you face the basilica, is the **Procuratorie Nuove** (Mauro Codussi, 1500; Bartolomeo Bon, 1512; Jacopo Sansovino, 1532) and on your left is the **Procuratorie Vecchie** (1582-1640, first by Scamozzi and then by Longhena). They are still used as offices.

Proceeding clockwise from the Museo Correr, past the Procuratorie Vecchie, you'll come next to the **Torre dell' Orologio** (dei Do Mori). Several houses were demolished to make way for this clock tower, which was designed by Pietro Lombardo and inaugurated in 1499. The clockworks, which were revised several times, caused the two "moors" (the handiwork of Ambrogio d'Ancona) to strike the bell with their hammers. One figure is an old man, representing the past, and the young man symbolizes the present. A very long-drawn-out restoration is still under way at the time of writing, and the or optical illusion treatment of the ceiling is impressive). Probably its greatest treasure is Fra Mauro's Mappamundo (1459), a map drawn by a friar of the Lagoon monastery of St. Christopher, which represents the culmination of all geographic knowledge by that date, just before Columbus's and others' voyages redrew the world map. It is occasionally on display.

Midway along the Libreria, at No. 17 is the entrance to the **Museo Archeologico,** with treasures—mainly Greek and Roman sculpture from the fourth and fifth centuries B.C.—that were collected by Cardinal Domenico Grimani (died 1523). They are not especially well displayed or identified, and of course they don't have much to do with Venice, but the quality is high.

One of the most distinctive landmarks on the skyline of San Marco is the **Campanile.** There has been a tower here since the seventh century; perhaps used for defense or as a lighthouse. The first bell tower was built between 888 and 912, but the present structure is by Bartolomeo Bon (1450–1509). It is not quite 300 feet (92 m) high, and is 36 feet (11 m) wide. The golden angel—it's also a weather vane—was placed on the top on July 6, 1513. The structure resisted earthquakes and lightning bolts till the morning of July 14, 1902, when it collapsed (no one was injured). It was rebuilt as it was. From the top you can see a spectacular panorama of the city and Lagoon (on clear days, obviously). Be warned: The bells ring at 9:30 a.m., noon, and 2 p.m., though if you should find yourself under them, the noise is not unbearable.

The Loggetta, the baroque raised platform that stands at the entrance, was designed by Jacopo Sansovino (1540). ■

Basilica di San Marco

"A PIRATE CATHEDRAL ENRICHED WITH THE SPOILS OF THE universe" and "the colossal reliquary of Venetian civilization" (Theophile Gautier). "Unreal, fantastic, solemn, inconceivable throughout" (Charles Dickens). Generations of writers have groped for words to describe this extraordinary creation representing a thousand years of artistic genius, political power, and religious faith. But they all understood that it is a place that is meant to be felt, and not merely to be seen.

Basilica di San Marco

-  Map p. 73
- ✉ Piazza San Marco
- ☎ 041 522 5205
- 💲 Loggia dei Cavalli: $, Pala d'Oro: $, Treasury: $
- 🚌 1, 51, 52 to San Zaccaria; 1 to Vallaresso; 82 to San Marco

The best way to visit the basilica is to come for a service. What you miss in adding to your list of masterpieces will be compensated for by having paused to let the magnitude of it seep into your pores. Even if this has to be your one and only visit, you will have added something deeper to your understanding of Venice's soul than could ever be found in a checklist of artworks.

Once officially the doge's chapel (it became the city's cathedral only in 1807), the basilica embodies Venice's unique position linking East and West both in war and peace. Its Greek cross form deliberately echoes the Byzantine grandeur of Constantinople's Church of the Twelve Apostles, but it is located in a city that was Latin, not Greek.

The first church on this site

(seventh century) was a modest structure dedicated to St. Theodore, the city's first protector. As the city grew in power, so did the desire for a more important patron saint. In 828, two audacious Venetian sailors found themselves (some say at the behest of Doge Giustiniano Partecipazio) in Alexandria, Egypt, where they contrived to acquire the body of St. Mark the Evangelist, hide it on a wagon under a layer of pork, and carry it away—the first, but hardly the last, stolen object to adorn the church.

In 829, Doge Partecipazio ordered the foundations laid for a worthy building to house this precious relic. The shrine almost immediately became one of Europe's foremost sites of pilgrimage. That building, as well as the Palazzo Ducale, was destroyed by fire in 976; it was replaced twice, the last version being consecrated in 1094. This is the structure we see today, though obviously it has been embellished over the intervening centuries, not least by the many doges who, after being elected, would offer a gift to the basilica.

From the outside, the church gives only a little hint of the grandeur within. In fact, on first sight you may even feel slightly let down, because it doesn't appear all that big. The five front doors are surmounted by **mosaic lunette panels** that are 18th-century replacements of the 16th-century mosaics that had already replaced the 13th-century mosaics (which can be seen in the background of Gentile Bellini's 1496 painting

Icon of Venice, the basilica lords over the Piazza San Marco.

of the "Procession in St. Mark's Square" in the Accademia Gallery; see pp. 183-87). The mosaics within the arches depict scenes from the adventure of stealing St. Mark's body, while the insipid mosaics (1617–18) in the arches above show moments from the life of Christ. But look at the mosaic farthest to the left. Its austere Byzantine style makes it clear that it is the oldest among them; it shows the facade of the basilica as it appeared in the 13th century, and depicts the doge, priests, and people bringing the saint's sarcophagus into the basilica.

It is the first complete "picture" we have of the church in the period 1265–1270 (showing the bronze horses already in place).

On the right-hand outer wall, facing the Bacino di San Marco, is an impressive portal, now closed. This was known as the *porta da mar*, or sea entrance, and was the doorway used for ceremonial entrances, which usually began from that direction. On this side

Ascension Dome

Pentecost Dome

Baldachino

Pala d'Oro

Rood screen

Pulpit

Mosaic pavement

Right: A lion of San Marco surveys the Piazza "where," one writer mused, "pigeons walk and lions fly."

there are several treasures to note. One is the dark red marble statue showing four men, commonly called the **Tetrarchs** (though they are probably four Roman emperors, including Diocletian). They are of fourth-century Egyptian design, and came either from Syria or Egypt, by way of Constantinople. Another is the pair of elaborately carved freestanding white marble pillars, which were brought from Acre, in Syria, after the Venetians defeated the Genoese (1256), and are of fifth-century Syrian design. The short red stone pillar, taken from Acre in 1256, is what remains of the **Pietra del Bando,** from which the sentence of banishment was announced (hence our word "bandit"). Lastly, look up to the space above the loggia, facing the water. Here is the 13th-century mosaic of the **Madonna del Navigante,** and the votive lamps on each side are always lit, fulfilling the vow of a thankful sailor who survived a storm by following a light in the piazzetta.

On the left-hand outer wall, on the stone pillar that forms the corner with the main facade, you'll see a little metal rod sticking out, and the faint outline of a vertical line carved into the stone column. This is all that remains of a simple astronomical device (early 13th century), and many churches had something similar to demonstrate their symbolic link between Earth and heaven. Turn the left-hand corner, toward the Piazzetta dei Leoncini, and in the far corner you will see a large sarcophagus inside a wrought-iron fence. This is the tomb of

Copies of the Horses of St. Mark

Loggia dei Cavalli

Romanesque carvings

Main entrance

Original facade mosaic: "Translation of the Body of St. Mark to the Basilica"

Daniele Manin, who led the failed uprising against the Austrians in 1848. Next to it is the doorway into the basilica called the Porta dei Fiori; above the door is a sculpted stone cross and a simple nativity scene dating from the 13th century.

Apart from the times when services are under way, you can visit the church by taking your place in line. There is one line for groups, and another for individuals. If you are not properly attired, the guard at the entrance may not permit you to come in. Women are not required to cover their heads, but arms, chest, and legs should not be too drastically revealed. Inside, a pathway has been cordoned off, and you have to follow it.

Just inside the front door, the L-shaped **narthex,** or atrium, contains some of the oldest mosaics (13th century) in San Marco, and is designed, like the space inside the sanctuary, according to a very precise storytelling scheme. Here, the scenes are all from the first five books of the Old Testament, whereas inside the basilica itself they are from the New. The creation is clearly visible on your right, depicting Adam and Eve and their adventures, as well as Noah and the Ark. The vignettes that show water (the creation of the fishes and the Great Flood) are particularly appealing in this watery setting. The modest mosaics of St. Matthew and St. Mark, in their niches flanking the central door-way, are from the early 12th-century basilica, and, having survived fire and earthquake, may be the oldest in the church.

Three doges and one dogaressa have been entombed in the walls of this area, but they draw hardly any attention to themselves. The most obvious tomb is that of Doge Ordelafo Falier (died 1118), located between the two main doors within

Left: Heroes of Christianity— here, St. Liberalis, canonized in A.D. 400—cover the acres of the basilica's walls.

a lighted niche that is covered by a stone screen carved in a somewhat Islamic style.

On the floor just inside the main door is a **commemorative stone,** a diamond-shaped piece of red marble marking the historic place where, on July 13, 1177, the Holy Roman Emperor Frederick Barbarossa knelt before Pope Alexander III, a peacemaking triumph by Doge Sebastiano Ziani.

As soon as you've caught your breath—taken away by your first sight of the interior—you'll note that there are five cupolas: three large ones and two smaller. The first one nearest the main entrance, the **Pentecost Dome**, is probably the oldest in the church (mid-12th century), and shows the descent of the Holy Spirit as a dove during the

feast of Pentecost, with the Apostles bearing the red "tongues of flame" of the Holy Spirit on their heads—an outstanding example of the skill of the Venetian mosaic masters in combining the Byzantine and Romanesque styles.

The central, or **Ascension Dome** (early 13th century) shows the risen Christ ascending to heaven. In the spandrels at his feet are 12th-century mosaics of the four evangelists: The winged lion of St. Mark, the angel of St. Matthew, the bull representing St. Luke, and the eagle of St. John. The Latin inscription shared out among them translates as: "These four are the sentinels of the church of Christ, and their sweet song reverberates from every part of the heavens." The scene of "Christ's Agony in the

San Marco is quintessentially Venetian in that its creators drew on many styles, but adapted them into something original.

The bronze horses that once crowned the racetrack in Constantinople have been Venice's pride since 1204.

Garden" is one of the most dramatic in the entire church. The **dome of the Prophets,** or **Emmanuel,** soars above the high altar, and the curving surface of the apse facing you shows the looming figure of Christ Pantocrator, a 1506 reproduction of the Byzantine original.

The right side of the church (connected to the Palazzo Ducale) was traditionally overseen by the doge, while the area to the left was the domain of the priests. In the **cupola of San Leonardo** above the right transept are Sts. Leonard, Basil, Clement, and Nicholas, the so-called political saints because each was added when Venice established an important political link with their native territory. The **cupola of San Giovanni** is above the left transept.

The **high altar** was built to contain the body of St. Mark, and features a remarkable baldachino resting on four carved alabaster columns which depict 90 scenes from the life of the Virgin and of Jesus. It is not certain whether they are sixth-century Byzantine or mid-13th century Venetian.

The **iconostasis,** or rood screen, that divides the nave from the choir is topped by statues representing the Virgin, the Apostles, and St. Mark, with a silver and bronze crucifix in the center—all notable examples (1394) of the work of Gothic masters Jacobello and Pietro Paolo delle Masegne.

The broad and squat 14th-century **pulpit** on the right, covered with red marble panels, some from Constantinople, was used primarily for the presentation of the new doge to the people (today, the cardinal patriarch of Venice uses it to preach his sermons on solemn festival days). The need for another pulpit for everyday use inspired the creation of the unusual **two-tier pulpit** to the left, which may be the only one of its type in the world. The required readings from the Bible during Mass are given from this structure (the Letter and Old Testament are read from the lower, and the Gospel from the higher).

The **Madonna del s'ciopo,** or Madonna of the rifle, is a tall, narrow relief carving on a square column with an array of the usual votive offerings in a glass case at her feet. But embedded in the column by her side is an old rifle, which was offered to her by a now unknown Venetian soldier in 1848 in thanksgiving for having survived a battle during the uprising of that year. The huge mosaic (1542–1552) on the wall in the left transept above the Chapel of the Nicopeia depicts the **Tree of Jesse,** or the Virgin's family tree; you can see her atop this elaborate design, holding Jesus in her arms. Designed by Giuseppe Porta, nicknamed Il Salviato, and executed by Vincenzo Bianchini, it is sometimes also called San Marco's "Sistine ceiling."

Extending across the main facade is the **Loggia dei Cavalli,** where doges used to stand to witness the tournaments in the piazza, and where the four bronze horses of San Marco keep watch—the originals are on display in a room inside. Other rooms just inside contain a small museum of early mosaic segments, tapestries, and the painted wooden covering for the Pala d'Oro by Paolo Veneziano (1345). From the interior balcony over the main doorway you have a splendid view of the nave from above, and you are closer to some mosaics, mainly of the Apocalypse. You also get a glimpse of the wending narrow walkways along the side, which were once the *matronie,* wooden-floored areas reserved for the ladies of the doge's family. They were closed after the fire of 1145.

If you can take even more splendor, the **Treasury** occupies a small area off the right transept and displays some of the most glorious Byzantine gold and silverware in the world. This, too, was part of the plunder from Constantinople in 1204 at the end of the Fourth Crusade. Note the incense burner in the form of a gilded silver Byzantine church. There was much more before the fall of the Venetian republic, including the crowns of Cyprus and Crete, but in 1797 Napoleon ordered the rarest and most valuable pieces to be broken up and melted down. ■

Christ is depicted on the Pala d'Oro in one of the greatest examples of religious enamel work ever made.

Three treasures

There is a small chapel in the left transept, in which a 10th-century Byzantine icon of the **Madonna Nicopeia,** "she who gives victory," is displayed. This image by an unknown painter came to Venice as part of the booty from the sack of Constantinople in 1204; it was carried into battle at the head of the Byzantine emperor's army (hence its name).

The four **Horses of San Marco** on the loggia outside the basilica are copies of the originals, now safely on view inside. This *quadriga* of gilded bronze probably drew a chariot, and may have surmounted the racetrack of the Emperor Constantine in Constantinople. They were possibly made in the second century by the famous Greek sculptor Lysippus, though some assert they are Roman work. They, too, formed part of the treasure taken from Constantinople in 1204, and are the only *quadriga* that has come to us from the ancient world.

The **Pala d'Oro** behind the high altar is Venice's most important work of religious art. Covered with gold and precious stones, and tiny religious scenes rendered in cloisonné enamel, it was made in Constantinople in 975 for Doge Pietro Orseolo, enlarged in the 12th and 13th centuries, and placed in its Gothic frame in 1342. ■

The "Madonna Nicopeia," always invoked by Venetians in times of crisis

Mosaics

The walls of the basilica, inside and out, are covered by some 2 acres (8,000 sq m) of mosaics, which date from the Byzantine to the Renaissance periods. That refulgent golden color? It doesn't just look like gold: It *is* gold, real gold leaf applied to an infinite number of bits of glass. And across this gleaming background, the symbolic color of heaven, march 181 figures of saints, prophets, Virtues, and myriad characters from the Bible, from Abraham to Joseph, Solomon to Salome, the sum of about 800 years of work.

Noah releases the dove to seek land, in one of the mosaics that depict the story of creation.

artists: Titian, Tintoretto, Veronese, Jacopo Palma il Giovane, Lorenzo Lotto, Sebastiano Ricci, and others. One example is the cycle by Tintoretto (1588–89) on the vault near the Ascension Dome that shows the life of Jesus, which replaced the earlier, damaged work. Not everyone considers that the Byzantine and the Renaissance mix very well, but they are all powerful testimony to the city's dedication to its basilica and its patron saint, who one Renaissance visitor said was adored more by the Venetians than by God Almighty.

The art of mosaic, though known in Rome and Ravenna, was preeminently Byzantine by the ninth century, but Venetian masters learned quickly from their Greek teachers. The layout of the figures follows a very deliberate scheme either by an unknown Venetian iconographer, or possibly by Iacobo Venetico Greco, a theologian at the church in 1136. They are roughly divided into the categories "biblical" and "hagiographical" (saints). The themes of the Old Testament scenes strictly corresponded with the sequence of weekly readings of the liturgy, and many images carried a symbolism that would have been clear to earlier Venetians. Worth noting in the creation sequence in the narthex are the two majestic lions, symbols of Venice, prostrate before their Creator. And the lion who gets precedence descending from the ark would have been understood to represent both the lion of Judah and Venice, his worthy successor.

You will already have noticed that the styles vary widely. The earliest mosaics followed the austere, static Byzantine formula, and were usually designed and made by the same person. As the High Renaissance flowered, the tasks became divided, and some of the more painterly mosaics of the 15th century were made to the cartoons by Venice's greatest

The tradition of mosaic at San Marco did not continue uninterrupted over the centuries. The basilica entered a period of crisis in the 15th century with the death in 1424 of the last mosaic master, Jacobello della Chiesa. An appeal by the Senate brought the Florentine artist Paolo Uccello to Venice to design and oversee new mosaic work, and two other Tuscans, Michele Giambono and Andrea del Castagno, also worked in San Marco. Though many of their designs are no longer extant, their contribution as teachers to the Venetian mosaic workers was vitally important. But their more dynamic "mosaic picture" style put an end to the great Byzantine tradition. Two centuries later, many mosaic masters died in the great plague of 1630, and the work undertaken in the following two centuries was of a flunctuating but generally lesser standard.

Perhaps less prized, but no less beautiful, are the intricate mosaics that cover the floor, some of them specifically designed to echo the mosaic above. ■

Joseph in Egypt covers three cupolas of the atrium, perhaps to honor the country from which St. Mark's body was brought.

Palazzo Ducale

IN 726 THE EARLY VENETIANS, WHO WERE STILL COLONISTS
of Byzantium, decided they wanted to be governed by a *doge* (duke),
and began to seek a suitable place for his residence. In 810, Doge
Agnello Partecipazio donated a small island on the palace's present
location overlooking the Bacino di San Marco, and construction
began on a wooden fortress that enclosed both his house and the first
church of San Marco.

During the course of the intervening centuries the Palazzo Ducale
(Doge's Palace) has obviously
undergone dramatic changes, but it
was always the seat of the Venetian
government—its importance could
be compared to the White House,
Capitol, and Supreme Court all
occupying the same building. The
building today gives a dazzling
insight into the sheer scope and
detail of how the Venetian empire
governed itself and its colonies, and
the viewer is left in no doubt that
no expense was spared in present-
ing the state as rich, powerful,
shrewd, and favored by God.

Only a few faint traces (not
visible to the visitor) remain of the
original structure; there were fires
in 976, 1094, 1483, 1574, and 1577,
and the expansion of Venetian
power continually called for more
rooms for the various governing
bodies. All this required a series of
reconstructions, the last of which
was completed in 1615. The airy
construction of the palace demonstrated how secure the Venetian
state really was—rulers here didn't
have to live in fortified castles such
as those in Florence and other cities
plagued by plots and rebellion.

Before entering, pause in the
piazzetta between the palace and
the Campanile, and look up at the
long balcony. You'll notice two pink
pillars contrasting with all the other
white ones. The doge would stand
between these pillars to officially
witness the execution of a criminal,
which would occur between the
two large columns with the statues
of the lion of St. Mark and St.
Theodore. Often, the victim's body
would be placed up here afterward,
as was the case with the mutilated
corpse of the traitorous Doge
Marino Falier (see p. 29).

Below: The Doge's
Palace reflects
Gothic elements
as well as touches
of the Levantine
that were not
common in
Europe.

Prison life

Venice was among the first cities in Europe to have an isolated, purpose-built state prison. Cells and passageways that may appear appalling today were actually in the vanguard of improved prison design. Prisoners were separated according to the severity of their crime, and there was even a space for those who had turned themselves in. Wealthy or aristocratic prisoners fared better.

The cells were subdivided, however, and overcrowding was a constant problem. Floors and walls were lined with wood to mitigate the damp and chill, but this created the perfect environment for fleas, cockroaches, and bedbugs.

Common complaints included the incarceration of sick and healthy prisoners together, corrupt guards, and unreasonable delays for trial. But many charitable organizations, particularly *scuole* founded for the purpose, worked to help the prisoners, from supplying food to paying their debts. ■

Charitable groups worked to improve prisoners' lives, but conditions were harsh, as shown by this prison inside the Doge's Palace.

Arguably the palace's most dramatic space is the **Sala del Maggior Consiglio** (Great Council Hall), the largest room in the world to have a ceiling that is unsupported by even one pillar. Lined up around the wall just under the ceiling are small portraits of the first 76 doges. Note on the west wall that there is a black curtain covering the space where the face of Doge Marino Falier ought to be; he was convicted of treason and executed in 1355, and no portrait of him has survived.

Originally, the palace also contained the prisons; when the "New Prisons" were built, detainees were led from the palace to their cells across the Ponte del Sospiri, or

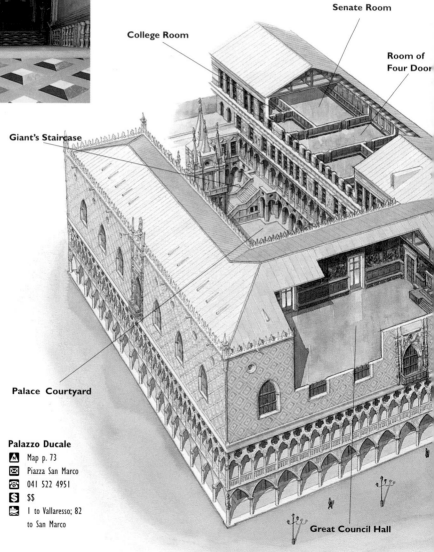

Senate Room

College Room

Room of Four Door

Giant's Staircase

Palace Courtyard

Great Council Hall

Palazzo Ducale
- Map p. 73
- Piazza San Marco
- 041 522 4951
- $$
- 1 to Vallaresso; 82 to San Marco

Left: The Golden Staircase was intended to impress dignitaries entering the Palazzo Ducale.

Bridge of Sighs, a late Romantic name that supposedly evoked their despair. It was built of Istrian stone in 1602 by Antonio Contin. In 1569 it had become obvious that more space and better conditions were called for, and the New Prisons were built on the other side of the canal between 1589 and 1614. They were designed by Antonio da Ponte and Zamaria de' Piombi, with the help of Zaccaria Briani, a prisoner serving a life sentence who was rewarded for his suggestions with three years of home detention. ∎

Bridge of Sighs

Casanova

His name is commonly associated with just one thing, but in many ways Giovanni Giacomo Casanova (1725–1798) was the epitome of the 18th-century self-made man, someone who instinctively appreciated the theatrical nature of life in the Europe of his day, and understood that an orphan could find success only by his own daring and imagination. He firmly believed, and often quoted, the Roman poet Seneca: "Follow your will," or, more simply, do as you please.

The son of an actress who abandoned him, he wasn't handsome, but he had an imposing build, "burning eyes," and an equally powerful intelligence. He translated Homer's *Iliad* from Greek into the Venetian dialect, and wrote his memoirs in French.

Casanova briefly sought a career as a priest, but somehow one thing just kept leading to another. He traveled across Europe, from London to Paris to Vienna, living by expedients: musician (he played the violin), gambler, diplomat, and finally spy. Some scholars have advanced the theory that at least some of his legendary exploits with women were information-gathering encounters. His autobiography gives an altogether different impression.

Probably his most famous escapade, recounted in excruciating detail in his autobiography, was his breakout in 1756 from the Piombi, the notorious area just under the prison roof that was supposedly escape proof. He claims to have cut his way through the roof, but it is possible that he simply bribed the guard. Casanova died in exile in Bohemia in 1798, bitter and alone. ∎

A walk north of Piazza San Marco

This area is essentially Venice's ground zero, where the most important sights and shops are clustered, and consequently it is also one of the busiest and most congested parts of the city. This, of course, makes it also the least suited for strolling, but if you pick a slightly off-center moment of the day—or even early in the morning—it can be a beautiful area for a ramble.

The stores in the Mercerie dell'Orologio prepare for Christmas.

Standing in front of the **Basilica di San Marco** facing the piazza, turn right toward the Torre dell' Orologio (Clock Tower). Passing under the tower, you enter the long street called Mercerie dell' Orologio. Venetians were once required to leave their horses here, in an effort to limit the confusion in the piazza.

At the first street on your left, the Sotoportego del Cappello, pause and look up. Over the arched passageway, there is a stone carving of a wizened little old woman and a marble mortar (for grinding salt and spices) which appears to be falling from her grasp. The Venetians informally call her **La Vecia del Morter,** or "the little old lady with the mortar." Her name was Lucia Rossi, and on the evening of June 15, 1310, she saved Venice from an attempted coup by Baiamonte Tiepolo and Marco Querini. Hearing the noise

of the soldiers' rushing toward the Palazzo Ducale, she leaned out her window and knocked her mortar into the street, where it struck the flagbearer on the head. In the ensuing melee, the doge's militia was able to overcome the rebels.

At the end of this street, turn right into the Campo San Zulian. The church of **San Zulian ❶** facing you is dedicated to the saint of the same name, an early martyr, but the statue on the facade is of a learned doctor named Tommaso Rangone, who paid for the restoration of the facade in 1553 on condition that they put up his statue. With similar bravura, he also added three inscriptions praising his accomplishments in Latin, Greek, and Hebrew.

Turn left and walk up the main street, the Mercerie San Zulian. Atop the next bridge, the **Ponte dei Bareteri,** you have two choices, both of which will bring you out at the same spot. Either keep going straight along the Mercerie del Capitello, or turn immediately right and walk by the canal under the Sotoportego de le Acque, which is prettier, then turn left. In either case, there are only shops to be observed.

You will emerge onto the **Mercerie San Salvador**. Continuing straight ahead, you will reach the intersection of two wide streets, which meet in the **Campo San Salvador**. The large but somewhat forbidding 12th-century church of **San Salvador ❷** was rebuilt in the 16th century by a series of architects, lastly Jacopo Sansovino (1534). Treasures inside include a painting, "Supper at Emmaus," which, during a recent restoration, was found not to be by Bellini, but rather Vittore Carpaccio (1524). The unusually powerful depiction of "The Annunciation" painted

by Titian (1564–65) features a threatening background of the Venetian skyline tormented by the billowing smoke and flames of a fire.

Walk toward the Grand Canal, which is clearly visible from the campo. When you reach the embankment, turn left and walk along the Riva del Carbo (where coal was once

⊠ See also area map pages 72–73
▶ Piazza San Marco
↔ 0.75 mile (1 km)
🕐 1 hour
▶ Piazza San Marco

NOT TO BE MISSED
- La Vecia del Morter
- Palazzo Loredan
- Teatro Goldoni
- Bacino Orseolo

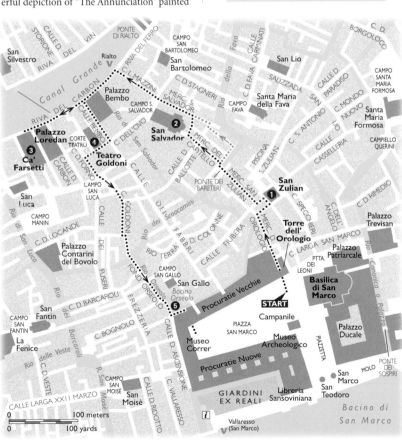

The Bacino Orseolo, behind the Piazza San Marco, is one of eight stations where gondolas are always ready for passengers.

unloaded) to the **Palazzo Loredan** and **Ca' Farsetti** ❸ (see p. 59). These two palaces are both in the 13th-century Veneto-Byzantine style. Ca' Farsetti (the brown one) and the Palazzo Loredan, its white twin, are now joined and serve as City Hall. On Saturday mornings it's not unusual to see bridal couples, just married by the mayor, posing on the balcony. At the corner of the Calle del Carbon, look at the palace wall: There is a small marble **Piscopia Plaque** in honor of Elena Lucrezia Cornaro Piscopia, who was born in this palace and on June 25, 1678, became the first woman in the world ever to earn a university diploma (at the University of Padua).

Retrace your steps to Calle Bembo, and turn right, then walk to the next open space, and turn right again. In front of you is the **Teatro Goldoni** ❹, named for Carlo Goldoni, the Venetian playwright (1707–1793) who specialized in comedies based on Venetian life written in the Venetian dialect.

The theater boasts three pairs of splendid bronze doors made in 1979 by Gianni Aricò. The pair farthest to the left represents the three most beloved Venetian festivals, from top to bottom: The Festival of the Redentore (see p. 198); the Feast of the Madonna della Salute (see p. 188), and the Regata Storica (see p. 188). The central pair shows a series of typical Venetian crafts, and the pair to the right shows Goldoni himself, smiling benevolently on many of his beloved characters.

Above the theater entrance is a series of small bronzes, also by Aricò, representing the six Venetian *sestieri*, from left to right: The Scuola di San Marco; the Basilica di San Marco; The Bridge of the Three Arches; San Giovanni in Bragora; San Giacometto at the Rialto; and Santa Maria della Salute.

Continue walking to the Calle de Forno, where you turn left and enter **Campo San Luca.** Cross the square diagonally leftward and walk down the Calle Goldoni, which with only a few little doglegs will bring you to a largish bridge and onto the Fondamenta Orseolo, and the **Bacino Orseolo** ❺. This small basin, named for Doge Pietro Orseolo II (R. 991–1009), is one of the eight official gondola stations—usually completely full. It's pretty interesting to watch how the gondoliers manage to maneuver their craft in what appears to be no space whatsoever. Pass under the covered arcade to your left, and reenter the Piazza San Marco. ■

Western San Marco

THE CONTINUATION OF WHAT MIGHT BE CALLED VENICE'S downtown area, this neighborhood contains many beautiful churches and campos. While a good number of the palaces are still in use, either as apartments or offices, the prevailing impression is that of an area that's more looked at than lived in these days. Nevertheless, the atmosphere can soften in the late afternoon, when the Campo Santo Stefano fills up with children at play.

Gondoliers can await you at many other places, usually by a bridge, such as here, just under the Ponte delle Ostreghe.

One of the saddest sights of western San Marco is the melancholy looming bulk of what was once one of the world's great opera houses, the theater for which Verdi composed *Rigoletto* and *La Traviata*. A terrific blaze gutted **La Fenice** on January 29, 1996, and, at the time of writing, the restoration work has only just begun. Predictions as to how long it will take continue to change. You could stop by to check on progress, but then turn your attention instead to the lovely churches in the area, some of which have stories to tell of local families and adventurers.

One of several churches dedicated to Old Testament figures,

San Moisè was rebuilt in 1682 by Alessandro Tremignon, who was commissioned by the Fini family to design the wildly baroque facade that celebrates the family's mercantile adventures. This is a building that's easy to ridicule, but perhaps not when it is compared with the hideous sterility of the Hotel Bauer-Grünwald just to the right. Inside, the extravagant altarpiece shows Moses receiving the Ten Commandments atop a Mount Sinai literally hewn and polished from a solid piece of rock.

The church of **Santa Maria del Giglio,** nominally dedicated to St. Mary of the Lily, is also known as the church of the

Western San Marco
- Map pp. 72–73

La Fenice
- Map p. 72
- Campo San Fantin
- 1 to Giglio or S. Angelo

San Moisè
- Map p. 73
- Campo San Moisè
- 041 528 5840
- Closed a.m.
- 1 to Vallaresso or Giglio

The 15th-century church of Santo Stefano has one of only four "ship's-keel" wooden ceilings in Venice.

Santa Maria del Giglio

- 🅰 Map p. 72
- ✉ Campo Santa Maria del Giglio
- ☎ 041 275 0462
- 💲 $
- 🚣 1 to Santa Maria del Giglio

Santo Stefano

- 🅰 Map p. 72
- ✉ Campo Santo Stefano
- ☎ 041 522 5061
- 💲 $
- 🚣 1, 82 to Accademia; 82 to San Samuele

Zobenigo (the Slavic family who contributed to its foundation in the 10th century), but it's the Barbaro family that is celebrated on its facade (Giuseppe Sardi, 1680–83). Front and center is Antonio Barbaro, with the baton and distinctive flat-topped hat of a *capitano da mar*. The jewel of the facade is the series of six marble relief panels showing Dalmatian or Italian fortified areas that were significant in Barbaro's career, from left to right: Zara, Candia (Crete), Padova (Padua), Rome, Corfu, and Split.

Renowned as a splendid example of Venetian High Gothic of the 15th century, the church of **Santo Stefano** is especially noted for its vast coffered wooden ceiling in the "ship's-keel" style. The church, which has always belonged to the Augustinian monks, contains monuments to some of Venice's most noted figures. Foremost is the bronze seal on the floor of the main aisle marking the tomb (by Filippo Parodi, 1630–1702) of Doge Francesco Morosini (1619–1694), victor of the wars in the Peloponnese. There are also three

paintings by Tintoretto from his mature period: "The Last Supper," "The Washing of the Feet," and "Christ in the Garden."

On the outside wall, to the left as you leave, there is a marble tablet dated June 20, 1663, one of many posted around the city bearing admonitions either from the government or various other civic bodies. This one warns that near the church it is forbidden to gamble, set up stands, "sell things," or blaspheme (a common occurrence in a market or gambling situation), and that transgressors risk prison, the galleys, or banishment.

In a side area just off the campo you will see the **Palazzo Pisani.** The Pisani family were wealthy businessmen who were the first, in the 14th century, to found an exchange bank at the Rialto, and in 1614–15, Alvise Pisani commissioned architect Bartolomeo Manopola to build his new residence here. The parties were legendary—in 1784 Almoro Alvise I gave a banquet and ball for 800 guests in honor of King Gustave III of Sweden. The dinner was served by 170 waiters, and the king dined off a massive dinner service of gold made specially for the occasion. On departing, he remarked that he would never have been able to offer the same welcome to Pisani in Stockholm. The eventual bankruptcy of the family came as no surprise, and, on the fall of the republic, their goods were distributed to their creditors, and the palace was divided into apartments. The city acquired the palace in 1940, and it now houses the Benedetto Marcello Conservatory of Music. ■

Fires & firemen

Fire, much more than water, has historically been Venice's mortal enemy. Catastrophic blazes destroyed the Palazzo Ducale and the Basilica di San Marco in 976 and 1479, half of Venice burned down in 1105, and the entire Rialto market area went up in flames in 1515. The most recent disaster was the destruction of La Fenice.

Venetian houses are connected, and often have highly combustible fill such as wood shavings in the spaces between the walls. Buildings can be full of complicated empty spaces that act as virtual chimneys, and firemen called to extinguish a blaze in one house frequently discover that the fire began several houses away.

There are 120 firemen in the Venice detachment. As anywhere, putting out fires is their least common task: They also rescue cats up trees, help old ladies who are locked out of their houses, capture swarms of bees, and secure areas where chunks of plaster have fallen off houses. They also respond to boats in distress and fish out floating debris that could be a hazard to navigation.

When there's a fire, they leap into boats specially designed to slip through the narrow canals, and they have to know not only the shortest route to the fire, but also how to get there in extreme tidal conditions—high tide makes it impossible to get under some bridges, and very low tides prevent the boat from getting anywhere. The water to quench the fire is pumped either straight from the canal, or from a hydrant. ■

Only the walls remain of La Fenice after the fire of January 29, 1996. Rebuilding has just begun.

More places to visit in San Marco

The "snailshell" staircase of the Palazzo Contarini del Bovolo illustrates both a love of decoration and engineering skill.

PALAZZO CONTARINI DEL BOVOLO

Hidden away down a side street from Campo Manin is this elegant palace with its distinctive spiral outer staircase, hence the Venetian nickname *bovolo,* or snail. The tiny garden, with seven ancient wellheads, sets it off beautifully. The palace is closed to the public, but you can climb the staircase, and the view from five stories up is charming.

🅰 Map p. 72 ✉ Corte Contarini del Bovolo
☎ 041 521 7521 🕐 Closed Nov.–March 💲 $
🚤 Sant'Angelo, Giglio

PALAZZO FORTUNY

In the half-hidden Campo San Beneto this 15th-century palace, formerly the Palazzo Pesaro degli Orfei, was originally built for the Pesaro family. In the late 19th century it was bought by the Catalonian artist Mariano Fortuny, who rediscovered the 15th-century techniques for dyeing fabrics and weaving gold and silver thread. His fabrics adorned such turn-of-the-20th-century divas as Eleanora Duse, Sarah Bernhardt, and Isadora Duncan. After a lengthy restoration, the palace now houses the **Museo Fortuny,** with permanent and changing exhibitions, and is again open to the public.

🅰 Map p. 72 ✉ Campo San Beneto ☎ 041
520 0975 🕐 Closed Mon. 💲 $$
🚤 Sant'Angelo

PALAZZO GRASSI

One of Venice's most impressive museums, the Palazzo Grassi may lack the warmth of the Accademia, but it offers state-of-the-art facilities and specializes in the sort of blockbuster traveling exhibitions—Scythian Gold, Art of the Maya—that no other museum in the city can, or will, take on. There are usually long lines to get in; it can be best to go at an odd hour, such as lunchtime, to avoid the worst of the crowds. The museum has an excellent shop.

🅰 Map p. 72 ✉ San Samuele ☎ 041 523
1680 💲 $$ 🚤 Sant'Angelo ∎

Entertainment history

If you venture down the Calle del Traghetto that branches off the Calle Larga XXII Marzo, you'll find yourself in the little Corte del Teatro San Moisè. No theater remains, but this is a historic spot in the history of entertainment. Two stone tablets on the wall commemorate the theater where the first opera by the 18-year-old Gioacchino Rossini was performed on November 3, 1810. Nearly a century later, on July 9, 1896, the same theater witnessed the first movies shown in Venice, brought here by the Lumière brothers. ∎

Venice's largest *sestiere*, Castello first took its name from the massive fortification that once defended it, and later also from the castle-like Arsenale. Here one can still sense the military and maritime muscle that made Venice great.

Castello & eastern districts

A Greek lion guards the Arsenale.

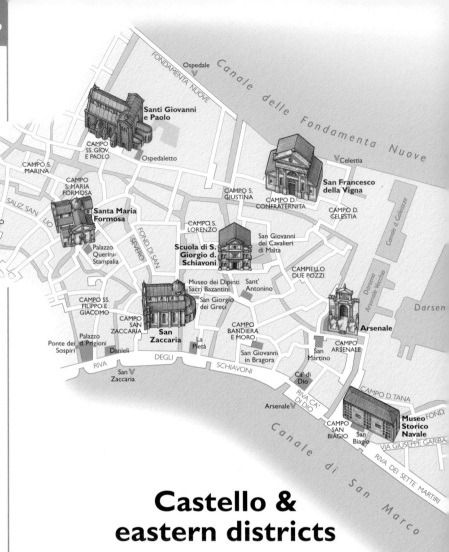

Castello & eastern districts

CASTELLO ARGUABLY BOASTS THE WIDEST RANGE OF SIGHTS IN ALL VENICE, from the splendor of the Basilica di Santi Giovanni e Paolo to the working-class reaches of the Via Garibaldi. And it is the perfect area for a walk in the green shady spaces of the Public Gardens, or for strolls along the breezy edge of the Lagoon, a breath of the country in a city whose stones can sometimes begin to weigh you down.

Even in Venice there is a north–south divide: The Castellani are those who live in Castello and, by extension, in the whole area on the northern side of the Grand Canal; the Nicolotti are the southerners, taking their name from the area surrounding the church of San Nicolò dei Mendicoli. The rivalry between the two was often intense, sometimes reaching

the point of street battles (either spontaneous or secretly fostered by the government).

Castello had reason to be proud: It was where the Arsenale was based, unquestionably the core (along with the Rialto Market) of Venice's power. But today, the farther east you go from San Marco, the less you feel the city's pull. Here you'll find campos without so much as a café or a public telephone, and little streets that are filled more with laundry flapping on the lines than with people. At the farthest edge, where San Pietro di Castello raises its lone white campanile, the crush of San Marco is long forgotten.

Castello has some of Venice's greatest Gothic and baroque masterpieces. The Basilica di Santi Giovanni e Paolo, with the tombs of 25 doges, is often called the city's Pantheon, but San Zaccaria and San Francesco della Vigna have their own glory. And for a refreshing blast of the bizarre, the Biennale (see box p. 46), the international exposition of modern art, fills the Public Gardens' pavilions with every sort of oddness. ■

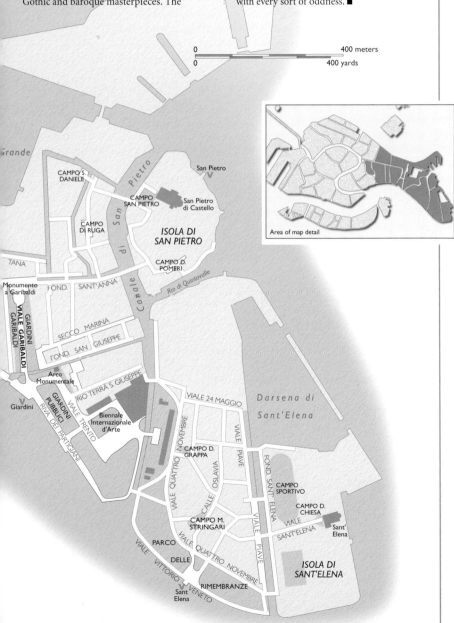

0 ———— 400 meters
0 ———— 400 yards

Area of map detail

Santi Giovanni e Paolo

THIS MAGNIFICENT CHURCH NAMED FOR STS. JOHN AND Paul is one of Venice's greatest marvels. It was begun in 1246 on land that was then on the edge of the Lagoon—land that Doge Jacopo Tiepolo had donated to the Dominican order. Nearly 200 years in construction, the church was finally consecrated in 1430. The largest Gothic church in Venice, Santi Giovanni e Paolo is 281 feet (85 m) long and 106 feet (32 m) high—almost the same size as its contemporary, the Franciscan church of the Frari. And though many consider the Frari to be more appealing, Santi Giovanni e Paolo is unquestionably in the premier league.

"San Zanipolo," as the Venetian dialect has it (though you never hear Venetians actually say that any more), is often termed the "Pantheon" of Venice because of the notables who are entombed here. You will see the tombs of Venice's greatest heroes: Vettor Pisani, victor over the Genoese at Chioggia (1380); Marcantonio Bragadin, martyred by the Turks after the siege of Cyprus (1571); Lazzaro Mocenigo, who vanquished the Turkish fleet in the Dardanelles (1656); Doge Leonardo Loredan, who shielded Venice from the attacks of the League of Cambrai (1508); and the monument to Sebastiano Venier, victor of the Battle of Lepanto (1571).

The facade, now plain brick, was originally covered with multi-colored marble slabs. The marble entrance (made in 1459 by Bartolomeo Bon) incorporates pairs of columns that were made for the Cathedral of the Virgin at Torcello. Six ancient sarcophagi flank the doorway; the second and third from the left contain the remains of Doge Jacopo Tiepolo (died 1249), appropriately the first to be buried here, and his son, Doge Lorenzo Tiepolo (died 1275).

Inside, the nave gives a striking impression of length and height, with the typically Venetian

combination of stone and brick. The central area once contained the friars' wooden choirstalls, an echo of the arrangement that still exists at the Frari; they were removed in 1682 to make more room for the public religious ceremonies, particularly doges' funerals.

One surprising fact is that the interior you see today is, in many respects, different from the one the doges knew. A large number of the paintings as well as the elaborate tombs themselves have been moved around over time, switching places with each other for various reasons. And not a few of the artworks and monuments were brought here from other churches, mainly those that were closed or destroyed by Napoleon in 1807.

The circuit of the interior starts along the right-hand wall. First, look for the tomb of Marcantonio Bragadin, flayed alive by the Turks after the fall of Cyprus in 1571; the urn contains his skin. The monument is by Vincenzo Scamozzi (late 16th century) and the bust by Tiziano Asetti (1607), but the black-and-white fresco depicting his torture is of uncertain attribution.

The magnificent nine-section painting, "St. Vincent Ferrer" (Giovanni Bellini, 1465), depicts a variety of saints, with the great healing saint in the center. Note the

Santi Giovanni e Paolo

🅰 Map p. 100

✉ Campo Santi Giovanni e Paolo

☎ 041 523 5913

🚊 41, 42 to Fondamenta Nuove; 51, 52 to Ospedale

striking effect of the light in the painting, which appears to come from slightly below the faces, one of Bellini's innovations. The three scenes on the bottom row show miracles wrought by the saint, fascinating genre scenes often overshadowed by the main figures.

Then you come to two chapels. The first is Our Lady of Peace, dedicated to a Byzantine icon brought to Venice in 1349. The overwhelming baroque monument to the Valier family here is the work of Andrea Tirali (1737); "The three seem to be taking a majestic 'curtain' like the leading actors in the theater," wrote Da Mosto in his history of the doges. The other is the chapel of San Domenico, which contains Giambattista Battista Piazzetta's "Glory of St. Dominic"

(1727)—one of the best works of 18th-century Venice. It was damaged by an Austrian bomb in 1916.

The right transept has a splendid Gothic stained-glass window, probably the most beautiful product of the Murano glass furnaces. The upper part is from drawings by Bartolomeo Vivarini; those of the Virgin, St. John the Baptist, and St. Peter are by Cima de Conegliano; those along the bottom are by Gerolamo Mocetto (1531). Below the window, to the right, is a painting of "The Charity of St. Antonino Pierozzi of Florence" by Lorenzo Lotto (1480–1556). Note the crowd scene, with monks and townspeople scrambling for the saint's alms.

The **Chapel of the Crucifixion,** to the right of the high altar, was the seat of the Scuola

The Dominican order still tends the splendid Gothic basilica, which boasts the monuments of 25 doges.

"St. Vincent Ferrer" altarpiece, by Giovanni Bellini (1465)

di San Girolamo, or of "The Condemned," as this charitable group devoted itself to the care of those sentenced to death (see the stone to the right of the altar). On the right wall is the tomb of Vettor Pisani (died 1370), who defeated the Genoese fleet at Chioggia. Only the statue, by an anonymous sculptor at the end of the 14th century, is original; the rest is a modern reconstruction of the tomb which was originally in the church of St. Antonio in Castello.

The **chancel** contains some of Venice's supreme funerary art. Facing the high altar, from right to left counterclockwise, you will see first the 15th-century tomb of Doge Michele Morosini (he died in 1382), which Ruskin called the "richest monument of the Gothic period in Venice." Next comes the tomb of Doge Leonardo Loredan (died 1521), designed by Girolamo Grapiglia in 1572, which celebrates the valor of Venice in resisting the League of Cambrai. The statue is also by Girolamo Grapiglia (1572). Most art historians regard the monument of Doge Andrea Vendramin (died 1478; monument 1493 by Pietro and Tullio Lombardo) as the masterpiece of Venetian Renaissance funerary art.

Starting down the left aisle, from the high altar toward the main entrance, you will see over the sacristy doorway two monuments to the Venier family: The tomb of Doge Antonio Venier (R.1382–1400), one of the earliest doges' tombs in the church, is the work of an unidentified follower of the Dalle Masegne family (early 15th century); the other is the monument to Doge Sebastiano Venier, victor of the Battle of Lepanto in 1571 (see pp. 34–35). The bronze statue (1907) is by Antonio dal Zotto.

The **Chapel of the Rosary** was built by the Confraternity of the Rosary in thanksgiving for the victory of Lepanto on the feast of the Madonna of the Rosary in 1571. A fire on the night of August 15, 1867, destroyed 34 masterpieces, among which was the ceiling painting by Tintoretto, a painting by Giovanni Bellini, and one by Titian which had been put there for safekeeping. One of its greatest treasures is the "Annunciation, Assumption and The Adoration of the Shepherds" by Paolo Veronese, placed here in 1925 after years in the Vienna Gallery. Not only is his idea of placing the Christ Child's back to the viewer powerfully effective, but the man leaning down toward the donkey is the artist himself.

The **Monumento a Colleoni** (Colleoni Monument) dominates the campo outside. This is one of the masterpieces of Renaissance bronze sculpture—originally gilded—an imposing if idealized portrait of Bartolomeo Colleoni, a mercenary commander from Bergamo depicted in all his ferocity by Florentine sculptor Andrea Verrocchio. It was cast in Venice and set up in 1496. This was 25 years after Colleoni's death, which was a good thing because he would not have wanted to know that his monument ended up here thanks to a deft Venetian maneuver. Colleoni had bequeathed the money for a commemorative statue on condition that it be erected "at San Marco." He obviously intended the Piazza di San Marco, and the Venetian government, which would never have placed a statue to anyone in the piazza, agreed—but then placed it here instead, in front of the Scuola Grande of San Marco. Venetians love this story.

The **Scuola Grande di San Marco** faces the Campo San Giovanni e Paolo at right angles to the church. Founded in 1260, it was one of the six "great" Venetian scuole, and the building reflects the work of several outstanding architects, notably Pietro Lombardo and his sons Tullio and Antonio, who began the reconstruction after a fire in 1485, and Mauro Codussi, who finished it in 1495. With its lavish marble decoration and characteristic crowning lunettes, it is one of the most significant examples of the Lombardo period of the Renaissance. Note the two fine marble lions that guard the entrance (guarded in turn by transparent shields), by the Lombardo workshop. When the scuola was suppressed in the early 19th century, the building became the city hospital, which it remains today. The cloister can be visited.

Leaving the campo along Salizzada Santi Giovanni e Paolo,

Verrocchio's statue of mercenary captain Bartolomeo Colleoni (1496)

then following the signs for Santi Giovanni e Paolo, you will soon come to the church of **Santa Maria dei Derelitti,** or **Ospedaletto,** on the corner of Calle Torelli. Founded in 1572, it was restructured by Baldassare Longhena in the 17th century, and like several others, it was attached to a "hospital," or hospice. These were founded by rich families to benefit the infirm or the elderly, or to give shelter and some education to poor young women. The church's primary fame rests on Longhena's astonishing facade. This looming baroque extravaganza, wildly out of proportion with the narrow street that it faces, bears four huge "grotesque" stone masks such as those Ruskin so detested at Santa Maria Formosa. ∎

Santa Maria dei Derelitti (Ospedaletto)
- Map p. 100
- Salizzada Santi Giovanni e Paolo
- 041 520 0633
- Closed Sun.–Wed. & Oct.–March
- 1, 82 to Rialto; 1, 51, 52 to San Zaccaria; 41, 42, 51, 52 to Fondamenta Nuove

**Campo Santa
Maria Formosa**

 Map p. 100

**Santa Maria
Formosa**

Map p. 100

Campo Santa Maria
Formosa

041 523 4645

$

1, 51, 52 to San
Zaccaria; 1, 82 to
Rialto

Campo Santa Maria Formosa & around

THE CAMPO SANTA MARIA FORMOSA IS ONE OF THE
lovelier large campos, and its charm derives to some extent from its
graceful proportions. Added to this, however, is the atmosphere
provided by the fruit and vegetable stands that offers a glimpse of the
day-to-day bustle once typical of virtually every campo in the city.

The church of **Santa Maria
Formosa** is the most obvious
treasure in the campo that shares
its name. It was founded in the
seventh century, and was the first
church in Venice to be dedicated to
the Virgin Mary. The name comes
from the legend that she appeared
as a *formosa* (buxom) woman to
St. Magnus, and asked him to
construct a church where she

indicated. The present building,
the latest of several, was begun in
1492 by Renaissance architect and
artist Mauro Codussi. With its elegantly unified style, it represents
his first important work. He
respected, to a certain extent, the
Greek-cross form of the earlier,
11th-century building, which had
imitated the central part of the
Basilica di San Marco. The cupola

was rebuilt in 1668 after an earth-quake and again in 1921 after suffering damage from Austrian bombing during World War I.

The facade on the canal was erected in 1542 and dedicated to the *capitano da mar* Vincenzo Cappello, and the frontage that faces the campo (1604) contains portraits of various members of the Cappello family. The small doorway that leads into the bell tower (1688) is guarded by a huge grotesque face (not uncommon, except for its size), which John Ruskin, the English art historian, described as "leering in brutal degradation…too foul to be either pictured or described, or to be beheld for more than an instant." Some experts believe it may have been a representation of an actual person.

One of the church's greatest treasures is the painting, "The Madonna of Mercy" (1473), by Bartolomeo Vivarini, a particularly graceful version of a common pose. Its vibrant, jewel-like colors were recently restored, thanks to a fund raised by two young Venetian tour guides. Over a period of several years, they gave a series of after-work lectures on Venice in the church hall, then donated the sum they had collected in admission fees to the cost of two restorations, as a mark of their appreciation of this work of art.

BEYOND THE CAMPO

On the side of the campo toward the hospital is a modest cream-colored palazzo. On its second-floor facade is a simple tablet saying that this is the **birthplace of Sebastiano Venier,** "the victor of Lepanto" (see pp. 34–35). The Venice empire heaped every conceivable honor upon him, electing him doge virtually by acclamation, rather than by the regular, long-winded election

Right: Carnival masks come in a variety of styles and materials, from traditional papier-mâche to ceramic, leather, and even glass.

Palazzo Querini-Stampalia

⬛ Map p. 100
✉ Campiello Querini-Stampalia
☎ 041 271 1411
🕐 Closed Mon.
💲 $$
⛴ 1, 82 to Rialto; 1, 52 to San Zaccaria; 41, 42, 51, 52 to Fondamenta Nuove

system (see p. 30), but it soon became clear that the qualities that made him a great naval commander also made him almost impossible to deal with as doge.

Stand in the campo facing the main entrance to the church, and behind the church, on the other side of the canal, you will see the Renaissance **Palazzo Querini-Stampalia.** Dating from the early 16th century, it was donated to the city by Giovanni Querini in the 19th century. In spite of the stringent laws that restrict alterations to the exteriors of city buildings, the palazzo's facade has been inexplicably permitted to display neon signs to promote the museum's contents. Its main attraction is the rich collection of naive but highly detailed genre paintings of 18th-century Venetian life by Pietro Longhi. One of the best known is his scene of duck-hunting in the Lagoon. You should put off visiting this collection until you have been in Venice for a few days—you'll be surprised how many of the places you have seen can be recognized here. ∎

The Riva degli Schiavoni was once hectic with ships unloading straw, wine, and other goods. Today it is perfect for a sunset stroll.

A walk along the waterfront

The Riva degli Schiavoni (Slavs) is one of Venice's most beautiful promenades—or would be, if it were not now so cluttered with trinket hawkers, taxi stands, and waterbus stops. Stretching from the Ponte della Paglia nearly to the Arsenale, it was enlarged on landfill several times beginning in the ninth century, using mud dredged from the Grand Canal. As the name indicates, it was the customary landing place for ships belonging to Dalmatian merchants, who imported cured fish and meat.

Begin at the **Palazzo Ducale** (see pp. 88–91), facing the Bacino di San Marco, and begin walking left toward the Arsenale, with the water on your right. Cross the Ponte della Paglia, so named because straw used to be unloaded along the shore here. Pause at the top and look left: You will see the **Ponte dei Sospiri ❶** (Bridge of Sighs) suspended over the canal, linking the Palazzo Ducale and the Prisons. This very poignant name was a late Victorian invention, intended to evoke the sadness of condemned criminals crossing the bridge with a heavy heart to begin their terms of imprisonment.

Next on your left are the **Palazzo delle Prigioni** (New Prisons, see p. 91). On a more cheerful note, the next building is now one of Venice's most luxurious hotels, the **Danieli ❷**.

The bland white annex was built in the late 1950s on land where construction of houses taller than one story had been forbidden for centuries, as it had been the site of the assassination of Doge Vitale Michiel II (1172).

Cross the next bridge; you're now facing an agglomeration of huge bronze statues in the middle of the street, topped by an equestrian hero: This is the monument to **Vittorio Emmanuele II,** the first king of a unified Italy. It is an elaborate homage to Italy's new-found independence, sculpted by Ettore Ferrari (1887) and typical of the grandiose style of its era, but totally out of tune with the more subdued grandeur of Gothic Venice. The church of Santa Maria della Visitazione, better known as **La Pietà ❸** *(Riva degli Schiavoni, tel 041 523 1096, open only for*

cross and immediately turn left onto the Fondamenta dei Furlani. At the end of this small stretch you will come to the **Scuola di San Giorgio degli Schiavoni** ❹ (see p. 113), which is the goal of your little detour.

Coming out of the scuola, walk straight ahead back along the Fondamenta dei Furlani to the end, where it joins the broad street, Salizzada Sant' Antonino, onto which you turn left. The large white church of **Sant' Antonino** is closed for extensive restoration and looks rather derelict. Follow the Salizzada Sant' Antonino to the end and turn right. You will arrive in a spacious campo with two names: Campo Bandiera e Moro, or more

Below: The 14th-century Dandolo family palace is now the Danieli Hotel, converted in the 1950s by a man named Da Niel.

concerts & Mass; vaporetto 1, 51, 52 to San Zaccaria), is more simply called Vivaldi's Church. It was here that Antonio Vivaldi (1677–1741), the master of 17th-century Venetian music, composed many of his masterpieces, which were performed by the young women of the adjoining orphanage and hospice. Over the main doorway outside is a simple but very moving 19th-century relief of "Charity" by E. Marsili that shows the Madonna holding the infant Jesus on her lap; instead of the usual formal pose, the baby here has turned around and thrown his arms spontaneously around his mother's neck. On the outside right wall of the church, down the Calle della Pietà, is a square, dark brown tablet. The inscription (1548) threatens everything from "thunderbolts of God" to excommunication to anyone who, "having the means to care for them," might think of shuffling off their illegitimate children into the care of the hospice.

Keep going along this street, the Calle della Pietà, to the end; take a left, then a right, and go straight along Calle Bosello until you reach a broad street called the Salizzada dei Greci. Turn right here and wander along this hidden neighborhood artery, lined with useful stores selling fresh meat, pasta, housewares, and plumbing supplies. You'll come to a bridge, which you should

commonly San Giovanni in Bragora. The first name refers to three Venetian martyrs of the uprising against the Austrians in 1844, the second refers to the church of **San Giovanni in Bragora** ❺ *(Campo Bandiera e Moro, tel 041 520 5906; vaporetto 1, 82, 51, 52 to San Zaccaria, 1 to Arsenale),* which may have been founded as early as the eighth century. It was completely rebuilt in 1475 by Mauro Codussi, who bridged the Gothic and the Renaissance. One of the church's many treasures is the "Baptism of Christ," by Cima da Conegliano (1492–95), who added one of his typically enchanting Veneto landscapes as the background. Recent work has restored the marble to its earlier brightness; look closely at the left wall of the apse surrounding the main altar: The black rectangle that you will see on the narrow carved trim was left to indicate how severely the centuries of candle smoke had stained the stone.

The font in which composer Antonio Vivaldi was baptized is in the alcove in the left aisle with a copy of his baptismal certificate.

As you come out of the church, cross the campo and take the narrow street to the left, the Calle del Dose (Venetian dialect for "doge"). When you reach the Riva degli Schiavoni, pause for a moment and try to imagine the scene, in 1819, when an elephant escaped from its cage here. Fleeing the rifle shots of its pursuers, it took refuge in the nearby church of Sant' Antonino. The elephant was finally felled by a cannon blast from the artillery corps.

From the Riva degli Schiavoni, turn left and continue to the next bridge, which you cross. The building immediately on your left is known as the **Ca' di Dio** ❻, or "house of God," as pilgrims' hostels were called during the Middle Ages. There has been a hospice here since 1272; ancient documents also record that in 1360 several friars from Genoa

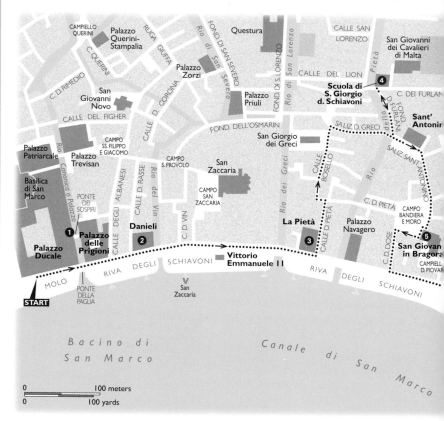

stayed here while on assignment to blow up the Arsenale (they failed). Today it is a private nursing home for the elderly.

Turn left up the next street, the Calle dei Forni (Street of Bakeries). The large building on your right was once the bakery for the Arsenale, and provided bread for the Venetian sailors; it is now used by the navy as offices. At the next corner, turn left onto the Calle di Fondamenta Pegola, and take your next right onto the Fondamenta Pegola. At the next corner on your right is the church of **San Martino** ❼ *(Campo San Martino, tel 041 523 0487; vaporetto 1 to Arsenale).*

This church is dedicated to St. Martin of Tours, who cut his cloak in half and gave it to a poor beggar (see the Gothic relief carved over the doorway on the church's right corner). The first church on the site was built in the seventh century, but the present structure is the result of several rebuildings, the latest by

The church of San Martino is two steps from the Arsenale, as the saint was patron of many of the shipbuilding craft guilds.

Jacopo Sansovino (1540). The house next door, facing the canal, was where the Armenian abbot, Mechitar de Sebaste, stayed in 1717 while establishing the monastery on the island of San Lazzaro (see p. 210).

Coming out of the church, turn right along the Fondamenta di Fronte and continue to Campo Arsenale, where you will find yourself in front of the Arsenale (see pp. 116–17). ∎

▲ See also area map p. 100
➤ Palazzo Ducale
⟷ 1 mile (1.6 km)
⊕ 1 hour
➤ Arsenale

NOT TO BE MISSED

- Ponte dei Sospiri (Bridge of Sighs)
- La Pietà
- Scuola di San Giorgio degli Schiavoni
- San Giovanni in Bragora

San Zaccaria

Among the myriad paintings in the church of San Zaccaria, the greatest is surely Giovanni Bellini's glowing "Madonna and Child with Saints" (1506).

THIS IMPOSING CHURCH, WHICH MAY HAVE BEEN founded in the seventh century by St. Magnus, is another of the few named for Old Testament prophets—Zachariah, the father of John the Baptist, whose body was donated to Venice by the Byzantine emperor Leo V. The doges Agnello and Giustiniano Partecipazio (810–827 and 827–29, respectively) added a Benedictine convent to the church to house the relic.

San Zaccaria

🅰 Map p. 100

✉ Campo San Zaccaria

☎ 041 522 1257

🚊 1, 41, 42, 51, 52 to San Zaccaria; 1, 4-G2 (summer only) to San Marco "Vallaresso"

There are two approaches to the Campo San Zaccaria, the more beautiful being from Campo San Provolo, with its carved relief of the Madonna and Child on the portal. The campo also belonged to the convent, and the gates were locked at night—you can still see the heavy metal hooks for the hinges in the stone doorposts. The convent (see p. 132) was abolished in 1810.

The church was rebuilt after a disastrous fire in 1105, but the present edifice was designed by Gothic architect Antonio Gambello in 1458; in 1483 the Renaissance master Mauro Codussi took over the project and it was finally completed in 1515. On the right

side of the church are two chapels that have been created from the earlier church. The **Chapel of St. Athanasius** was once the central part (1505), and contains relatively rare wooden choir stalls by Francesco and Marco Cozzi (1455–1464). The **Chapel of St. Tarasius** was originally the apse of the earlier church, and you can still see the 12th-century mosaic floor around the altar, as well as the crypt of the very first ninth-century church.

Most of the paintings are unremarkable, but there is an admirable marble statue of San Zaccaria by Alessandro Vittoria (16th-century) over the main doorway. ■

Scuola di San Giorgio degli Schiavoni

One of Vittore Carpaccio's paintings for the scuola of the Slavs, "St. Jerome conducts the lion to the monastery" (1507–1509)

THE MERCHANTS OF THE DALMATIAN AND ISTRIAN coastline prospered in Venice ever since the year 1000, when Venice acquired these territories as Venetian colonies. Istrian stone, a form of white marble well suited to taking heavy wear, was a major import from the eastern Adriatic because it was ideal for use as palace foundations and in the borders of the embankments. In 1451 these traders established their own confraternity dedicated to Sts. George, Tryphon, and Jerome.

The small, square building was reconstructed by Giovanni de Zan in 1551. Over the doorway outside is a relief of St. George and the dragon (1552) by Pietro da Salò, who also sculpted the Gobbo di Rialto. It houses one of the most engaging cycles of pictures to be found in Venice, or anywhere—Vittore Carpaccio's scenes from the lives of Dalmatia's patron saints (1507–1509). The large panels, brimming with color and sharp detail, are full of appealing little touches: the pathetic groveling of the subdued dragon; the panic-stricken friars fleeing from St. Jerome's very placid lion; and, perhaps the best known, the scene of St. Augustine at work in his study being watched by his irresistibly alert, tiny white dog (see pp. 164–65). The rooms, compact but richly decorated, are typical of the scuole of smaller organizations. There is also a small adjacent room displaying various artifacts pertaining to the still active community. Upstairs is a large meeting room also used as the chapel, with art representing scenes and characters from Dalmatian history. ■

Scuola di San Giogio degli Schiavoni

🅰 Map p. 100
✉ Calle & Fondamenta dei Furlani
☎ 041 522 8828
🕐 Closed Mon.
💲 $
⛴ 1, 51, 52 to San Zaccaria

San Francesco della Vigna

Below: Palladio's classical facade is guarded by imposing statues, not of St. Francis, but of Moses and St. Paul.

ONE OF VENICE'S MOST IMPOSING AND IMPORTANT churches is just enough off the beaten track to add an air of remoteness to its appeal. In fact, in the 13th century, when the first Franciscan monastery was built here, the *vigne* (vineyards) were still plentiful in this area. One cloister, unfortunately closed to the public, is still full of vines.

San Francesco della Vigna

- Map p. 100
- Campo della Confraternita
- 041 520 6102
- 1 to Arsenale; 41, 42, 51, 52 to Celestia

Opposite: God the Father was added 50 years later to Negroponte's "Madonna and Child" (1463–69). The sky resembles ocean waves.

Popular legend maintains that St. Mark took refuge from a storm on this island, and an angel appeared to him, predicting the future founding of Venice and saying "Pax tibi, Marce, evangelista meus" ("Peace to you, Mark, my evangelist"). This is the motto that traditionally has been inscribed, with only a few exceptions, on the book that the lion of St. Mark holds with his paw.

When the original church, dating from 1253, was in danger of collapse, Jacopo Sansovino was entrusted with the rebuilding project and designed what many consider to be the first example of Renaissance architecture in Venice (1543). The facade was added in 1569 by Andrea Palladio in his typical Greek-temple style.

Both the right and left sides of the nave are lined with chapels, but rather than being dedicated to saints, each is devoted to a particular noble family, whose names read like a litany of Venetian fame (and philanthropy, as they paid for the space). Primary among them, with two magnificent tombs flanking the high altar, is the Gritti family. Doge Andrea Gritti (1523–1538) not only commissioned the rebuilding, but also laid the foundation stone. Among other exploits were his many liaisons, which led to some opposition when his name was initially put forward for the office of doge.

Among the numerous works of art are paintings by Giorgione, Veronese, Vivarini, and Giovanni Bellini (in the sacristy), but possibly the most memorable painting is the "Madonna and Child" (1463–69) by one of the friars, Antonio Falier da Negroponte. This elaborate and vivid work is a mesmerizing mix of Renaissance and Gothic elements (and even contains bits of painted paper). The effect is heightened by the fact that it is illuminated only when money is dropped into the lighting machine; the blast of brilliance makes it fairly leap to life.

To the left of the high altar is the small chapel of St. Jerome, or Badoer-Giustinian, recently restored, with beautiful marble relief carvings of Old Testament prophets lining its walls. Those on the right and left walls nearest to the altar, depicting the four evangelists, are by Tullio (died 1532) and Antonio Lombardo (died 1516). Carvings of the Twelve Prophets and the 18 stories from the life of Jesus are by Pietro Lombardo and helpers (1435–1515).

Beyond the sacristy you will find the only one of the monastery's several cloisters that is accessible to the public. The numerous tombstones are now mostly worn away, but on the south side is a slab bearing the simple outline of a shored-up ship. It marks the grave of the *Gastaldo*, or leader, of the *Calafai* (shipcaulkers) who were active in the Arsenale. ∎

One Italian nobleman once declared that he would rather be lord of Venice's Arsenale than of the four fairest cities in Italy.

Arsenale

VENICE WAS GREAT BECAUSE IT WAS POWERFUL, AND from 1104 its power depended on the ships that were built in the Arsenale. All sorts of craft were produced here, from the slim galleys that fought naval battles to the doughtier vessels that carried merchandise in convoys throughout the Mediterranean (and even as far as Flanders and the Black Sea). All had their part to play in Venice's prosperity and power, but the most splendid was undoubtedly the *Bucintoro,* the doge's fabulously carved and decorated ceremonial barge.

Arsenale

- Map p. 100
- Campo Arsenale
- Not open to the public
- 1 to Arsenale; 41, 42, 51, 52 to Celestia

The Venetian government had a rich appreciation of its dependence on the Arsenale, and the *Arsenalotti,* or workers, enjoyed an unequaled array of rights and privileges. Special security forces would patrol the premises at night, rowing along the encircling canals to check the nearly 2 miles (3 km) of fortress-like brick battlements. The deep-voiced bell in the campanile of San Marco, nicknamed the *marangon* (carpenter), still tolls every day at 2 p.m. as it did for centuries to signal the end of the lunch break in the Arsenale.

A then revolutionary system of assembly-line construction was

around a vat of boiling pitch, of all the workers who are caulking a ship (the *calafai;* see p. 114), those who are making oars, hammering away on the prow or the stern, or repairing rudders.

The Arsenale is the property of the Italian Navy, and the public is not admitted. However, you can step inside the foyer of the entrance building; on the left-hand wall is a long metal ruler, one of the few remaining examples of the "Venetian measure," which was the

The Arsenale is still Navy property, as attests this *quadriga* of lieutenants.

dazzlingly efficient, and a famous anecdote recounts that Doge Alvise Mocenigo I, to impress the visiting Henry III of France and Poland, had a galley completely built during the time it took to consume the official banquet. Apparently, this was not an isolated example of this particular display of efficiency, but it was often carried out for the benefit of visiting dignataries, not least to remind them how quickly Venice could get ships and men to sea in time of war. In fact, during the late 16th century, in preparation for another conflict with Turkey, the Arsenale turned out a galley a day for a hundred days. Dante, in *The Divine Comedy,* referred to the *Arzana* in a famous stanza, now carved on a marble plaque to the left of the main doorway; he describes the frenetic labor

shipbuilders' own particular standard of dimensions.

The Renaissance entrance (Antonio Gambello, 1460) is flanked by two very stately lions, taken as spoils of war from the port of Piraeus by Francesco Morosini in 1687 when he reconquered the Peloponnese. Note the fading runic letters on the shoulder of the lion to the left of the entrance, which were carved by a Norse soldier fighting in Greece for the Byzantine emperor (11th century). The other lion, much more archaic, may be from the Lion Terrace at Delos.

Looking into the Arsenale from atop the wooden bridge, you can see the rows of what remain of some of the boathouses. Though some ship repair still goes on here, most of the vast area is unused. ■

This is a model of the *Bucintoro*, the doge's state galley, which was kept in the Arsenale between state occasions.

Museo Storico Navale

AT THE POINT WHERE YOU MAY BEGIN TO THINK THAT Venice is all about churches and paintings of saints, spend a morning at the Museo Storico Navale. Here, in a sturdy building that was once the Arsenale's granary, is an astonishing array of nautical treasures that reflect one of the fundamental realities of Venice's existence: its supremacy at sea.

Museo Storico Navale

- 🗺 Map p. 100
- ✉ Campo San Biagio
- ☎ 041 520 0276
- 🕐 Closed Sun.
- 💲 $
- ⛴ 1 to Arsenale

Flanking the entrance are huge anchors, taken from two Imperial Austro-Hungarian battleships of World War I. Inside, the first floor has rooms dedicated to artillery and forts of the Venetian empire, World War II assault weapons, and a small room dedicated to Admiral Angelo Emo (1721–1792), last hero of the Venetian navy. The second floor also has some impressive exhibits, including a vast triangular

silk flag of the Morosini family (16th century), delicately drawn 17th-century parchment maps of the Mediterranean, and two huge wooden sculptures that may have adorned the galley flagship of Admiral Morosini (1684).

Probably the museum's greatest claim to fame is its wealth of wooden ship models, beautifully finished and perfect in every detail, some almost full size. Virtually every type

is represented, from sleek, arrow-like warships to tubby merchant ships; from sailing vessels to those powered only by oars. Pride of place goes to the large model of the *Bucintoro*, the doge's ceremonial galley. Putting the scale of these models into perspective are a reproduction of a galley oar that stretches almost the length of the room and a massive carved tiller from a 17th-century Genoese galley.

The third floor has a fascinating array of non-military lagoon boats, either full size or models, with an assortment of traditional fishing gear. Other displays include regatta pennants from the early 19th century, fanciful 17th-century *ferri*, the metal decorations for gondola prows, the black hat with silver decoration once worn by the gondolier

in the service of a noble family, and three gondolas, one of which belonged to the art collector Peggy Guggenheim. Assorted other treasures include the bronze bell that for centuries signaled the beginning and end of the day's work. An echoing building just outside the museum contains yet more boats. ■

The many models of both warships and merchant vessels impress even the casual viewer with the Venetians' nautical skill and ingenuity.

More places to visit in Castello & eastern districts

MUSEO DEI DIPINTI SACRI BIZANTINI

Lest you think you may risk being overwhelmed by icons, this museum is a small treasure-house—essentially one and a half rooms upstairs in the Institute for Hellenic Studies. The collection of 16th- to 18th-century icons, from the hands of artists from Crete, mainland Greece, and the Veneto, is refreshingly varied and shows some subjects rarely depicted even by better known artists. Among them is a very fanciful "Noah's Ark" (17th century), which, apart from the animals boarding the vessel, shows a very distracted and dubious Mrs. Noah dressed like a Flemish matron as painted by a Greek; "Doubting Thomas" (17th century), a powerful image in which Jesus, more than inviting his hesitant apostle to touch his wounds, has actually gripped him by the wrist and is literally

A vendor at Viale Garibaldi sells produce the Venetian way—by boat.

forcing the hand into his side. In the "Returning of the Blind Man's Sight" (1686), the artist has rendered the miraculous moment with extraordinary tenderness, showing Jesus barely touching the eyelid as the man trustingly holds his face up to meet the delicate reaching finger. The small adjacent room contains a number of liturgical vestments and other church treasures; there is also a long, tattered parchment written in cursive Greek which dates from the fifth century.
🅜 Map p. 100 ✉ Ponte dei Greci ☎ 041 522 6581 🚤 1, 51, 52, 82 to San Zaccaria

SAN GIORGIO DEI GRECI

Located in Castello—but only just—this Renaissance-style church is what remains of Venice's Greek community, which rose to as many as 5,000 after the fall of Constantinople in 1453. This is the oldest Greek church in the West, paid for by contributions from the Greek community. Most notably these were Greek seamen, but there were also many from Crete, a Venetian colony for 400 years, who formed an important commercial and artistic presence in the city. The church, dedicated to Sante Lombardo (1539–1561), is still used for the Greek Orthodox liturgy. Be sure to walk around the right side of the church outside; the side door is surmounted by a splendid mosaic of St. George slaying the dragon, which in this portrayal looks strangely like a turkey. The schedule of services for each month is posted on the door, in English and in Greek.
🅜 Map p. 100 ✉ Ponte dei Greci ☎ 041 522 5446 🚤 1, 51, 52, 82 to San Zaccaria

VIALE GARIBALDI

This is the main street of the far end of Castello, connecting the Riva dei Sette Martiri (so named for seven partisans who were executed here during World War II) to the Island of San Pietro. Viale Garibaldi is not the only place in Venice where you can see real life being lived beyond the tourist crush, but it's one of the best; the small stores, cafés, and school all seem made for the locals, who pay very little attention to you. Best of all are the fruit and vegetable barges floating at the far end of the street. It's worth noting the triangular house at the corner where the street begins; it bears a stately marble tablet commemorating the residence here of the two explorers, Giovanni Caboto (John Cabot) and his son, Sebastiano, who discovered Newfoundland, Labrador, and Greenland for King Henry VII of England during a 1497–98 voyage.
🅜 Map p. 101 ∎

S lotted into Venice's north-western corner, Cannaregio may seem to lack the grandest monuments and most appealing stores, but the city's second largest *sestiere* has a powerful, haunting appeal that may make it your favorite part of the city.

Cannaregio

A merchant of Venice, possibly one of the Mastelli brothers, on Tintoretto's house

Cannaregio

"CANNAREGIO" PROBABLY COMES FROM THE WORD *CANNE*, OR REEDS, which centuries ago lined the shores of the Cannaregio Canal, at that time usually just muddy beaches. Bunches of Lagoon reeds are still the traditional tool for certain tasks in wooden boatbuilding and repair, particularly when set afire as a sort of torch for stripping old varnish or slowly bending wooden planks, and at least one street name— Calle delle Canne—reflects their once abundant presence.

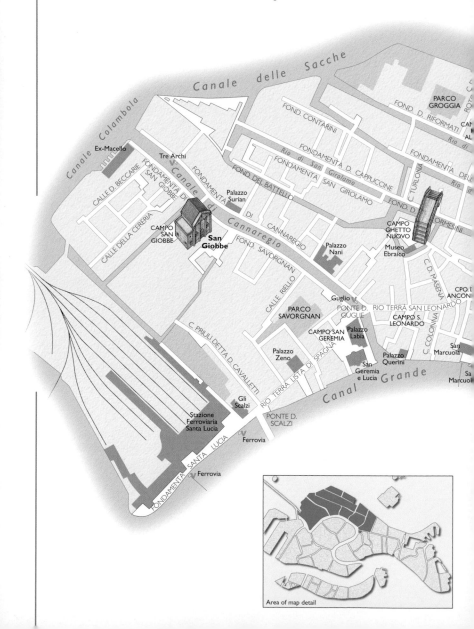

Area of map detail

This area, close to the mainland, was one of the first to be settled, but the city developed faster around Rialto and San Marco and Cannaregio retains an air of remoteness. This is the perfect area for seeing ordinary neighborhood life: old ladies doing their shopping, flocks of children coming home from school, and small stores busy catering to the locals.

Three parallel, long, straight canals rake like fingers deep into this *sestiere*. These were once the main arteries for delivering merchandise that came by boat from the mainland; everything from stone to hay to live animals destined for the slaughterhouses would be

The tranquil Rio de la Sensa

unloaded along these canals. Before the bridge connected Venice to the mainland, this was the main entrance to the city from terra ferma. Now its peak moment of glory each year is one Sunday morning in May, when more than a thousand rowing boats of every type reenter the city in the Canale di Cannaregio at the finish of the annual Vogalonga, after which it returns to the daily routine—the world of mothers and schoolchildren, store workers, and visitors who are passionate for Tintoretto. ∎

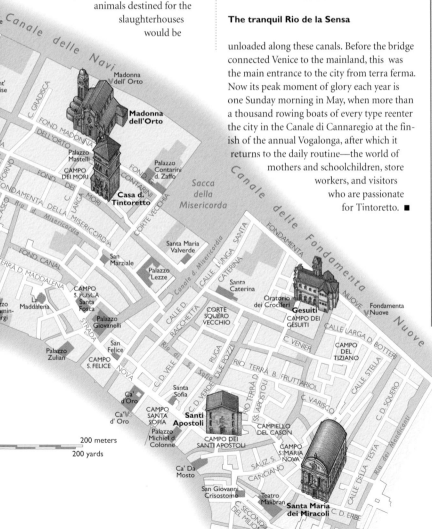

The Ponte dei
Gesuiti is one of
some 400 bridges
in Venice. Until
the 19th century
most Venetian
bridges were of
wood, and
without railings.

Gesuiti & district

THE THREE SMALL STREETS IN FRONT OF THE CHURCH OF
the Gesuiti give a hint of how life around the square used to be—
there is the street of the Cadene (chains), Legnami (carpenters), and
Botteri (barrelmakers.) Not the grandest of locations, for sure, but
the church of the Gesuiti is, as one famous French guidebook would
characteristically say, "worth the voyage," if not to Venice, at least
to Cannaregio.

Gesuiti

- Map p. 123
- Campo dei Gesuiti
- 041 528 6579
- 1 to Ca' d'Oro; 41,
  42, 51, 52 to
  Fondamenta Nuove

The Gesuiti, or Jesuits, had a very
prickly relationship with the
Venetian empire on the basis of a
feud between the pope and La
Serenissima (see p. 34), but their
members were prized as teachers of
the children of noble families. The
church that was built here in the
12th century for the Order of the
Crociferi was rebuilt in 1715 for

the Jesuits by Domenico Rossi,
totally baroque in all its glory, or
horror, depending on your taste.

What you'll find unforgettable is
the interior: The white marble
columns and stone draperies have
been inlaid with green marble to
render the perfect impression of
flocked velvet, totally deceiving the
senses—you will not credit that

Titian painted the "Martyrdom of St. Lawrence" (1558) in honor of Lorenzo Massolo. It was his first attempt to depict a night scene with torch light.

they could be made of stone. The baldachino, or canopy, over the main altar (by Fra Giuseppe Pozzo) echoes that in St. Peter's in Vatican City, with ten twisted columns of green marble inlaid with lapis lazuli. The exquisite stonework of the flooring has been restored. Paintings by Titian ("The Martyrdom of St. Lawrence," 1558) and Tintoretto ("The Assumption of the Virgin Mary," 1555) echo the dramatic nature of the setting. Many famous people of elevated taste have judged this church to be inexcusably excessive, but whatever your view, you could not fail to be impressed by the incredible skill involved in its creation.

The long building attached to the church was once the monastery, but it now serves as a barracks for the *carabinieri* (military police).

The immediate vicinity of the Gesuiti offers relatively little in the way of notable sights or treasures. There were once a large number of monasteries and convents here, and you can still admire their carved portals and enjoy a glimpse into their gardens, but mostly they have been converted to state schools. If one afternoon you happen to pass the former convent and church of Santa Caterina (the closest to the Gesuiti, on the Fondamenta Santa Caterina), the guardian may possibly be prevailed upon to let you have a quick peek at the garden, where various segments of Roman columns lie scattered around.

Just behind the Gesuiti, along the Calle Larga dei Botteri, is a long brick wall surrounding what was the house and workshop of the painter Titian. Over the doorway is a stately plaque bearing his name in Latin, *Vecellius*. If you go around either corner you'll come to the Campo del Tiziano; Titian's house was at Nos. 5181–82, and is marked by a modest plaque. ■

Santa Maria dei Miracoli

Santa Maria dei Miracoli

🅰 Map p. 123

✉ Campo Santa Maria Nova

☎ 041 275 0462

💲 $

🚤 1, 82 to Rialto; 41, 42, 51, 52 to Fondamenta Nuove

The church's best view may be from Campo Santa Maria Nova across the canal.

ONE OF VENICE'S MOST DISTINCTIVE CHURCHES, THE church of St. Mary of the Miracles is more Tuscan than Venetian in style, but its exquisite stonework and its lovely canalside setting make it irresistible. It is also one of the very few Venetian churches that you can see from all four sides.

An exhaustive ten-year restoration effort, funded by the American committee, Save Venice, has unquestionably saved the church and given it a new freshness. The building had been ingeniously designed with cavity walls, allowing humidity to disperse, but when an Austrian team filled in the cavity in the 19th century, the resulting dampness put the entire structure at risk. Today the building is sound again, but the atmosphere has lost its accumulated warmth and it now feels more like a perfectly maintained museum than a church.

This Renaissance gem was consecrated on December 31, 1489, the handiwork of the Tuscan architects Pietro and Tullio Lombardo, which they built to house a miraculous image of the Virgin with Child. The facade is clearly a close relative of their other landmark, the Ca' Dario on the Grand Canal. An old tradition holds that it was decorated with bits of marble left over from work on the Basilica di San Marco.

You, like every other visitor, will undoubtedly want to voice the impression that it's like a little jewel box—and it is. It forms a simple rectangle, with elegantly decorated marble walls and a coffered ceiling showing portraits of some 50 patriarchs and prophets (Pier Maria Pennacchi, 1528). The dramatically raised high altar, reached by steep steps, is clearly reminiscent of San Miniato in Florence. The carvings flanking the steps are small masterpieces, also by the Lombardo family. On the right-hand pilaster at the foot of the altar steps, you'll see one of the Renaissance art works which so outraged (never difficult to do) English art historian John Ruskin (1819–1900): "The man who could carve a child's head so perfectly must have been wanting in all human feeling," he huffed, "to cut it off and tie it by the hair to a vine leaf." ■

Santi Apostoli

YET AGAIN A CHURCH STANDS WHERE A VISION TOLD
St. Magnus to build one—one of eight in Venice, including Santa
Maria Formosa (see p. 106). In this case, it was the Twelve Apostles
who appeared to the saint, advising him to build at a place where he
saw a gathering of twelve cranes.

Santi Apostoli
- Map p. 123
- Campo dei Santi Apostoli
- 041 523 8297
- Closed Sun.
- 1, 82 to Rialto; 41, 42, 51, 52 to Fondamenta Nuove

The seventh-century church was
remodeled several times, and most
of what we see today is the result of
renovations undertaken by Guisto
Pedolo in the mid-18th century.
The bell tower from 1672, is
notable for the antics of an elderly
priest, Domenico Longo, who acci-
dentally fell from it—somehow his
clothing snagged on the clock's
minute hand. Legend maintains
that it slowly carried him to safety.

Inside, the Chapel of the Corner
family is attributed to Mauro
Codussi (1552), and this was the
resting place of the body of the
unfortunate Caterina Corner, the
thwarted and finally deposed
Queen of Cyprus, until her remains
were moved to an even more splendid tomb in the church of San
Salvador. The chapel's altarpiece,
"Communion of St. Lucy," by
Giambattista Tiepolo (1748), is an
almost seductive portrait of an
enchanting young woman oblivious
to the symbol of her martyrdom,
the two eyes resting on a plate in
the foreground.

The church contains a number
of other interesting works: the "Last
Supper" by Cesare da Conegliano
(1583), its background showing
the courtyard of the Doge's Palace
with the Foscari staircase, which
was destroyed in the early 17th century; an exquisite marble sculpture
by Nicolò di Pietro Lamberti (late
14th century) which shows the
Madonna and Child flanked by
small trees; and an otherwise standard scene in which the Blessed
Virgin and Child with various

saints are all completely upstaged
by a large white sheep looking at
them from the foreground.

Outside, the inscription on the
lintel over the doorway stipulates
that a visit here carries equal value
as one to San Giovanni Laterano in
Rome, good news except for the
carver's obvious uncertainty as to
how to spell "Laterano." ∎

**In 1579 a fiery
sermon at this
church railed
against revealing
necklines worn by
Venetian ladies.**

Strada Nova walk

The "New Street" was carved out of a jumble of houses extending from the church of the Santi Apostoli to the church of San Felice in 1872. You take a direct route along a series of strung-together neighborhood streets until you reach the train station, but the entire length is not technically known as the Strada Nova (watch for changing street names). There are shops of almost every sort lining both sides, selling everything from fresh pasta to eyeglasses, which means that what this street may occasionally lack in charm, it more than makes up for in usefulness. Because it's long and in most places fairly wide, the Strada Nova is a favorite spot for many Venetians to come for their cool-of-the-evening stroll, the *passeggiata,* especially on Sundays.

Start in front of the church of the **Santi Apostoli** *(Campo dei Santi Apostoli, tel 041 523 8297, closed Sun.; vaporetto 1 to Ca' d'Oro, 41, 42, 51, 52 to Fondamenta Nuove).* Take the broad boulevard stretching ahead of you, which is the Strada Nova proper. You will pass the walls of a few palaces, now used either as offices or apartments. The church of **Santa Sofia ❶** *(Campo Santa Sofia, closed Sun., except for attending Mass, vaporetto: 1 to Ca' d'Oro, 41, 42, 51, 52 to Fondamenta Nuove)* is so small and simple it doesn't at first strike you as a church, but there has been a church here since 866, possibly because of its nearness to the Rialto. It was heavily restored in 1836.

Beyond the church of San Felice, you'll cross a bridge. Just on your right you can peek through the gate into the brick-walled garden of the **Palazzo Giovanelli ❷** *(closed to the public).* It opens onto the Campiello Chiesa, the site of a stonemason's workshop, crammed with statues and other carvings awaiting restoration.

The next building on your right is the church of **Santa Fosca,** and in the little campo in front of it is the **statue of Fra' Paolo Sarpi,** a monk-historian (1552–1623). Among other deeds, such as discovering the mechanics of the iris of the eye, he became a hero in the long-drawn-out power struggle between Venice and the papacy (see p. 34). All Europe watched their doctrinal battles, until Sarpi, as a consultant to the Venetian state, came up with the solution that everyone could agree on: "God has instituted two governments in the world," he stated, "one spiritual and the other temporal, each of which is supreme and independent of the other." This may not sound very remarkable now, but it is highly probable that this simple and sensible statement averted war. Not surprisingly, the solution didn't satisfy everyone, and a few months later three men attacked Fra' Sarpi near Santa Fosca, stabbed him in the face and left him for dead. He survived, and lived another 16 years.

Go over the next bridge, and you'll see the perfectly round church of **La Maddalena ❸** *(Campo della Maddalena, open for special events*

only; vaporetto 1 to San Marcuola) immediately on your left, dominating its eccentric little campo. A small neoclassic gem, it was built in 1760 by an amateur architect named Tommaso Temanza, who wanted to echo the design of the Pantheon in Rome. Not an active church, it is usually closed.

In the next small campo, called **Campiello dell' Anconetta,** look up at the building on the corner of the Calle dell' Aseo. You'll see a beautiful mosaic image of the Virgin, familiarly referred to as an *anconetta* (little icon). It was first installed in the church of San Marcuola by the Confraternity of the Holy Face, but the brothers moved it here in 1623 after an argument with the parish priest. It survived the disastrous neighborhood blaze of November 28, 1789, when a nearby warehouse full of olive oil caught fire.

From here it's a short stretch to the **Ponte delle Guglie ❺,** a wide stone bridge

decorated at its four corners by *guglie* (obelisks). This crossing point, once traversed by a ferry-raft, was spanned by a wooden bridge in 1285 that was replaced in stone in 1580 and then in 1777 with the present version. At this point you can either cross the bridge and go as far as the train station, or turn right for the Ghetto (see pp. 136–37). ∎

🗺 See also area map pp. 122–23
▶ Church of Santi Apostoli
🔁 0.6 mile (1 km)
🕐 45 minutes
▶ Ponte delle Guglie

NOT TO BE MISSED
- Santi Apostoli
- Statue of Fra' Paolo Sarpi
- La Maddalena
- Ponte delle Guglie

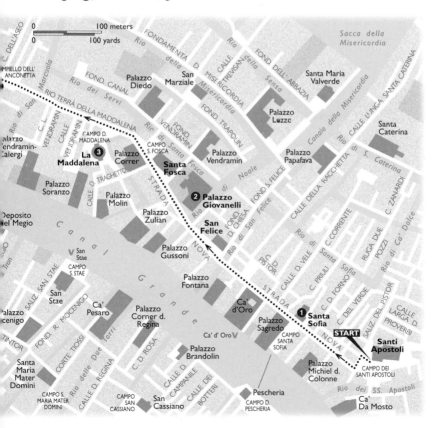

Madonna dell'Orto

Opposite: The courtyard of bricks laid in a herringbone pattern is one of the few surviving examples of a once common paving style in Venice.

THIS MID-14TH CENTURY GOTHIC CHURCH WAS ONCE dedicated to St. Christopher, but then changed to "Our Lady of the Garden" for the statue of the Virgin and Child by sculptor Giovanni de' Santi. He kept it in his garden nearby, but so many pilgrims came, convinced of its miraculous power, that it was moved in 1377 to the church, where it now resides in the chapel of San Marco. The church itself is something of a pilgrimage site for admirers of Tintoretto.

Madonna dell'Orto

🗺 Map p. 123

✉ Campo Madonna dell'Orto

☎ 041 719 933

💲 $

🚍 41, 42, 51, 52 to Orto; 1, 82 to San Marcuola

Madonna dell'Orto is an elegant, self-confident late Gothic structure, rebuilt between 1399 and 1473, with the same brick-and-Istrian-stone treatment typical of the Frari (see pp. 158–63) and Santi Giovanni e Paolo (see pp. 102–105). The Twelve Apostles in the niches of the facade have been attributed to the Dalle Masegne family, but other sources will only commit to "various Tuscan masters." Whoever sculpted them created a form of decoration that is unique in Venice. The doorway, with a statue of St. Christopher between the Virgin Mary and the archangel Gabriel, is by Bartolomeo Bon (1460).

The interior, which has a beautifully spacious simplicity, has been restored within an inch of its life by the British committee, Venice in Peril. The space seems now to have been sanitized for its protection, working against the spiritual power of the paintings, which appear as guests in the church rather than family members. Better, though, than how the church must have appeared in the mid-19th century, when the occupying Austrian forces used the building as a storehouse for straw.

As for Tintoretto, he not only was born and lived in this neighborhood, and is buried here in a simple, strangely modern chapel to the right of the high altar, but also produced a number of impressive paintings for his parish church. On the left side of the high altar is "The Making of the Golden Calf" (the men helping to carry the calf are said to be, left to right, Giorgione, Titian, Veronese, and the artist), and on the right is "The Last Judgment," infinitely more dramatic and affecting than his painting of the same subject in the Great Council Room of the Palazzo Ducale. In the apse are also "St. Peter's Vision of the Cross" and "The Beheading of St. Christopher." Most enchanting, though, is the dream-like "Presentation of the Virgin in the Temple," gleaming with the young girl's inner grace.

Two other treasures deserve a mention, though only one of them can still be seen. That is the painting "Sts. John the Baptist, Mark, Jerome and Paul" by Cima da Conegliano (1494), whose background shows his trademark Venetian landscape, complete with the castle of Conegliano; the colors and calm are a welcome relief from all the brooding contortion of the Tintorettos. The other was a Madonna and Child by Giovanni Bellini, but all that remains today is a photograph of the painting over the altar where it hung before it was stolen in 1993. Venice, like most other cities in Italy, is constantly under attack by art thieves, and this is a poignant reminder of what theft actually means: There is now a hole in the heart of the place where it belongs, and wherever it is now, it will never be as beautiful as it was. ■

Above: Tintoretto's "Presentation of the Virgin in the Temple" (1552) is unusually dramatic, even for him, with strong effects of light and shadow.

Convents & monasteries

At its peak of wealth and power, Venice contained some 123 churches—a figure that is now reduced to a mere 95—and a good many of these were connected with monasteries and convents. The reasons for this abundance came, over time, to have less to do with faith, and somewhat more to do with establishing a simple solution to some thorny family problems.

Beginning in the Middle Ages, religious orders throughout Europe served many crucial social functions: feeding the poor, tending the sick, providing hospitality for pilgrims, and so on. But in Venice, two factors eventually came to bear on this hard but simple world, and made Venetian vocations come to mean something scandalously different.

Money was at the root of the first. Many of the noble families, who over the centuries had become vastly wealthy, were reluctant to divide their fortunes among many sons, let alone see them disappear as dowries to enrich other families. Thus, many offspring were consigned to religious institutions, particularly daughters, who were sent to convents rather than allowed to marry, thus populating the places with a large number of women who would never have willingly chosen that life.

Power was the other significant factor. Venice always had a very testy relationship with the Vatican, resisting every effort of the papacy to direct Venetian policy—the entire city was actually excommunicated on more than one occasion, an edict that was generally disregarded by priests and the population alike. Piety almost always finished a distant second behind self-interest.

By the 16th century, many Venetian convents were hardly recognizable as such. The nuns wore makeup, curled their hair, gave parties and masked entertainments (even puppet shows), and received male visitors with absolute freedom. The case of the Benedictine nuns at San Zaccaria became notorious. Already intransigent in 1514, when the patriarch's vicar came to close the parlor where they enjoyed the company of their gentlemen friends, they drove him away with stones.

The case of Suor Maria, the abbess of Santa Maria Maggiore in Dorsoduro, was another example of how far standards had deteriorated. In 1502 it came to light that she had been conducting an affair with a priest named Francesco of San Stae—many of her gifts were confiscated from his house, sold, and the money given to his church. Interestingly, they were both tried in a civil court; Francesco was sentenced to ten years in prison, and Suor Maria was sent to Cyprus, evidently permanently, "on bread and water."

When Napoleon seized Venice, he suppressed the monasteries and tore down a good number of them, along with their churches. Today the city still contains a few convents and monasteries, but they are few indeed compared to their pre-Napoleonic number. They are gradually being converted to schools, or even hotels. ■

Above: Nuns today, though more scarce than in the past, live a more exemplary life than their sisters under the Venetian empire. Below: Francesco Guardi illustrated those less pious times in "The Nun's Visiting Day" (17th century).

Around Madonna dell'Orto

THE MADONNA DELL'ORTO AND ITS ENVIRONS AREN'T
really on the way to anywhere, which means it is still a tranquil neighborhood that is busier with locals leading their ordinary lives than
with visitors. Because this is the area closest to the mainland, hence
once an important transit point for goods and people, the families
who lived here left fascinating historic traces and works of art.

Madonna dell'Orto
🅰 Map p. 123

San Marziale
🅰 Map p. 123
✉ Campo San Marziale
☎ 041 719 933
🕐 Closed Sun.
🚤 41, 51, 52 to
Madonna dell'Orto;
1 to Ca' d'Oro

The long narrow campo, more
street than square, that leads to the
Madonna dell'Orto is called the
Campo dei Mori. Attached to the
corner of the building where the
campo joins the Fondamenta dei
Mori is a curious stone statue of a
man with a darkened, metal nose—
a replacement for the original stone
version, which was either worn or
broken off. He came to be called

"Sior Antonio Rioba," and he and
his two companions, each depicted
as an exotically dressed statue
attached to a house on the fondamenta nearby and in the campo,
are not Moors, as one might be
tempted to guess, but three merchant brothers—Rioba, Sandi, and
Afani Mastelli—who came in 1112
from what used to be called the
Morea, now the Peloponnese, in

factory of the Mastelli family. Tintoretto lived here from 1574 until he died in 1594. The Latin inscription on the plaque over the doorway says: "Do not ignore, passerby, the ancient home of Jacopo Robusti, called 'Il Tintoretto,' who spread innumerable paintings abroad from here to every place, admirable both publicly and privately, masterfully executed with the fine skill of his brush. The zeal of the current owner makes this known to you. 1842." It is not open to the public.

Exactly three canals and three bridges southeast from the Madonna dell'Orto is the church of **San Marziale.** St. Martial doesn't loom very large in the list of saints, and the church, built in 1133 and renovated in 1693, isn't memorable. Its fame is based on a wooden statue of the Virgin, now on the second altar to the left, which was reputedly carved by a shepherd near Rimini in 1286, placed in a boat, and left to drift where it would; it eventually came ashore right here.

This sturdy camel and his solicitous master adorn the wall of the Palazzo Mastelli, a proud emblem of the family's trade as spice merchants.

Greece. The family participated in the Fourth Crusade and, presumably, the Sack of Constantinople.

Two noteworthy buildings nearby are connected with the Mastelli family. One is their home, the **Palazzo Mastelli,** its facade clearly visible across the Rio Madonna dell'Orto if you walk to the left of the church. The palace is unmistakably identifiable by the large relief carving of a heavily loaded camel being led by a man—a reference to their business as spice importers—and is familiarly known as the Camel Palace.

The other building to note is **Casa del Tintoretto,** on the Fondamenta dei Mori at No. 3399. A plaque and a bust of the artist decorate the modest exterior of what was once the spice warehouse/

The two ceiling paintings by Sebastiano Ricci (painted 1700–1705) show "God the Father with Angels" and "St. Martial in Glory."

For some odd reason, this parish seems to have been more than usually prone to tragedy. One Sunday in October 1545 one of the famous "battles" between Castellani and Nicolotti took place on the bridge by the church. The Nicolotti were clearly losing, and a priest, a barber, and his friend started throwing roof tiles at the Castellani. By the time the fight was over 30 people were dead, either stabbed, suffocated, or drowned. And in 1575 it was discovered that the terrible plague that struck the city had started in the house of Vincenzo Franceschi in this parish; he happened to have had a guest from Trento who carried the disease. ∎

Ghetto

Ghetto

Map p. 122

THE TERM "GHETTO" HAS ACQUIRED MALIGNANT overtones, but it didn't start out that way. It's a Venetian word, and connotes both the foundry that once stood in this neighborhood (*getar* means "to cast") and the custom of sequestering a particular ethnic group. Venice welcomed numerous creeds and nationalities, and many congregated in their own specific areas. All were kept under strict surveillance, but the Jews were the only ones to be locked in.

The Ghetto was surrounded by water and patrolled by Venetian police at night.

The Jews had been in Venice since 1152, probably living first on the Giudecca. After various vicissitudes, in 1516 they were given land in the "New Ghetto," which was the island we see today, and the entrances were closed by gates at night. Armed guards patrolled the encircling canal. The "Old Ghetto," oddly, was added later, in 1541, and the "Newest Ghetto" joined on in 1633. Because space to expand outward was nearly nonexistent, the houses soon rose to one-third taller than the rest of the city, some with up to eight stories.

Here three different communities coexisted: the Alemagni (who came from areas of Germany, Poland, and other parts of Eastern Europe), the Levantine, and the Spanish. They were forbidden to practice any "noble" profession except medicine (Jewish doctors were permitted to leave the Ghetto at night), and any manual art, which meant that the five synagogues were all designed by Christian architects. They were also forbidden to own houses. However, many grew wealthy in banking, shipping, and business, as well as printing and dealing in antiques. In various periods they were required to wear a distinguishing token, often something in yellow.

You can enter the Ghetto from three different points: From the Fondamenta degli Ormesini, crossing over the wrought-iron bridge into the Campo Ghetto Nuovo; from the Strada Nova by taking the Calle Nuova; or—perhaps the most evocative approach—from the Fondamenta di Cannaregio near the Ponte delle Guglie. Entering by the small passageway here, you can see the holes in the stone doorposts for the

heavy metal hinges that once held the wooden doors.

There are still a few Jewish businesses, a nursing home, and two active synagogues (one for summer, the other for winter), but only some 200 people still live here. However, you can gain some appreciation of how busy it once was by reading all the names of the Venetian Jews, either soldiers or victims, on the various memorials. In the Campo Ghetto Nuovo are two large and very poignant bronze memorials to the Holocaust by Arbit Blatas (1979).

Two other plaques are worth noting: Just inside the entrance from the Fondamenta di Cannaregio, look high up at the left-hand wall. A very worn stone tablet from the days of the Venetian empire elucidates in great detail the specific punishment to be given Jews who pretend to have converted to Christianity, but who are discovered to be secretly practicing Judaism. A few steps farther along, on the left-hand wall of the winter synagogue, is a stone tablet in Italian with this inscription:

"1939–1945/Two hundred Jews of Venice/Eight thousand Jews of Italy/Six million Jews of Europe/ hunted, martyred, suppressed by blind barbaric hatred in distant lands/The memory of the most atrocious offense to human civilization/Recalls all men/To the holy law of God/To the feelings of brotherhood and love/which Israel was the first to affirm among the peoples."

Even if you normally don't like to take part in guided tours, a visit to the Ghetto really needs to be rounded out by joining one of the scheduled tours of the synagogues, which are only accessible to visitors in these groups.

A visit to the small but very beautiful and well-designed **Museo Ebraico** is also highly recommended. It contains a fascinating array of religious objects and textiles, and the bookshop and café (kosher) are exceptionally attractive and well organized. Unfortunately, many of the books are not in English. Orthodox services are held on the Sabbath in the Spanish synagogue *(summer)* and the Levantine synagogue *(winter)*. ∎

Arbit Blatas created one of the Holocaust memorials in the Campo Ghetto Nuovo that record the fate of Venetian and European Jews.

Museo Ebraico

🗺 Map p. 122

✉ Campo del Ghetto Nuovo

☎ 041 715 359

🕐 Museum closed Sat. & Jewish holidays

💲 $. Guided tour of museum & synagogues: $$

🚏 51, 52 to Guglie; 41, 42, 51, 52 to S. Alvise; 1, 82 to S. Marcuola

San Giobbe & around

JOB SEEMS AN UNUSUAL CHOICE FOR A SAINT, BUT A hospice dedicated to him was founded here in 1378. In 1450, Antonio Gambello was called upon to redesign its church, but the only remaining traces of his late Gothic structure are the bell tower, the three acutely arched windows on the southern facade, the remaining wing of the cloister with the portico, and the "capital room."

When Pietro Lombardo was asked to continue the work in 1470, he changed course and designed one of Venice's earliest Renaissance buildings, its facade reminiscent of that of San Giovanni in Bragora. The statues over the doorway, by Pietro Lombardo and his assistants, show Sts. Bernardino, Antonio, and Ludovico; the lunette depicts San Giobbe and San Francesco.

Inside, perhaps the most interesting chapel is that of the Martini family, Tuscan merchants from Lucca who had the chapel ceiling covered with polychrome terra-cotta tiles from the school of Della Robbia; perhaps very fine, but oddly garish in a city accustomed to more subtle colors.

Doge Cristoforo Moro (1390–1471), whose tomb is on the

Above: Ladies and laundry give a solid domestic foundation to the neighborhood along the Canale di Cannaregio.

San Giobbe
- Map p. 122
- Campo San Giobbe
- 041 524 0889
- Closed Sun.
- 41, 42, 51, 52 to Tre Archi Giobbe

Ex-Macello
- Map p. 122
- Fondamenta di S. Giobbe

right-hand side, was a difficult and extravagantly pious man. His record as doge wasn't very good, leading Venice to a number of humiliating defeats at the hands of the Turkish Army. When he died, he not only requested that he be buried in the habit of a Franciscan friar, but he also left money for the rebuilding of the church. His tomb is located in the chapel of his friend, San Bernardino of Siena. The ponderous baroque monument inscribed in French in the right aisle is to Renato de Voyer de Palmy, Signore d'Argenson, the Sun King's ambassador to Venice, who died here in 1651.

At the end of the Fondamenta di San Giobbe, on the corner facing the Lagoon, is **Ex-Macello,** a long building with several doors, with the remains of dilapidated ramps sloping down into the water. This is now the Economics Department of the University of Venice, but the buildings were the Venetian *macelli* (slaughterhouses). Until the 20th century Venice operated one of the busiest abattoirs in Italy, with animals being off-loaded from boats onto these ramps. The streets around San Giobbe once teemed with livestock, and work would start at 2 a.m. Notice the beautifully carved bovine skulls above the doorways. At the time of writing, a few of the spaces have yet to be converted to classrooms and are still being used as boathouses by a number of small Venetian rowing clubs, which will eventually move to another facility.

On the corner of the Grand and Cannaregio Canals, the magnificent 18th-century **Palazzo Labia** has one of the best locations in the city. However, its fame rests more on its residents than its splendid baroque architecture and the usual art treasures. The Labia family, originally from Catalonia in northern Spain,

Right: Stone skulls still decorate the facades of the former slaughterhouse, now part of the University of Venice.

Palazzo Labia

- Map p. 122
- Campo San Geremia
- 041 781 1277
- Closed, except by appt. Wed., Thurs., & Fri. at 3–4 p.m.
- 1, 41, 42, 51, 52, 82 to Ferrovia; 41, 42, 51, 52 to Guglie

came to Venice in the middle of the 1500s, and were admitted to the nobility after having contributed 300,000 ducats toward the war to save Crete. They were unfathomably rich, and Francesco Labia felt he needed a palace in keeping with both his wealth and his new status. They spared no expense in entertaining on a scale that astonished even the luxury-loving Venetians, and Paolo Antonio Labia offered sumptuous banquets with food served on solid gold plates—which he would then throw out the windows into the canal crying, "Le abia, o non le abia, sarò sempre Labia." ("Whether I have them or not, I will always be Labia.") It eventually became known that he— possibly mad, but not completely stupid—had arranged for nets to be stretched across the canal under the water to make it easy to recover the plates later. After the family's inevitable decline, the palace passed through several owners. It is now the headquarters of the RAI, the national broadcasting company, but the Salone di Tiepolo is open to the public. ■

More places to visit in Cannaregio

CORTE PRIMA & CORTE SECONDA DEL MILION

Tucked just behind the church of **San Giovanni Grisostomo,** these two little courtyards take the name of Marco Polo's famous memoir of his travels. The Byzantine arches on the facade on the Teatro Malibran, which are still undergoing extensive reconstruction, are said to have formed part of the Polo family house. It is possible that they may have lived in the smaller house facing the canal, but this is not certain. It's likely that they owned it, in any case.

🅰 Map p. 123   🚤 1, 82 to Rialto

SAN GEREMIA E LUCIA

San Geremia e Lucia was founded in the 11th century, rebuilt in 1174, and rebuilt again in 1753 to the design of a priest named Carlo Corbellini. There are two distinctive elements

***Capitelli,* or small shrines, are common especially on street corners, where they once provided faint illumination at night.**

on the side facing the Grand Canal, which you can see as you pass in any vaporetto: One is the large tablet announcing the presence of the body of St. Lucia, virgin and martyr of Syracuse, who "implores light and peace." As she is the patron saint of those with eye problems, this is appropriate. Her body was moved

here from her own church when it was demolished to make way for the train station (still termed "Santa Lucia"). The second is an elaborate carving with a skull. This was the sign of the confraternity of the Blessed Virgin of Aid to the Dead, who met in this church to pursue their chosen mission, which was the arranging of funerals for those who couldn't afford them. In the 18th century this campo was a favorite place for bull-baiting, a popular sport that appears in some paintings of Venetian life of that epoch.

🅰 Map p. 122   ✉ Campo San Geremia
☎ 041 716 181   🚤 1, 82 to Ferrovia; 41, 42, 51, 52 to Guglie

SANT' ALVISE

The austere facade of this late Gothic church (1380s) is hauntingly beautiful. The interior was renovated in the 17th century, and contains some early paintings by Giambattista Tiepolo, particularly his huge "Road to Calvary" (ca 1740), admirable for its brilliant color and sense of drama that shows the influence of Tintoretto on the young artist. In the sacristy are eight naive tempera paintings of Bible stories. English art historian John Ruskin attributed them to Vittore Carpaccio, but they are not by him at all; he would have been only eight years old at the time. All the same, everyone calls them the "Baby Carpaccios." The probable artist was an unknown student of Lazzaro Bastiani, who was Carpaccio's teacher.

🅰 Map p. 123   ✉ Campo Sant' Alvise
☎ 041 524 4664   🅢 $ 🚤 41, 42, 51, 52 to Sant' Alvise

ORATORIO DEI CROCIFERI

Near the Gesuiti, this was once the headquarters of the 13th-century order which built the original church (it was eventually suppressed after flagrant misconduct continued unabated). A cycle of paintings by Palma il Giovane (1583–1591) depicts events from the order's history.

🅰 Map p. 123   ✉ Campo dei Gesuiti   ☎ 041 270 2464 (administrator's office)   ⊕ Closed Mon.–Thurs., Fri.–Sun. p.m., & Nov.–March
🚤 41, 42, 51, 52 to Fondamenta Nuove ∎

These two *sestieri* contain the city's second largest campo, two of its greatest monuments, and one of the most famous markets in the world. It is entirely possible that you will spend some of your very best moments here.

San Polo & Santa Croce

At the Rialto fish market

San Polo & Santa Croce

ANYONE WHO GOES TO VENICE WILL BE BRIMMING WITH STORIES ABOUT this district dedicated to St. Paul and the Holy Cross—the magnificent Franciscan Gothic church consecrated to Santa Maria Gloriosa dei Frari; the Scuola Grande di San Rocco, with its overwhelming Tintorettos; the Rialto Market, at one time both the historic core of Venice and one of Europe's great financial centers. There are still a surprising number of seemingly forgotten corners, too, not to mention a few marvelous churches that deserve greater fame than they get. Leisurely exploration here will be well rewarded.

The name Santa Croce comes from the Benedictine monastery and church consecrated to the Holy Cross in 774 on what was then a very remote piece of land, now next to Piazzale Roma. In 1470 two nuns founded their own small religious order, and their church was named for Santa Chiara. Both foundations were suppressed in 1810 following Napoleon's order, and the churches were demolished. The only remnants to be seen today are the Gothic arches attached to the Hotel Santa Chiara at Piazzale Roma (the convent itself is now used as the central police headquarters), and the Giardino Papadopoli (Papadopoli Gardens).

San Polo, on the other hand, has always been a busy area; the relatively high, hard terrain and activity of the Rialto Market made the district attractive to merchants, bankers, and artisans, and the large campo served from earliest times as a major gathering point, useful for

Map labels:
Cana...
CAMPIELLO SAN SIMEON PROFETA
PONTE D. SCALZI
San Simeon Grande
CAMPIELLO DELLA COMARE
C. LARGA LA...
FOND. RIO MARIN O GAH...
FOND. SAN SIMEON PICCOLO
San Simeon Piccolo
FOND. RIO MARIN
Palazzo Diedo
SANTA
CORTE CANAL
FONDAMENTA
CORTE CASE NUOVE
C. L. CONTARINA
FONDAMENTA SANTA CHIARA
Santa Chiara
Piazzale Roma
Stazione Autobus
Autorimessa
GIARDINO PAPADOPOLI
CAMPO D. LANA
C. D. LACA
CROCE
DEI
CORTE D. AMAI
C. D. CAMPAZZO
PIAZZALE ROMA
FOND. COSSETTI
C. D. CHIOVERE
C. DIETRO
L'ARCHIVIO
CAMPO D. TOLENTINI
CAMPIELLO LAVADORI
TOLENTIN
San Nicolò da Tolentino
San Rocco
FOND. SANT'ANDREA
Rio Nuovo
FONDAMENTA
FOND. MINOTTO
FOND. FABBRICA TABACCHI
FOND. DELLE BURCHIELLE
RIO TERRÀ DEI PENSIERI
FOND. RIO NUOVO
CORTE GALLO
C. FALIER
Scuola Grande di San Rocco
C. VINANTI
C. DEI PRETI CRO...
FONDAMENTA RIZZI
Rio di S. Maria Maggiore
Rio Nuovo
CAMPIELLO MOSCA
CAMPO SAN PANTALON
San Pantalon
C. LARG...

0   200 meters
0   200 yards

everything from an archery practice and military parade ground to all sorts of festivals, markets, public balls, bull-baiting, and even the occasional murder.

When English traveler Thomas Coryat wrote his account of his visit to Venice in 1608, he mentioned that the campo, similar to many others, was "all greene." It was first paved with bricks, then much later, in the 19th century, with stone. A canal once flowed through it, right in front of the imposing facade of the fine Renaissance Palazzo Soranzo, on the side of the campo opposite the church. ∎

Palazzo Loredan

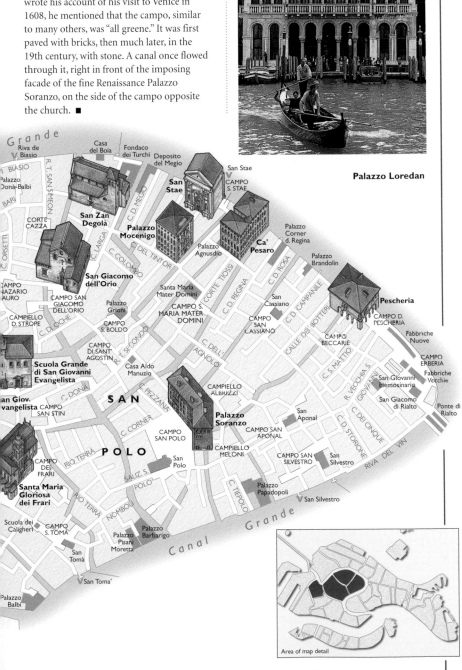

Area of map detail

Campo San Polo

THE CAMPO DEDICATED TO ST. PAUL HAS SEEN MORE THAN its share of drama, though the doughty saint himself unfortunately came to be associated with the earthquake on his feast day in 1343 which, according to one chronicler, lasted 15 days, dried up the Grand Canal, and caused a thousand houses to fall.

San Polo

Map p. 143

Campo San Polo

041 275 0462

Closed Sun.

$

1, 82 to San Tomà; 1 to San Silvestro

Opposite: Shops offer ever more fanciful masks year-round. During Carnival, the campo has entertainment and plenty of booths selling masks.

A market was held here every Wednesday until the end of the Venetian empire; nowadays, during Carnival, the scene is re-created, with booths selling masks and tents offering refreshments and entertainment, and during the summer you can watch movies under the stars in a temporary theater.

On July 26, 1450, a monk named Fra' Santo, intending to excite sudden excesses of wild penitence among the wealthy and the unscrupulous, lit a huge fire like the "bonfire of the vanities" and threw into it "a great quantity of silk fabric, elaborate fringes, and even women's tresses." Among the various spectacles organized in the campo was a Carnival *festa* held by the masked Florentine merchants in 1497; an elaborate celebration by the guild of the Calza in 1503 with bull-baiting, dancing, and fireworks; and two public balls in 1507 to celebrate the weddings of several patrician families.

And here, on February 26, 1548, Lorenzino de' Medici and his uncle were murdered after having fled the vengeance of the Duke of Florence. The two paid assassins discovered where Lorenzino was living under a false name and slew them both one day when they came out. Lest we feel too sorry for them, just remember that Lorenzino was wanted for having killed the Duke's cousin.

Prominent in the campo is the church of **San Polo** and its campanile. The first church, built in 837, was rebuilt in the 15th century and then drastically restored and

altered in the 19th century. But it is not for its architecture that the church is known—people come here to see its outstanding works of art.

The 14-picture "Stations of the Cross" by the young Giandomenico Tiepolo (1747–49) in the Oratory of the Crucifix (entrance beneath the organ) is one of those magnificent portrayals of the Venetian nobility in all their splendor to which the sacred story line has been flimsily attached. These paintings quickly showed the artist to be the worthy successor to his father, Giambattista, who also contributed several paintings to this church. There is also the inevitable Tintoretto, a dramatic "Last Supper" (1568–69) portraying the instant of consternation following Jesus's announcement that one of the disciples would betray him.

The fine wooden "ship's-keel" ceiling is one of the few that remain in Venice—the others are in Santo Stefano (see p. 96) and San Giacomo dell' Orio (see p. 154).

Across the street from the entrance, the campanile (1362) is decorated by two 12th-century lions just above eye level, a rare Venetian example of Romanesque art. Though their dates would make it impossible, popular tradition holds that the serpent that is being devoured by one lion represents the traitor doge, Marino Falier, beheaded in 1355, and the man's head gripped by the other lion is that of Count Francesco Carmagnola, who in 1402 was also decapitated for treachery. ■

The Rialto fish market is the place to buy the freshest local and foreign fish.

Rialto Market

THE ISLAND KNOWN AS RIVOALTUS, OR HIGH BANK, HAD obvious appeal to the earliest settlers, who, by 810, had already decided this would be an ideal spot for the necessary city market. More than just offering food, the area was also the site of the very first ducal residence, the courts and prisons, the city storerooms, and the barracks of the military guards. If San Marco was Venice's political heart, the Rialto was unquestionably Venice's commercial nerve center: "What news on the Rialto?" Shylock asks in *The Merchant of Venice*, just as thousands had done before him.

Rialto Market
 Map p. 143
 Open Tues.–Sat. a.m.
1, 82 to Rialto; 1 to San Silvestro

By the 12th century the powerful Venetian financiers at the Rialto had established Europe's first state bank, and for at least 300 years they served businessmen across Europe.

A catastrophic fire in 1514 razed virtually all of the Rialto area, so most of what we see today dates from the Renaissance period and later. A number of buildings reflect the area's earlier importance as a municipal center. The buildings in the Naranzeria flanking the Palazzo dei Camerlenghi were built in 1525–28, probably by Guglielmo Bergamasco, as the residence of the

Marco Polo

Marco Polo in a German woodcut portrait (1477)

three *camerlenghi*, or state treasurers. The "Fabbriche Vecchie" stretching along the side of the Campo di Rialto was once the residence of the officials overseeing trade, navigation, and supplies. The similar building along the Grand Canal, with its back to the fruit and vegetable stands, is still the criminal court, and launches still bring prisoners to trial here.

The Rialto is still a working market, but is notably diminished from what it was even ten years ago. Supermarkets and more stringent laws on sanitation and storage have made the area increasingly expensive and inconvenient for the merchants, but shoppers and vendors still exchange vivid comments over stands of fresh fish, fruits, vegetables, and flowers. ∎

He may be the most famous Venetian ever, whose name is emblazoned on everything from the Venice airport to a Parisian restaurant. It is a name that reeks of what we imagine to be the glamour of exploration. But Marco Polo's travels to China revealed qualities that were quintessentially Venetian: He was a trader first and foremost, curious, resourceful, and tough. He was also apparently a man of considerable charisma, and a born storyteller.

Marco was born in 1254 to a family of Venetian jewel merchants. His father and uncle, Niccolò and Maffeo, had already undertaken a trading venture that had led them as far as the court of Mongol ruler Kublai Khan, and when they were ready to return in 1271, Marco went with them.

Il Milione, Marco's account of the 17 years that he spent in China as a trader and even diplomatic emissary for the khan, is a book that still arouses debate among scholars. Some dispute that he could have done all that he claimed, but most agree that the major points are not improbable. He died in 1324. ∎

The Rialto is still full of merchandise, but these days it is mostly souvenirs.

Walk around the Rialto

This walk explores the heart of Venice's historic commercial and trading center, and you will see evidence of its former importance all along the way. It begins by the Grand Canal at the foot of the Ponte di Rialto, or Rialto Bridge, facing the market area.

Walk away from the bridge, going straight ahead under the porticoed walkway that is just to your left. Although it is not identified as such, this is the **Ruga degli Orefici.** Look up at the vaults, whose colorful frescoes have recently been restored. Note, too, the heavy iron grilles over the third floor windows, protecting the storerooms of the goldsmiths below.

At the end of this passageway (signposted as "Sotoportego di Rialto"), you will be standing on a wide street called Ruga Vecchia San Giovanni. Immediately turn left, and a few feet along on your left you will see the vaulted and frescoed entrance to the church of **San Giovanni Elemosinario** ❶ *(closed to public).* The church is undergoing major restoration, but work on the frescoes is complete.

Turn around and take your first right,

walking back up the open main street. Just before the **Ponte di Rialto,** pause at the church on your left. This is dedicated to **San Giacomo di Rialto** ❷ *(Campo San Giacomo, tel 041 522 4745, closed Sun.; vaporetto 1 to San Silvestro or Rialto),* but is usually called San Giacometto. This is the only building to have survived the fire that leveled the area in 1514, and stakes a good claim (difficult to prove) to being the oldest church in Venice. It may have been founded in 421, 428, or 540, and has been rebuilt and renovated numerous times, most recently in 1600, though always according to its earliest plan. Note, too, the covered porch at the entrance surmounted by a round blue clock, a feature that was typical of the Gothic era, though in this case both were added in the 15th century.

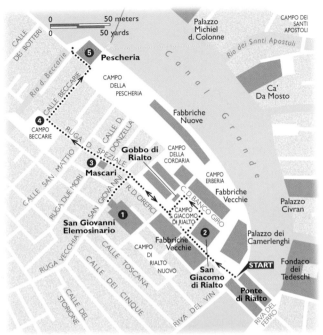

Map labels:
0 50 meters
0 50 yards

Palazzo Michiel d. Colonne
CAMPO DEI SANTI APOSTOLI
Rio dei Santi Apostoli
Canal Grande
Ca' Da Mosto
⑤ Pescheria
Rio d. Beccarie
CALLE DEI BOTTERI
CALLE BECCARIE
CAMPO DELLA PESCHERIA
Fabbriche Nuove
④ CAMPO BECCARIE
RUGA D. SPEZIALE
CALLE D. DONZELLA
Gobbo di Rialto
CAMPO DELLA CORDARIA
CAMPO ERBERIA
Fabbriche Vecchie
Palazzo Civran
CALLE SAN MATTIO
RUGA DUE MORI
③ Mascari
C. D. BANCO GIRO
Palazzo dei Camerlenghi
San Giovanni Elemosinario
SAN GIOVANNI
R. D. OREFICI
① CAMPO S. GIACOMO DI RIALTO
②
Fabbriche Vecchie
START
Fondaco dei Tedeschi
RUGA VECCHIA
CALLE TOSCANA
CAMPO DI RIALTO NUOVO
Fabbriche Vecchie
San Giacomo di Rialto
CALLE DEI CINQUE
CALLE DEL STORIONE
RIVA DEL VIN
Ponte di Rialto
RIVA DEL FERRO

⊠ See also area map p. 143
▶ Ponte di Rialto
⟷ 0.33 mile (0.5 km)
⊕ Half an hour
▶ Pescheria

NOT TO BE MISSED
- Ruga degli Orefici
- San Giacomo di Rialto
- "Gobbo di Rialto"
- Mascari
- Pescheria

Drogheria Mascari, recalling the era when spices were termed "drugs," still offers the exotic wares of the Venetian traders.

The square in front of the church, complete with many-spouted fountain, is the **Campo Erberia,** which from 1097 till only a few years ago was the wholesale fruit and vegetable market. It wasn't paved until 1758.

At the far end of the campo, you'll see a white stone pedestal with steps, being supported on the shoulders of a kneeling man. This is called the **"Gobbo di Rialto,"** or hunchback of Rialto, sculpted by Pietro da Salò in 1541. This platform served as the place from which official announcements were made to the public. Ordinary Venetians would

also use this pulpit to decry negligence, abuses, and various other injustices. Some scholars have noted that, far from being a hunchback, this figure is an accurate representation of a common laborer from Bergamo, of the sort who flocked here to find work when Venice conquered that region in the 15th century, and who were well-known rustic characters in Venetian satires.

The "Gobbo di Rialto" was the ideal platform for public announcements.

Note the few small streets stretching back from behind the Gobbo, whose names bear witness to the once powerful financial dealings that were centered here: Calle de la Sicurità, Calle de Banco Giro. Venice was also the first place where the idea of insuring ships and their cargo became common, and, of course, profitable.

Turn left from the Gobbo, then right, and walk down the Ruga degli Speziale, street of the spice merchants. At the next corner on your left is **Drogheria Mascari** ❸ (*381 San Polo, Ruga degli Speziali, tel 041 522 9762, closed Sun.; vaporetto 1 to San Silvestro or Rialto*), one of Venice's most evocative shops. For more than 50 years it has sold an array of spices, coffees, and teas, beautifully displayed in the window—a rare glimpse of the exotic bounty that once characterized the entire market.

Continuing straight ahead, you'll soon reach the **Campo Beccarie** ❹, which is named for the many workmen's taverns that once lined its confines. A few still remain where you can pause for a quick drink and small fresh-cut sandwich. Those who love fresh fish will want to see the **Pescheria** ❺, or fish market, which bustles every morning except Sunday and Monday under the covered pavilion stretching toward the Grand Canal. This structure appears to date from the Gothic era, but was actually built in 1907 to replace an earlier shelter. If you walk toward the Grand Canal down Calle Beccarie turn left at the first and only street you come to; it leads to a smaller bridge. Before the bridge, on the canal-side facade of the fish market, you'll see a large old marble tablet inscribed with the names of the fish on sale (in Venetian) and their minimum legal sizes. Although these are several hundred years old, they're still valid. ∎

Ca' Pesaro

Detail of "The Princesses and the Soldier" (1914) by Vittorio Zecchia, based on "The Thousand and One Nights," in the International Gallery of Modern Art

THIS PONDEROUS PALACE OF THE PESAROS WAS FORMERLY three medieval palaces that the family acquired between 1558 and 1628, the year in which Baldassare Longhena was commissioned to renovate them. The work went on until 1710, long after both architect and patrician were dead. The result in any case is one of the masterpieces of Venetian baroque, though its sheer mass doesn't coexist very happily with its Gothic neighbors.

Today the palace is home to the **International Gallery of Modern Art,** which belongs to the Venice Biennale. Its collection consists of pieces that were bought following their showing at one of the exhibitions. When the museum reopens, it will again be a lovely place to see late 19th- and early 20th-century masters such as Henri Matisse, Marc Chagall, Gustav Klimt, Paul Klee, Henry Moore, and many important Italian artists. "Giuditta" by Klimt and "Rabbi from Vitebsk" by Chagall are are among the most remarkable works on display.

The **Museum of Oriental Art,** also in the Ca' Pesaro, is one of the world's most important collections of Japanese art; it was gathered by Prince Enrico II, Count of Bardi, during his travels in Japan. ■

Ca' Pesaro
- Map p. 143
- Fondamenta Ca' Pesaro
- 041 520 0970
- Closed for renovation
- $
- 1 to San Stae

San Stae

San Stae

- Map p. 143
- Campo San Stae
- 041 275 0462
- Closed Sun.
- $
- 1 to San Stae

THE FIRST CHURCH ON THIS SITE, DEDICATED TO St. Eustachius (San Stae in the Venetian dialect), was founded in 1107. It was demolished in 1678 and a new church built by an otherwise unknown architect named Giovanni Grassi who, among other things, turned the church round so its facade would front onto the Grand Canal. The facade itself was added in 1710 by Domenico Rossi, who won a public contest for this commission.

Restored in 1979 and closed to worship, the church is now used as a hall for baroque music concerts.

The small but airy church shows all the hallmarks of the Palladian aesthetic: The interior is a single room, not divided by columns; it is painted a calm, creamy white; the half-moon windows along the edge of the ceiling let in plenty of light, and there is a sense of simplicity and symmetry, ideal for showing the paintings to their best advantage.

The most important works are found on the walls around the high altar. Most notable are: on the right, "St. Jerome the Greater" by Giambattista Piazzetta (1717) and "The Martyrdom of St. Andrew" by Giovanni Antonio Pellegrini (1722–23). On the left are "St. Peter Freed From Prison" by Sebastiano Ricci (1717–1724) and "The Martyrdom of St. Bartholomew," a powerful work by the young Giambattista Tiepolo (1722) in which the huge knife about to strike the fatal blow contrasts dramatically with the old man's vulnerable white skin. The positions of victim and executioner, though, give no hint as to exactly how the execution is going to be carried out. As is often the case, the few paintings (and a very modest marble statue) representing the church's patron saint are lost amid the welter of more famous martyrdoms. The melodramatic "Fall of the Manna" by Giuseppe Angeli (1722) looks remarkably like a set design for a Hollywood epic.

The Foscarini chapel to the left of the high altar contains a superb marble crucifix (Giuseppe Torretto, ca 1700). Not only is the position of the crucified Christ unusual, with a strong twist of the shoulders, but there is something about the expression, particularly the mouth, that gives the impression that it is a portrait of a real person. ∎

Palazzo Mocenigo

The palace of the "old" Mocenigos, as opposed to the "new" branch of the family that lived on the Grand Canal

THE MAIN APPEAL OF THIS RENAISSANCE PALACE IS AS A residence more than a museum, which can offer a peaceful wander through the rooms, with their frescoed walls and Venetian glass chandeliers. Here, you may sense the dimensions of life in such a place, confirming the truth of Henry James's comment in *Italian Hours:* "A Venetian palace...that is not overwhelming by its mass makes almost any life graceful that may be led in it."

The Mocenigo family name was one of Venice's greatest, and like many patricians they accumulated several palaces as the family continued to branch out. They not only contributed ambassadors, generals, and a good seven doges, the main family line shone in the reflected glory of Alvise Mocenigo, a captain general of the navy who fought many battles against the Turks in the mid-1600s. "This hero," one source recounts, "was mourned not only by his own, but by his adversaries too, who, at the moment of his funeral draped their ships with black flags, and in sign of mourning trailed their banners along the waves."

A palace was already here in the 15th century, as can be seen in Jacopo dei Barbari's famous detailed aerial view of the city (1500). The current palace, however, was gradually expanded and renovated until the point at which we see it today, which dates from the beginning of the 17th century. No information remains concerning the name of the architect or how long the work took. It now houses the **Center of Studies of the History of Textiles and Costume,** founded in 1985, with a collection of textiles gathered from the Civic Museums. There are also paintings showing some of the Mocenigo family's exploits. ■

Palazzo Mocenigo
- Map p. 143
- Salizzada San Stae
- 041 721 798
- Closed Mon.
- $
- 1 to San Stae

San Giacomo dell'Orio

San Giacomo dell'Orio

🅰 Map p. 143

✉ Campo San Giacomo dell'Orio

☎ 041 524 0672

🕐 Closed Sun.

💲 $

🚤 1 to Riva de Biasio

The "ship's-keel" church ceilings reflect the city's boatbuilding tradition.

THE CURIOUS NAME OF THIS CHURCH IS GENERALLY agreed to have come from *alloro*, or laurel, as there was once a laurel tree in the campo here. This is one of that small group of early Venetian churches (founded in the 10th century, rebuilt in 1225) that still reveals its sturdy Veneto-Byzantine outlines despite the inevitable later accretions of Romanesque and Gothic elements.

This is just a fancy way of saying that it's an irresistibly appealing jumble of styles and dates and it still feels very much like a parish church, which it is. Among its many treasures is a sixth-century green granite column that came from Byzantium (probably from a church, though some experts attribute it to a pagan temple, both plausible themes) easily visible on the right as you face the high altar. The splendid Gothic "ship's-keel" wooden ceiling is one of the very few in Venice.

To the left of the high altar is a small but exquisite 14th-century marble statue of the Annunciation, a subject more often painted than sculpted. The room along the wall to the left of the high altar is the old sacristy, and is covered by paintings which Palma il Giovane produced between 1580 and 1581. Amid more predictable sacred subjects are such Old Testament events as "Elijah Fed by the Angel," "The Descent of the Manna," "The Serpent of Bronze," and "The Passage Through the Red Sea."

In the adjacent chapel dedicated to St. Lawrence is an altarpiece by Veronese, "St. Lawrence, St. Jerome and St. Prospero" (ca 1581), his skillful coloring making this a much more interesting painting than the title might imply. Look closely at the painted wooden pulpit next to one of the columns and see if you can find which of its panels can be opened to allow entry.

Just as deserving of a visit to the church would be a pause for coffee in the campo outside, a real neighborhood meeting place that children convert into their own playground in the afternoon, making it something of an obstacle course for people passing through on their way to the train station or Piazzale Roma. ■

San Zan Degolà

Byzantine frescoes uncovered during a recent restoration show St. Helen above Sts. John, Peter, Thomas, and Mark.

NOT QUITE ON THE WAY TO ANYWHERE, THIS LITTLE GEM dedicated to St. John the Beheaded is a real delight, another of that select group of the very oldest churches (and therefore smallest and richest in atmosphere) in Venice.

San Zan Degolà

🅰 Map p. 143

✉ Campo San Zan Degolà

☎ 041 524 0672

🕐 Closed Sun. & p.m.

🚤 1 to Riva de Biasio

It was built in 1007 following the recognizable Byzantine design. The eight 11th-century columns of Greek marble are topped by Byzantine capitals, and the ship's-keel ceiling is as remarkable as a work of engineering as it is an impressive work of art. It is incomprehensible that it had been abandoned and remained dilapidated, until 1983, when a small group of parishioners from San Giacomo dell'Orio raised a protest and urged the restoration of this treasure. The work was completed in 1994.

The most striking works of art are the frescoes, which the restorers uncovered, somewhat unexpectedly—little remains in Venice of what was a common art form here, usually a victim of the humid climate. In the chapel to the left of the high altar are frescoes that, though now incomplete, are treasures of Veneto-Byzantine art: On the ceiling is a cross, and around it are the symbols of the four evangelists (15th century); on the right-hand wall frescoes showing "The Annunciation," "St. Helen and Four Saints" (St. John, St. Peter, St. Thomas, and St. Mark, 11th century). There is also a wonderful fresco on the ceiling of the transept showing "Christ Among the Evangelists" (early 13th century) and in the chapel to the right of the high altar is a powerful fresco in a Gothic stone frame showing "St. Michael the Archangel" (14th century) as he triumphs over Satan. This simple but elegant church, which has lost many of its treasures along the way, is now the perfect setting for these haunting images that resemble so strongly the great mosaics of the same epoch. ∎

The church of "little" St. Simeon makes a great impression on first-time visitors exiting the train station.

San Simeon Grande & San Simeon Piccolo

CURIOUSLY, SAN SIMEON GRANDE (LARGE) IS SMALL AND its neighbor, San Simeon Piccolo (small) is large, but perhaps this, in its convoluted way, makes it easy to remember which is which. The fact that for quite some time now San Simeon Grande is the only one that is open helps to clarify matters.

San Simeon Grande

- 🅰 Map p. 142
- ✉ Campo San Simeon Profeta
- ☎ 041 718 921
- 🕐 Closed Sun.
- 🚊 1 to Ferrovia or Riva de Biasio

San Simeon Piccolo

- 🅰 Map p. 142
- ✉ Campo San Simeon Piccolo
- 🕐 Closed for restoration
- 🚊 1 to Ferrovia

San Simeon Grande, officially named San Simeone Profeta, may rest on a tenth-century church, but it was altered extensively in the 18th century. Two works of art inside deserve a look: "The Last Supper" by Tintoretto (possibly his favorite theme), in which the white-robed priest who commissioned the painting is shown standing to the side, and a statue of St. Simeon by Marco Romano (1317), who is known only for this piece. In the 18th century the city ordered a new floor to be built in this church because a plague victim had been buried here in 1630; later restoration work revealed that the previous floor, with its tomb coverings, was still intact.

In the second chapel on the left aisle is an altar that is dedicated to the Scuola dei Garzotti, the guild of the wool-carders.

San Simeon Piccolo is now deconsecrated and seems to be undergoing permanent restoration. It is the monumental building that forms your first view of Venice when you exit the train station, and the impression is quite unforgettable, with its huge green dome dominating the Grand Canal at its feet. A closer look at the building reveals that it comprises an interesting assortment of architectural elements that were cleverly combined as part of the reconstruction undertaken by Giovanni Scalfarotto in the 18th century. ■

Scuola Grande di San Giovanni Evangelista

THE SETTING OF THE CHURCH AND SCUOLA IS ONE OF THE most attractive in Venice, facing each other across their own little campo guarded at one end by a passageway under a house, and at the other by a splendid carved marble portal.

The emblem of St. John and a representation of the True Cross adorn the portal by Pietro Lombardo.

It was thanks to a relic of the True Cross that the **Scuola Grande,** founded in 1261, became one of the wealthiest religious societies in Venice and was able to commission Mauro Codussi to design a larger building in 1454. Codussi's majestic double-ramp grand staircase is a Renaissance masterpiece, and leads to the *albergo,* or main committee room, richly decorated with paintings depicting the life of St. John by Giorgio Massari (1727). Of the more unusual episodes seen portrayed here, all but two dating from the 16th century, are (from right) "Fall of the Temple of Ephesus by the Prayers of St. John," by Domenico Tintoretto, "Martyrdom of St. John Immersed in a Cauldron of Boiling Water," by S. Peranda,

"St. John and the Philosopher Craten," by Andrea Vicentino, and "St. John Revives Two Dead Men," by G. Cignaroli (18th century). The ceiling is covered with large 18th-century panels, the work of various painters, that portray scenes from the Apocalypse.

The relic of the True Cross is still kept in its reliquary on the altar of the oratory in the Hall of the Cross. The paintings by Gentile Bellini and Vittore Carpaccio depicting the miracles of the True Cross, made for this scuola, are now in the Accademia Galleries.

Across the campo is the church of **San Giovanni Evangelista,** which is a small, appealing 15th-century building that has been restored several times. ■

Scuola Grande di San Giovanni Evangelista

- 🅰 Map p. 143
- ✉ Campiello della Scuola
- ☎ 041 718 234
- 🕐 Church closed p.m. & Sun.; scuola closed except for special events
- 🚤 1 to Riva de Biasio

Opposite: Color
and light bring
alive Titian's
painting of "The
Assumption of the
Virgin" (1518).

Santa Maria Gloriosa dei Frari

THIS IS ONE OF THE PLACES YOU ABSOLUTELY SHOULDN'T miss, imposing yet warm, an assortment of mismatched elements that retains a haunting simplicity, and with enough Renaissance masterpieces to qualify it as a museum in itself. They say that aficionados of Venice tend to prefer either this church or that of Santi Giovanni e Paolo, but it is rare to hear anyone speak of the latter with the affection—"love" might not be too strong a word—they feel for the Frari.

**Santa Maria
Gloriosa dei Frari**
- Map pp. 142–43
- Campo dei Frari
- 041 522 2637
- May be closed for weddings or other services
- $
- 1, 82 to San Tomà

Followers of St. Francis of Assisi arrived in Venice in 1222 and by 1250 they were able to ask architect Nicolò da Pisa to build them a monastery and church dedicated to Glorious St. Mary "of the friars," which was consecrated in 1280. The growing importance of the Franciscan order in Venice (odd, for such a worldly city) eventually required a more impressive edifice, and the distinctive Gothic structure we see today dates from the mid-15th century. The **campanile,** the highest in the city after that of San Marco, was built between 1361 and 1369.

When the religious orders were suppressed for a period in the early 19th century, part of the monastery was converted to house the **State Archives,** which you see today beside the church's main entrance.

You probably won't enter by the main door facing the canal, as it is used only for special ceremonies, but rather from the side door next to the campanile. This obviously blunts what would be the visual impact of seeing the whole 335-foot (102 m) nave, but in compensation, on your right, you immediately find Titian's "Pesaro Madonna" (1519–1526), which is a marvelous welcome. The oblique position of the Madonna, St. Peter, and members of the Pesaro family and the gleaming, still fresh colors give this painting a sense of life often missing from depictions of similar

Titian

A later engraving of Titian's self-portrait

His Venetian noblewomen were ravishing, his skill in composition masterful, but "color" is the word that comes first to mind when considering the work of one of Venice's greatest artists.

Tiziano Vecellio was born about 1490 in Pieve di Cadore in the mountains of the Veneto region, and studied with the Venetian masters Giovanni and Gentile Bellini before working with Giorgione.

Titian was famed for his gifts as a portraitist, even in paintings that

were clearly of sacred subjects. Above all, however, he was admired for his sumptuous, sensual colors. Toward the end of his life, the artist's style changed to a darker, more brooding palette, with some paintings that appear surprisingly modern to our eyes.

He died in 1576 of the plague—ironically, so did his lifelong rival, Tintoretto, though not until 18 years later—and according to his dying wish is buried in the church of the Frari. ■

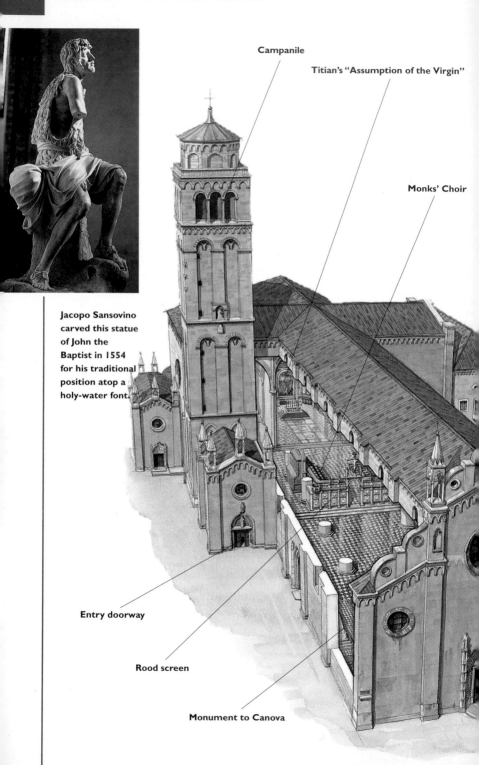

Jacopo Sansovino carved this statue of John the Baptist in 1554 for his traditional position atop a holy-water font.

Campanile

Titian's "Assumption of the Virgin"

Monks' Choir

Entry doorway

Rood screen

Monument to Canova

Franciscan churches were often huge, as demonstrated by the nine apses of Santa Maria's high altar, seen here from the street.

sacred groups. This was the first time a Venetian artist had painted the subject asymmetrically, and it was by no means greeted with universal enthusiasm.

Be sure to notice, to the left of the Pesaro altar, the small slim bomb that has been attached to the

Cloisters

wall. This was placed here as an offering of thanks, as it fell on the church's roof on February 27, 1918, and didn't explode.

The huge doorway immediately next to it is surrounded by the massive funerary monument to Doge Giovanni Pesaro by Baldassare Longhena, Melchior Barthel, and Bernardo Falcone da Lugano (1660–69). More impressive than the Latin inscriptions are the four massive statues of black men with torn clothing bearing the monument on their shoulders.

The "Monument to Canova" (1827) was carved by a whole squad of students of the sculptor Antonio Canova (1757–1822) according to the design their teacher had already made. The vase held by the heavily draped figure about to enter the pyramid's half-open door contains Canova's heart, while his other mortal remains are interred in the mausoleum near his home in Possagno. Lest it seem a little morbid for an artist to plan his own tomb, not to mention one so extremely melancholy, the fact is that Canova actually designed it to be a mausoleum for Titian.

It is probably safe to say that Canova and Titian were not exactly equals, but their fate brought them together in the Frari. As he was dying of the plague in 1576, Titian asked to be buried in the Frari, where two of his greatest masterpieces are found, and so he was. But Titian's monument, which is directly across from Canova's, was carved

Santa Maria's inlaid choir stalls are rare in Venice, not only for being made of wood, but also because monks still use them.

more than two centuries later in a strangely chilly baroque style by two of Canova's students, Luigi and Pietro Zandomenighi, who had also worked on their master's final resting place. Experts have commented that the vigorous, muscular statue of St. Jerome by Alessandro Vittoria next to Titian's tomb is probably a more accurate likeness of the great painter than the remote, Greco-Roman patriarch sculpted by the neoclassic disciples of Canova. And why Canova would have wanted to bestow an Egyptian pyramid on Titian does seem odd, though this finally explains the magnificently mournful lion of St. Mark prostrate at the pyramid's entrance—symbolizing the grief of Venice at the loss of one of her greatest geniuses

(which would not describe Canova). The reason for this switching of designs isn't clear, but evidently Canova's disciples thought his design more appropriate for him than for Titian.

The **monks' choir** (1468) is the only one in Venice that is still intact; its 124 seats of wood were fantastically carved and inlaid by Marco Cozzi. The outer shell of the choir is covered with rows of late 15th-century marble reliefs of Old Testament prophets, mainly produced by the Lombardo brothers' workshop.

Just to the left above the entrance to the sacristy is the stiff but dignified mounted statue of Commander Paolo Savelli by an unknown Tuscan artist (mid-15th century), who was the first

mercenary soldier to be given an equestrian monument in Venice.

The **sacristy** contains its own treasures: The altarpiece, "Madonna and Saints" by Giovanni Bellini (1488), whose exquisite light and jewel-like colors make it seem startlingly three dimensional, and the "Madonna with Child, St. Francis and St. Elizabeth who accompany the doge and the dogaressa" by Paolo Veneziano (1339). This painting seems vividly alive despite its obvious connection with the restrictions of Byzantine art; you can almost see the Renaissance beginning to break through the shell of convention in the lifelike gestures and varied positions of the principal characters. Some of its liveliness seems attributable to the fact that each person seems to be looking in a different direction.

In the **Florentine chapel** immediately to the right of the high altar is Florentine sculptor Donatello's wooden statue of John the Baptist (1438), originally intended for a merchant's chapel in his native city. Its gaunt power influenced generations of artists after him.

First among all these masterpieces, though, is the painting that dominates the high altar, and in a sense the whole church: The "Assumption of the Virgin" by Titian (1518). Its airy, swirling grace make it one of the happiest sacred works anywhere, its gold an echo of the traditional Byzantine color for heaven, and a fitting tribute to the church's namesake. ∎

St. Mark gives his blessing from the altarpiece painted by Bartolomeo Vivarini in the chapel that Giovanni Corner dedicated to his uncle, Marco.

Scuole

During the Middle Ages, social assistance to the poor, sick, and dying wasn't considered the responsibility of the State, but rather of the pious, whether monks and nuns or devout laymen. Often wealthy citizens would endow hospices—in Venice the Pietà and the Ospedaletto were examples of institutions founded to help the poor learn a trade, or to provide dowries. The *scuole*, though, were something else. Not literally "schools," they were confraternities, or charitable societies, founded by members who paid annual dues to meet a specific need.

The "minor" scuole, of which there were more than 300 by the fall of the empire, were guilds founded to protect the interests of a particular trade: The scuola of the furriers, the shoemakers, the sausage-makers, and so on, can still be seen. There were also numerous scuole which aided members of a particular foreign community, such as the Albanians, Greeks, Germans, and Dalmations.

The six "grand" scuole were rich and influential, each with several hundred members who gave generously to aid the suffering and deprived. They were dedicated to: San Giovanni Evangelista, Santa Maria della Carità, San Marco, Santa Maria della Misericordia, San Teodoro, and San Rocco. Such confraternities were common throughout Europe, but the Venetian ones had a crucial difference: Here they were civil organizations which were approved by the State (in this case, the Council of Ten), and, despite their religious devotion and patron saint, had no official connection whatsoever with the Roman Catholic Church. They were, as one scholar put it, "a state within a state," governed by a grand guardian and elected officers. Members paid annual dues, and were expected to provide rowers for the Venetian galleys when required (later, they sent a contribution instead). They paid taxes on their property, and could be audited by the State. They provided an almost unparalleled opportunity for various Venetian social classes to mingle; every member was equal, from the poorest to the most wealthy, and although

patricians could join, they were forbidden any official position. And as yet another indication of the scuola's orientation to the State and not the Church, it was the doge, and not the patriarch, who would be invited to attend the solemn Mass on the feast day of the scuola's patron saint.

Not all confraternities could afford their own building, but were usually content with an altar dedicated to their patron saint in whatever church they had chosen. The church of the Carmini contains the altar of the fish vendors; the church of San Trovaso has the altar of the *squeraroli* (gondola-makers). Although the guild itself no longer exists, there is still a working *squero* just outside. The

great scuole, however, took pride in their splendid buildings, which were designed like small palaces, and consisted of an entrance hall, a main hall (often with an altar for religious services), and a smaller *albergo* (meeting room) where the officers met.

The six grand scuole were proud of their independence, but would always participate in each other's festive celebrations. On St. Mark's Day (April 25), the most significant feast day of the state calendar, all of the scuole were expected to join the massive procession that wended around the piazza and through the surrounding streets. Jealous of their rights, the members were known to engage in scuffles for precedence on these solemn occasions; more than once the Council of Ten had to punish representatives of the scuole for hitting each other with their silver candelabra.

Napoleon suppressed the scuole with the same determination with which he closed churches and monasteries, and confiscated large amounts of their silver, jewels, and works of art. But the Scuola di San Rocco reopened after only two months, when its officers managed to persuade the French viceroy that to crush their confraternity would invite civil violence. The scuole of San Giovanni Evangelista, the Carmini, and San Teodoro were refounded in the early years of the 20th century, and are still very active in pursuing their mission in aiding the poor and disadvantaged. ■

"Vision of St. Augustine" (1502), one of a series of seven paintings by Vittore Capaccio that he painted especially for the Scuola di San Giorgio degli Schiavoni

Scuola Grande di San Rocco

Below: Although sumptuous, the Renaissance-style Scuola Grande is much less famous than the paintings inside.

PEOPLE COME FROM AROUND THE WORLD TO THROW themselves into this torrent of Tintorettos, probably the crowning achievement of the artist's long and prodigious career. Henry James wrote, "We shall scarcely find four walls elsewhere that enclose within a like area an equal quantity of genius. The air is thick with it and dense and difficult to breath...."

Scuola Grande di San Rocco

🅰 Map p. 142

✉ Campo San Rocco

☎ 041 523 4864

💲 $$

🚤 1, 82 to San Tomà

Opposite: Tintoretto's ceiling of the Great Hall was part of his cycle of biblical events depicting the hardships that the *scuola* labored to relieve.

The French St. Roch, patron and protector of plague victims, understandably had a fervent following in Venice, which, being a seaport, often suffered from outbreaks of this usually fatal disease. (Ironically, Tintoretto himself died of it.) The Venetians had few qualms about appropriating the saint's body and placing it in the church dedicated to him, which is across the campo from the scuola.

The confraternity of San Rocco was among the last of the six "great" scuole to be founded in Venice (see pp. 164–65). During the plague of 1478 the members began to build their headquarters, and were officially registered by the Council of Ten in 1481. By 1516 the number of members had grown to 500, and a larger and more splendid building was required. Completed in 1549, it is the handiwork of three successive architects: Bartolomeo Bon, Sante Lombardo, and finally Antonio delli Abbondi, called Lo Scarpagnino. Despite the grandeur of the structure, the confraternity existed (and still exists) to aid the poor, and as one of the richest has succeeded to a notable degree.

Several artists tried for the commission to provide the decoration, but Tintoretto won it, in part by an audacious maneuver: Instead of providing the requested sketch showing his plan for a painting of San Rocco, he unveiled the finished work already placed on the ceiling of the *albergo* (meeting room), where it remains today. He then

spent the next 24 years (1564–1588) covering the scuola's walls and ceilings with some of his greatest masterpieces.

As you enter the first-floor hall, it may seem rather dark; pause to let your eyes adjust. On the wall facing you, near the left corner, is "The Annunciation," a startling and original image of this oft-painted moment. In a brilliant but characteristic insight, Tintoretto has painted Mary as a farm girl. Her rough hands and sturdy build are a radical departure from the typical representation of her as a pale, aristocratic lady. And the angel, instead of politely approaching, appears to be literally bursting through the wall. For once one can understand why the angel said "Fear not."

As you climb the staircase, be sure to notice the large painting to your right on the second flight of stairs. "The Virgin Appears to the Plague-Stricken," by Antonio Zanchi (1666) is a striking scene of the pestilence in Venice, complete with muscular boatman, limp cadavers, and a man holding a cloth over his nose. This would have represented the terrible plague of 1630, for deliverance from which the church of Santa Maria della Salute (see p. 68) was built.

The main room, or upper hall, is literally covered with 23 paintings showing scenes from the Old and New Testaments. (Hand mirrors are provided to help you view them in some comfort.) The room at the end farthest away from the altar is

Concerts are frequently given in the scuola's entrance hall.

the meeting room, and on the ceiling is Tintoretto's "audition" painting of San Rocco in glory. But the true glory of the small room is the "Crucifixion," a painting that covers the whole wall and which is justly one of the artist's best known works. Before you leave, be sure to notice the painting on a freestanding easel of "Christ Carrying the Cross." Scholars are still divided as to whether this is by Titian or Giorgione, but the power of its faces make such debates immaterial to most of those who stand before it. ■

Tintoretto

Tintoretto's self-portrait shows characteristic drama.

Jacopo Robusti was the son of a dyer, and so was destined to be endowed with the nickname "little dyer"—Tintoretto.

He was born in 1518, and except for a what may have been a brief period in Titian's studio, he never studied under a master. At the age of 30 he launched his prodigious career—you would swear that every church in Venice has at least one of his paintings—which was marked by intense productivity and a style tinted by the new "mannerism." His scenes are dramatic, characterized by powerful emotions and gestures, strong contrasts of light and shadows, and he often appears to be more sympathetic to the calloused, work-stained common folk than the aristocrats.

His greatest undertaking was the painting of the Scuola Grande di San Rocco, to which he dedicated 24 years of labor. His "Paradise," painted for the Great Council Room of the Palazzo Ducale in 1590 but drastically restored more than once, is now more noted for being the largest canvas in the world than for its beauty. All the same, for psychological insight Tintoretto's frank and fearless eye is still unmatched. He died of the plague in 1594, and is buried in his parish church of the Madonna dell'Orto. ■

San Pantalon

THERE HAS BEEN A CHURCH HERE SINCE BEFORE THE 11TH century, rebuilt at various times before being demolished and replaced from scratch by Francesco Comino between 1668 and 1686. San Pantalon has one of the few unfinished facades in Venice, but that is not its main claim to fame.

In a triumph of trompe l'oeil, the ceiling appears to soar up into the sky, the optical illusion created by Gian Antonio Fumiani's representation of "The Martyrdom and Apotheosis of St. Pantalon." It took him from 1680 to 1704 to create what is the largest canvas painting ever used for a ceiling—a dizzying composition filled with characters significant to the life and death of the saint. Unlike other ceiling paintings, this doesn't have the cus-tomary gilded frame, which makes it appear that the events depicted are swooping up from the walls.

The San Pantalon chapel con-tains "The Miracle of San Pantalon" by Paolo Veronese (1587), one of his more melancholy last works, while the chapel of the Sacred Nail houses a relic of one of the nails used in the Crucifixion and a paint-ing of the "Crowning of the Virgin" by Antonio Vivarini and Giovanni d'Alemagna (1444). ■

It took 20 years to create the 40 separate paintings of the saint's life that were assembled for the ceiling.

San Pantalon
- Map p. 142
- Campo San Pantalon
- 041 523 5893
- Closed a.m. & Sun.
- 1, 82 to San Tomà

More places to visit in San Polo & Santa Croce

PALAZZO AGNUSDIO

This pretty little 14th-century house just across the canal from Palazzo Mocenigo is decorated with reliefs showing the Annunciation and the evangelists' customary symbols. It was once the home of a *luganegher*, or sausagemaker, who was raised to the status of patrician in the 17th century.

Map p. 143 ✉ Calle del Forner

The **Giardini Papadopoli** occupies the former site of the medieval church and convent of Santa Croce, near Piazzale Roma.

SAN CASSIANO

This isn't a church you'd be likely to make a pilgrimage across town to visit, but if you're in the neighborhood you might do well to stop in to see Tintoretto's "Crucifixion" (1568).

Map p. 143 ✉ Campo San Cassiano
☎ 041 721 408

CASA ALDO MANUZIO (ALDUS MANUTIUS HOUSE)

Venice became one of Europe's foremost centers of printing and bookbinding thanks largely to Manutius (1547–1597) and his Aldine Press. He virtually invented books as we know them today, small and reasonably portable, printed in octavos. His house, where Erasmus stayed in 1508, is on Rio Terrà Secondo at No. 2311.

Map p. 143 ✉ Rio Terrà Secondo, near Campo Sant' Agostin

SANTA MARIA MATER DOMINI

The Byzantine church erected in 960 in honor of St. Christina (and not, as the current name states, the Mother of God) was rebuilt in the 16th century probably to a design by Giovanni Buora. It's thought that Jacopo Sansovino completed the facade of Renaissance Tuscan forms. Its most beautiful painting is "The Martyrdom of St. Christina," (1520) by Vincenzo Catena, a follower of Bellini. Despite the vivid color, the painting has a mystical air heightened by the pale sky—is it dawn?—over the brooding background of lake and mountains.

Map p. 143 ✉ Campo Santa Maria Mater Domini ☎ 041 721 408

PALAZZO SORANZO

Dating from the beginning of the 15th century, the Palazzo Soranzo dominates the Campo San Polo on the side opposite the church. At first glance, it seems strange that the principal facade (which was once covered by frescoes by Giorgione) should be facing land rather than the water, but this wasn't always the case, and you can just see the traces of the canal that ran in front of this building until 1761. The Florentine poet Dante Alighieri (1265–1321) was an unofficial guest of Doge Giovanni Soranzo, and there are also connections with Casanova. The young Giacomo Casanova (see box p. 91) was hired as a violinist for a three-day ball here, at which he was befriended by an elderly senator who adopted him as his son. It still belongs to the Soranzo family.

Map p. 143 ✉ Campo San Polo ■

The "hard back" *sestiere* probably got its nickname from the firmer soil here. The wealth of galleries give an arty, uptown feel to the eastern half, while students make the scene at Campo Santa Margherita one of the liveliest in Venice.

Dorsoduro

Figure outside the Mondo Novo mask shop

Dorsoduro

DORSODURO REALLY HAS EVERYTHING, FROM HIGH ART TO RAUCOUS (FOR Venice) nightlife. This fact has not been lost on the people with money who have a mind to own a Venetian residence; east of Campo Santa Margherita many palaces or apartments have been bought by foreigners, raising property values even beyond their normal stratospheric level—unfortunate, considering that a good percentage only come here for a few weeks each year.

This area, along with Rialto, was popular with the earliest settlers because its terrain was noticeably firmer than many other islets. It's popular again because of the young and the foreign, who flock in ever increasing numbers to the Peggy Guggenheim Collection (see pp. 65–67), which not only continues to boast one of the finest modern art collections in Europe, but keeps expanding its gift and book shops. It appears that people who may not want to spend

all that much time in the gallery are willing to dawdle indefinitely among the stuff for sale.

The appeal of Campo Santa Margherita is easier to grasp: Unless you are impossibly demanding, it's safe to say there is something here for everyone. Food for all palates, from pizza-by-the-slice to an excellent full meal, shopping (no Murano glass yet,

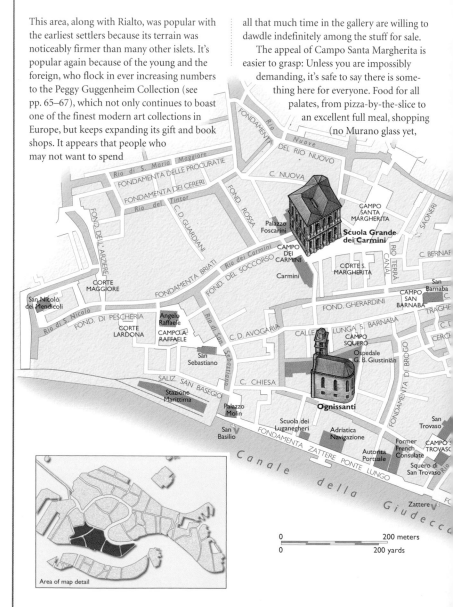

0 _____ 200 meters
0 _____ 200 yards

Area of map detail

though a very fancy Carnival mask shop is just on the fringe), and some of the best people-watching in the whole city, since it's on a direct trajectory between the university and the stations. If only the live music on summer evenings wasn't quite so loud, and didn't go on quite so long; residents spend their sleepless hours writing distraught letters to the newspaper.

Ca' Rezzonico (see p. 64) is one of Venice's marvelous palace-museums, and is well worth a visit. In 1687, the filthy rich Rezzonicos from Como were able not only to buy their way into the *Libro d'Oro* of aristocratic families, but also to buy the half-finished

The Zattere is a promenade perfect for strolling, running, or just sitting still.

palace of the destitute Bon family and hire Giorgio Massari to redesign it. They were also well placed to marry their son Lodovico to the daughter of one of Venice's oldest families, the Savorgnan, and the wedding in 1758 called for a wealth of celebratory frescoes by Tiepolo, far brighter and happier than the motives inspiring the event.

To relieve some of the pressure of day-trippers in Piazzale Roma, a boat from Fusina docks at the Zattere. This, added to the groups from cruise ships, can give parts of Dorsoduro the aspect of a migratory corridor. But, once the moment has passed, the *sestiere* returns to its contented and busy daily round. ■

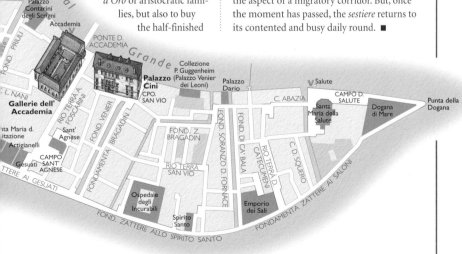

Campo Santa Margherita & around

THIS COMFORTABLY LARGE CAMPO HAS LATELY EVOLVED
into *the* place to be for young people, either students or visitors,
attracted by the live music offered by the various cafés in summer,
the inexpensive bookstores and pizzerias, and, of course, each other.
The residents are also much in evidence to meet each other, let their
children and dogs frolic, and do a useful amount of shopping.

**Campo Santa
Margherita**
Map p. 172

The truncated campanile at the far
end was once attached to a church
which was founded in 853. Since
then the church has lived through
various other phases, even serving
as an Evangelical church and a
movie theater. It's now an attractive
small auditorium of the University
of Venice. Occasionally concerts

given here are open to the public.
At the other end is a freestanding brick building dating back to
1725. This was once the scuola of
the *varoteri*, or furriers, then after
World War II was used by the
Christian Democratic Party as a
political meeting house. It is currently closed. Note the marble

tablet (carved in 1501 and brought here from the previous scuola) on the side of the building facing the campo; like the one at the Rialto (see p. 150), it lists the fish for sale at the nearby stands by their Venetian name and their minimum allowed length.

Just outside the southeast corner of this building you can see a squat, very battered stone column about knee high. For years women used this for pounding their soaked salt cod, or *baccalà*, to soften it before cooking. From this point, if you look toward the church of the Carmini, you can clearly see the white stone outline of the canal, now filled in and paved, that once reached this far inland.

The Carmelite Order was based in the convent attached to the church of the **Carmini,** and its confraternity established the **Scuola Grande dei Carmini,** which was built in 1663 to a design by Baldassare Longhena. It is richly decorated with paintings by Giambattista Tiepolo (1740s)—his first-floor ceiling fresco, "St. Simon Stock Receiving the Scapular from the Virgin" is considered one of his masterpieces (the scapular is the distinguishing garment of the order). The 14th-century church, altered in the 16th century, contains more modest works of art, though the ponderous funeral monument to the Foscarini family framing the main door includes beautiful reliefs of Venetian galleys at sea. On the right-hand aisle is Tintoretto's wonderful "Presentation," above an altar dedicated to the fish-vendors' guild.

Carmini & Scuola Grande dei Carmini

Map p. 172

Campo dei Carmini

041 522 6553

Closed Sun. a.m.

1 to Ca' Rezzonico; 51, 52, 61, 62 to Zattere; 62, 61, 82 to San Basilio; all lines to Piazzale Roma

The Scuola Grande dei Carmini contains some exceptional paintings by Tiepolo.

San Sebastiano

🅰 Map p. 172

✉ Campazzo San Sebastiano

☎ 041 275 0462

🕐 Closed Sun.

💲 $

🚤 1 to Ca' Rezzonico; 51, 52, 61, 62 to Zattere; 62, 61, 82 to San Basilio; all lines to Piazzale Roma

Anyone with the slightest attraction to the work of Paolo Veronese makes the pilgrimage to the church of **San Sebastiano** where he made his name. Virtually every painting here shows him at his powerful and lyrical best, but most interesting are the ceiling paintings showing three moments from the story of Esther ("Esther Taken to Ahasuerus," "Esther Crowned Queen by Ahasuerus," and "Triumph of Mordecai"), dramatic scenes hardly ever chosen as themes for church decoration. The artist and his brother are buried near the organ.

The little Veneto-Byzantine church of **San Nicolò dei Mendicoli** has a good claim to being one of the oldest in Venice. It was founded in the seventh century,

and various later alterations haven't concealed its simple 13th-century outlines and appealing proportions. The portico, which was once a common feature of Venetian churches, is one of only two that remain in Venice, though like the one at San Giacometto it wasn't added until the 15th century. Fans of the murky mystery film *Don't Look Now* will immediately recognize the church from certain scenes.

St. Nicholas "of the beggars" was first built by refugees from Padova; for centuries the neighborhood was the province of modest fishermen, if not actual mendicants, as it has remained till very recently. (This church gave the name Nicolotti to all those living on this side of the Grand Canal.) The campanile dates from the 12th century.

The interior, which was extensively restored in the seventies by the British committee, Venice in Peril, is beloved more for its homely clutter of art and artifacts from what appears to be almost every century of its life than for any individual work of art. It does have a dark, rather grottolike atmosphere brightened by the 16th-century organ painted by Paolo Veronese's son. The apse contains a large wooden statue of St. Nicholas dating from the mid-15th century, possibly by the workshop of Bartolomeo Bon. Parts of the apse as well as a few columns remain from the 12th century, though the capitals atop the pillars are 14th-century work.

This is the parish church of a decidedly working-class neighborhood and, like all churches, is best appreciated during a religious service, especially when the regular congregation is swelled by reinforcements from the two other nearby parishes. It takes on a glow at the Easter Eve midnight Mass that can't be attributed entirely to the candles.

Standing in the small campo, you are facing the long brick facade of the **University of Architecture;** if it seems like a factory, that's because it was—cotton thread was manufactured here from 1883 until only a few years ago, when it closed down and was converted. And before there was the factory, there was a brushy, muddy beach, with only the Lagoon between this spot and the equally brushy, muddy mainland shore. ■

The church of San Sebastiano is noted for its many works by Veronese, such as this showing the saint's martyrdom.

San Nicolò dei Mendicoli

🅰 Map p. 172

✉ Campo S. Nicolò

☎ 041 275 0382

🕐 Closed Sun. a.m.

🚢 41, 42, 51, 52 to Santa Marta; 61, 62 to San Basilio; all lines to Piazzale Roma

Walk along the Zattere

Zattere means "rafts," and it was here that huge tree trunks, lashed together, were landed after floating down the rivers from the alpine forests or from the Dalmatian shore, to be used for ships, buildings, and furniture. This spacious promenade, which extends along the Giudecca Canal from the Maritime Station all the way to the Punta della Dogana (Customhouse Point), was ordered to be built in 1519, and this was the only place where timber was allowed to be unloaded. Today the Zattere is one of Venice's most pleasant walks, especially during a summer sunset, when everyone seems to creep out of hiding to stroll in the cool of the evening.

Start at the western end, at **San Basilio,** so named for a monastery that has long since been demolished. A few houses along, at No. 1473, is a pale yellow palazzo; the two marble tablets flanking the statue of St. Anthony the Abbot explain that this was once the **Scuola dei Luganegheri,** or sausagemakers guild (the saint is associated with agricultural matters, in particular the pig). There were once many of these mountain-born artisans in Venice who made prosciutto, salame, sopressa, and other cured-pork wonders, but these products are now made elsewhere and this building is home to the Riviera Restaurant.

Several of the imposing palaces have done useful service recently as offices; you'll pass the ornate Gothic facade of the 15th-century Palazzo Molin with its fine ogee windows, now the home of the **Adriatica Navigazione,** the **Autorità Portuale,** a Renaissance-style modern building, and the **former French Consulate,** once the 16th-century Palazzo Priuli Bon, whose right-hand door bears an elaborate bronze door-knocker of Neptune with two winged horses at his feet.

As you walk, you may notice dark splotches on the stones near the edge—these are traces of the ink ejected by angry cuttlefish who've been caught by some of the neighborhood men who stand here fishing on spring or fall evenings when the tide is coming in.

Two steps after you cross the Ponte Lungo,

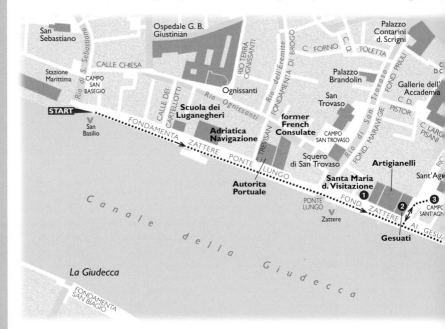

or "long bridge," you'll reach the church of **Santa Maria della Visitazione** ❶ *(Tel 041 522 4077; vaporetto 51, 52, 61, 62, 82 to Zattere, or 1, 82 to Accademia)* by Mauro Codussi or Tullio Lombardo (1423). Its main beauty is the painted coffered ceiling with 58 portraits of prophets and saints by an unknown Umbrian artist. This is all that remains of the church's works of art—the rest were stripped by Napoleon.

The next doorway along is the entrance of a former monastery, which until recently was used as a school to train young artisans, hence its nickname, **Artigianelli.** On the left is one of the few remaining stone lion's faces, whose mouth is open to receive anonymous accusations. The inscription specifies that this was reserved for complaints concerning public health in Dorsoduro; notice that the word here is spelled "De Ossoduro," a variation that in the Venetian dialect also connotes soil that is firmer than usual.

The church on the corner is dedicated to Santa Maria del Rosario, but it's more commonly called the **Gesuati** ❷ *(Tel 041 523 0625; vaporetto to Zattere),* the name of a minor monastic order that joined the Dominicans in 1668. The present church was

built in 1743 by Giorgio Massari and decorated in exuberant baroque and even rococo style. The ceiling frescoes depicting events in the history of the Dominican order are by Giambattista Tiepolo (1737–39); they are not only among his most beautiful, but herald the return of fresco to Venice after two centuries of paintings on canvas.

Just to your left is **Campo Sant' Agnese** ❸, a small shady spot with benches. If you look at the church wall, and even farther on, you'll see a series of large marble half-arches, rising from the street level. These were once the entrances to boathouses, no longer needed

---

🅜 See also area map pp. 172–73
► San Basilio
⬌ 1.1 miles (1.7 km)
🕐 One hour
► Punta della Dogana

NOT TO BE MISSED
- Scuola dei Luganegheri
- Santa Maria della Visitazione
- Gesuati
- Emporio dei Sali
- Punta della Dogana

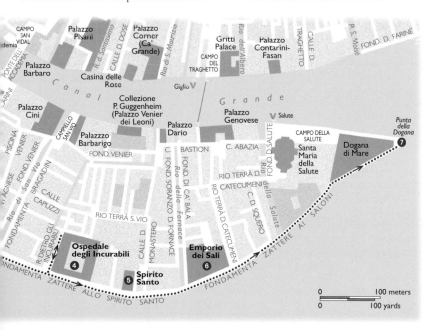

The Zattere was the only place in Venice where timber was permitted to be unloaded, hence the name, meaning "rafts."

when this street (once a canal) was filled in. Campo Sant' Agnese was the scene of one of the more interesting accidents in Venetian history. In 1866 the men who were drilling a new well in a brewery garden here unexpectedly hit an artesian well so powerful that a column of water shot 120 feet (36 m) into the air, not only covering the church and adjoining buildings with mud and sand, but threatening the area with subsidence. More serious was the fact that the terrifying plague of 1630, which inspired the church of Santa Maria della Salute, began here with an infected carpenter named Giovanni Maria Tirinello.

Cross the next two bridges, and you pass the former **Ospedale degli Incurabili ④**. If "incurables" sounds harsh, at least it's better than "syphilitics," which the patients mostly were. The hospital was founded by two noblewomen in 1522 and later it also aided orphans and poor young women by teaching them music and a trade. Formerly used as the Juvenile Court, it is now being renovated as the new seat of the Accademia of Fine Arts, the school connected with the gallery.

Turn left into the Ramo dietrogli Incurabili. When you reach the building at the end of the short street, look on the wall facing you, where you see a marble tablet forbidding card games, gambling, swearing, and other vices. There used to be a good number of sailors' bars along the waterfront here, and their favorite diversions usually became a neighborhood nuisance, hence the warning.

Return to the Zattere, where the next church on your left is a small one dedicated to the **Spirito Santo ⑤** (*Tel 041 523 7274, closed except for Mass 9 a.m. Mon.–Sat., 10 a.m. Sun., but may be open on special request; vaporetto 51, 52, 61, 62, 82 to Zattere, or 1, 82 to Accademia*). It was founded with an Augustinian convent in 1483, but is open only briefly, as it now belongs to the parish of the Gesuati and the rector is elderly. The nuns here were even more notorious for unseemly behavior than their sisters in the faith at the Ognissanti (see p. 181); not only was the founding abbess prone to pretend she was sick in order to have secret visits from a certain doctor, she was found to be pawning the convent's treasures. The sanctuary has a quiet, abandoned feel to it, but the trompe l'oeil effect of the ceiling decoration will almost certainly trick you into thinking that it is three-dimensional plasterwork and not painting.

As you cross the next bridge, you see the vast **Emporio dei Sali ⑥** stretching ahead and to your left by the canal. There have been salt warehouses here since the early 16th century; what stands today is the result of rebuilding by Giovanni Alvise Pigazzi in 1835–38. Its spaces are now used by various sports clubs, primarily the Bucintoro, the city's most venerable rowing club, but the Guggenheim (see pp. 65–67) has imminent plans to acquire the entire structure to use as additional exhibition space.

The end of the Zattere is the **Punta della Dogana ⑦**, or Customhouse Point. The curious figure standing tiptoe on a golden-colored ball, holding what appears to be a ship's rudder in its hands, is a 16th-century representation of Fortune by Bernardo Falcone which is also a weather vane. Here at Dorsoduro's Land's End you'll find what is probably the most spectacular view in all Venice: Across the entire Bacino di San Marco to the Piazza San Marco, the island of San Giorgio, the Palladian procession of churches along the Giudecca, and up the Grand Canal. ■

Ognissanti

A GROUP OF CISTERCIAN NUNS FINALLY ABANDONED the malaria-ridden island of Torcello toward the middle of the 15th century and settled here, to establish in 1472 a hospice, convent and church, dedicated to the Blessed Virgin Mary and All Saints.

The church was rebuilt in 1505, thanks to funds accumulated as offerings to a miraculous image of the Virgin, but her divine patronage availed them little, apparently, as they became notorious for loose living. To put it plainly, the abbess and several of her charges were discovered to be pregnant by a priest named Francesco Persegin; the patriarch came and had them taken away. The situation eventually improved, and the present church was consecrated in 1586.

The convent was converted to a hospital in 1960, which it remains today, albeit in reduced form, and it is a connection that gives this modest little church a particular appeal—it is maintained for the use of patients and their families. The church has recently been restored, and is occasionally used for concert performances. ■

Ognissanti

⬛ Map p. 172

✉ Fondamenta Ognissanti

☎ 041 529 4036

🚤 51, 52, 61, 62, 82 to Zattere, 61, 62, 81 to San Basilio

Veronese's "The Coronation of the Virgin" (1586) once adorned the high altar of the church of the Ognissanti; it is now in the Accademia.

Palazzo Cini

IF YOU'RE THE SORT OF PERSON WHO CAN TRULY SAVOR just one chocolate truffle rather than a dozen at a time, or merely feel the need of a quiet interlude in an exquisite setting among a small number of equally exquisite works of art, this little-known gallery near the Accademia will rest your eyes and soothe your spirit.

Palazzo Cini

- Map p. 173
- Piscina Forner, Dorsoduro 864
- 041 521 0755
- Closed Mon. & Dec.–Aug.
- $$
- 1, 82 to Accademia; 51, 52, 61, 62, 82 to Zattere

The wealthy industrialist Vittorio Cini bought the Palazzo Caldagno-Valmarana and filled it with his own collection of medieval and Renaissance religious art from Tuscany and Ferrara. Two floors of the palace have now been organized to exhibit these treasures.

A marble spiral staircase brings you, almost in secret, to the main floor. Even if art has small appeal, the palace itself will captivate you. The rooms are not too large, but have high, delicately stuccoed ceilings, with walls covered with brocade and lighted by chandeliers of Murano glass. Unlike more ornate palaces, one has no trouble imagining daily life in such a setting, though obviously a life that would be exceptionally gracious.

The **first room** contains one of the collection's highlights, the "Double Portrait of Two Friends" by the Mannerist painter Jacopo Pontormo (1494–1557). Almost stark in its simplicity, the painting concentrates attention on the two faces with their pale skin and arresting eyes. The **second room** contains "The Judgment of Paris" by Sandro Botticelli, whose goddesses exhibit his trademark features of flowing tresses and strangely almond eyes. More appealing than the ladies are the two large hunting dogs in the foreground, and the goat in the background that is scratching its ear with a hind hoof.

In the same room there is a "Madonna and Child" by maverick Renaissance genius Piero della Francesco, who has placed the two figures against a perfectly blank background and given the infant Jesus a strangely disturbing stare as he looks at you, but past you. The golden backgrounds and silent Byzantine gaze of most of the saints and angels may begin to seem repetitive, but in each painting you can discover something surprising and beautiful.

In the **last room** is a case containing some 20 pieces of carved ivory showing religious scenes. One—of Christ the King made in Sicily in the 13th century and bordered with Moorish geometric patterns—shows a surprisingly majestic figure, for its small dimensions, with a lush beard and powerfully expressive mouth. The "Death of the Virgin," also Sicilian from the 14th century, is a mass crowd scene of wildly grieving followers crammed onto an ivory tablet no more than four inches on each side. The deep folds of her robe and figure of a man clutching her body are superbly imagined and rendered. ■

"Allegone" was painted by Dollo Dossi (ca 1490–1542), who began his career as a court painter in Ferrara.

Gallerie dell'Accademia

Paintings from many a closed or demolished church have found a home in this gallery, which shows the best Venetian work from the 12th to the 19th century.

"IT WAS THE INEVITABLE DESTINY OF VENICE TO BE painted, and painted with passion," wrote American novelist Henry James in the 1880s. The Accademia Gallery is not only Venice's premier museum, but the most complete collection of Venetian art in the world, and although this probably shouldn't be your first stop in Venice—it's much more interesting to have already seen many of the places depicted in the paintings—it would be a pity to leave without having glimpsed at least a few of its wonders.

The gallery occupies the buildings that were once the scuola and the church of the Carità, one of Venice's oldest and wealthiest grand scuole (the art school is located in the former monastery). Over the cloister doorway facing the campo is an engaging relief of the "Coronation of the Virgin" (1445) by Bartolomeo Bon. The neoclassic facade on the gallery entrance was added in the 19th century when the scuola was converted to a museum. The church has no campanile because it fell on March 27, 1744; the records recount that not only did it damage two nearby houses, but also caused waves so big they threw a number of gondolas up onto dry land.

The Accademia was founded in the mid-18th century, and its second president was Giambattista Tiepolo. The core of its collection consisted of paintings by the 18th-century "academic" painters, but it later acquired many of the ecclesiastical artworks from churches and monasteries that had been suppressed by Napoleon.

The rooms are organized roughly in chronological order, beginning in the former assembly hall of the scuola, which displays the 14th-century paintings (sometimes called "Venetian primitives")

Gallerie dell' Accademia

- Map p. 173
- Campo della Carità
- 041 522 2247, OR 041 520 0345 (guided tours)
- $$
- 1, 82 to Accademia; 51, 52, 61, 62, 82 to Zattere

**Gallerie dell'
Accademia:
Key to rooms**

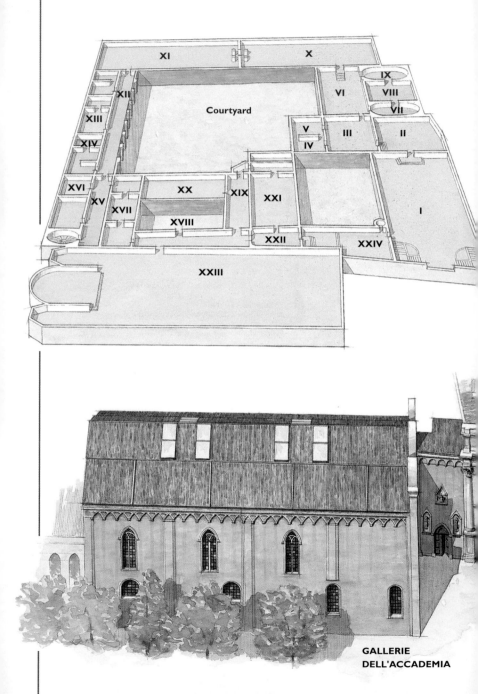

**GALLERIE
DELL'ACCADEMIA**

Above: The "Miracle of the Relic of the Cross on San Lorenzo Bridge" was painted by Gentile Bellini in 1500.

of such masters as Paolo Veneziano and Jacobello del Fiore. Static and frozen, but vibrant with color, these mark the transition between the Byzantine style and the more fluid Gothic approach.

In **Room II** you can see the three altarpieces that were originally housed in the church of San Giobbe: "Madonna Enthroned with Sts. Francis, John the Baptist, Job, Dominic, Sebastian, and Ludwig" by Giovanni Bellini (ca 1487); "The Presentation of Jesus" by Vittore Carpaccio (1510); and "Agony in the Garden" by Marco Basaiti (1516).

In the following four rooms the sense of a tidal wave of talent begins to rise; here are paintings by the Tuscan masters Andrea Mantegna and Piero della Francesca, as well as Giovanni Bellini and Titian. But, you'll be looking mostly for **Room V** and Giorgione's justly famous "The Tempest" (ca 1507). This enigmatic scene, with the soldier and the nursing mother immobile against a looming stormy backdrop, offers no explanation beyond its unmis-

takable fascination. It is one of the few paintings by Bellini's pupil that can be definitely attributed to him.

Room X contains one of Paolo Veronese's best known works, the enormous "Feast in the House of Levi" (1573), which he painted for the refectory of the monastery of Santi Giovanni e Paolo. It was originally titled "The Last Supper," but the Inquisition considered it close to blasphemous, seeing as it included dogs, a dwarf, drunks, and—worst of all—Germans, and demanded that he expunge them. In the end, all he changed was the title. The scene is obviously imaginary to a point, being a fantasy setting of Roman arches and marble platforms, but otherwise there are elements that would have been typical of a sumptuous 16th-century Venetian banquet: the luxurious clothing, the long table, the dogs underfoot, and people vying for attention.

Among the many masterpieces here, note especially Titian's last work, the "Pietà," (1576), which he intended to be hung near his tomb in the Frari. Strangely modern, almost devoid of his once trademark color, it makes a deep and disturbing impression.

In the following room are two works that are especially notable: The "Madonna of the Camerlenghi" by Tintoretto (1567), one of the multitude of paintings commissioned as gifts by outgoing financial magistrates (the bags of money make sure we understand this); and Paolo Veronese's "Mystic Marriage of St. Catherine" (1575), which shows his ravishing mastery of color, especially in the treatment of the sumptuous fabrics.

Subsequent rooms contain a welter of works by important, if non-Venetian, 17th-century artists such as Luca Giordano, Bernardo Strozzi, Sebastiano Mazzoni, and Francesco Maffei.

These are followed by Venice's 18th-century genius, Giambattista Tiepolo, with several paintings taken from various churches. "The Faithful Worshipers" is a survivor of the Scalzi, which was heavily bombed during World War I.

Wander on at your own pace, but the very best is ahead in **Rooms XX** and **XXI**—the huge, dazzlingly detailed Venetian narrative scenes painted by the Bellinis and Vittore Carpaccio for two great scuole. Here we see a Venice that is both fantastical and powerfully real, containing everything from miracles to angry gondoliers, deposed queens to flapping laundry.

The eight "Stories of the Holy Cross," by various artists between 1494 and 1502, were painted for the Scuola of San Giovanni Evangelista, which owned a relic of the True Cross. The "Corpus Domini Procession" (Gentile Bellini, 1496) not only dazzles us with its splendor, but also shows us the Piazza San Marco in a whole other light: note the mosaics over the basilica's doors, the brick pavement, the two procuracies still in their 12th-century Byzantine form, and the gold leaf on the then new Porta della Carta of the Palazzo Ducale.

Ponte dell'Accademia

Occasionally irresistible to Venetian skateboarders, the wooden bridge has recently been reinforced with steel girders.

The Accademia Bridge is one of only three that cross the Grand Canal, and, of the three, it unquestionably offers the most marvelous views. Upstream, you see the imposing Palazzo Balbi, with its two obelisks, at the sharp bend in the Grand Canal. Downstream the view sweeps away to the Bacino di San Marco, the sky pierced by Santa Maria della Salute and the Campanile of San Marco.

The chronicler Magno notes that on August 10, 1488, the council considered a proposal to build a bridge at this point, but as "the whole council laughed at it, it wasn't voted on."

A straight iron bridge was built by an English engineer named Neville in 1854, but it was superceded in 1932 by this higher structure that permitted the vaporettos to pass. It was made of wood because everyone thought it would be temporary, but the bridge has become a landmark in its own right, and, though reinforced several times, it has never been replaced. ■

In the "Miracle of the Cross on the Canal of San Lorenzo" (Gentile Bellini, 1550) Caterina Cornaro (or, Corner), Queen of Cyprus, is seen kneeling in the left foreground. The "Recovery of a Man Possessed by Demons" (Vittore Carpaccio, 1496) puts the old wooden Rialto Bridge front and center, as well as the Fondaco dei Tedeschi before the 1505 fire, how Ca' da Mosto once looked, and the campanile of the Santi Apostoli before it was rebuilt in the 17th century.

The great "St. Ursula Cycle" was painted by Carpaccio over 20 years (1475–1495) for the Scuola of St. Ursula, destroyed by fire in the early 19th century. The scenes relate the legend in which Ursula, a Christian princess of Brittany, agrees to marry the pagan king of Britain on the condition that she and 11,000 virgins first make a two-year pilgrimage to all the holy sanctuaries of the world (and he agreed). The story notwithstanding, the paintings show wonderfully realized vignettes illustrating dress, ships, and other aspects of late 15th-century Venice.

The next big room is part of what was once the church of the Carità. There are early triptychs by Giovanni Bellini in the apse.

The last room was the *albergo*, or committee room, of the scuola, with the only picture Titian ever painted for a confraternity, the "Presentation of the Virgin" (1534–38), still in its original position. The small girl mounting the steps, suffused in golden light, is beautifully imagined. ∎

Curiously modern in feeling, "La Tempesta," by Giorgione (1510), may be the painter's best-known work, though it has never been really explained.

Festivals & Carnival

During Venice's era of greatness, the daily drudgery of life was often interrupted by religious feast days, solemn civic ceremonies, and magnificent entertainments for visiting royalty. The government had a very clear sense of the usefulness of these celebrations as a way to reinforce the people's pride and sense of identification with their city-state, and the anniversaries of victories (and even defeats) were celebrated with fabulous pomp. The founding of Venice, the conquest of Friuli, the fall of Constantinople, the war with Chioggia…all were occasions for festivity.

The greatest of these was unquestionably **La Sensa,** or Ascension Day, which commemorated the departure in the year 1000 of Doge Pietro Orseolo II against the Narentani, or Dalmatian pirates; his victory assured Venice's consequent domination of the Adriatic. The symbolic "marriage of the sea," in which the doge led a vast boat procession to San Nicolò on the Lido to throw a gold ring into the water with the words, "I wed thee, O Sea, as a sign of true and perfect dominion," was not lost on the participants as a reminder that Venice fully intended to continue to rule the waves. La Sensa is still observed today with a boat procession to the Lido, with the mayor taking the place of the doge. The ring is no longer of gold, though.

Two other festivals are equally dear to the hearts of Venetians. First is the festival of the **Redentore** on the third Sunday in July, which commemorates their salvation in 1577 from yet another disastrous plague (see pp. 198–99). A pontoon bridge is built from the Zattere to the Giudecca that everyone crosses to visit the church of the Redentore. On the Saturday evening preceding the feast day everyone sets out in their boat, loaded up with friends, food, and drink, and anchors in the Giudecca Canal, ready to watch the midnight fireworks.

On November 21, the feast of the **Madonna della Salute,** a smaller pontoon bridge is built across the Grand Canal. The occasion is in thanksgiving for the city's deliverance from the 1630 plague, and every Venetian walks here in the late fall gloom to offer a candle, sold from the booths outside, to Our Lady of Health, and then to buy the children balloons and cotton candy.

The **Regata Storica** (Historic Regatta), which is held on the first Sunday in September, gives a glimpse of what the Venetian rowing races honoring visiting potentates used to be. Races in the Grand Canal began to be held in the 14th century, with the finish line always at the *volta de canal,* at Ca' Foscari. The present version, which lasts most of the afternoon, entails a ceremonial boat procession followed by four fiercely contested races, each involving a different type of boat. This is the Olympics of Venetian rowing, and families and friends of the participants, shrieking from their boats tied up on both sides of the canal, make no secret of their partisanship.

Carnival is the most touristic of the year's celebrations. This ten-day period preceding Lent, usually in February, has a long history throughout Europe, and in the Venetian 18th century, its customs offered a revealing glimpse of the city's social intricacy. For the non-scholar today it's enough to know that this is your chance to dress up however it suits you and stroll around the Piazza San Marco, looking and being looked at. Music and entertainments are organized in other parts of the city, too, as well as myriad parties in palaces and humbler private homes. The thrill of Carnival long ago lay in its permissiveness; social classes mingled freely and the rigid rules that controlled daily life were suspended, even mocked. Today, these strictures no longer exist, so Carnival has lost that edge of real daring and serves more simply as a happy excuse to get dressed up. The intense pressure of the tourist crowds, though, has inevitably made it a somewhat less festive experience for the Venetians themselves. ∎

The Regata Storica (above) begins with a boat procession led by the *Serenissima*, the most elaborate of the allegorical boats called *bissone*. The Redentore (right) reaches its supreme moment with the fireworks display at midnight over the Bacino di San Marco. Carnival (below) fills the city for ten days with elaborately costumed revelers.

More places to visit in Dorsoduro

ANGELO RAFFAELE

If you come as far afield as this to see either San Sebastiano or San Nicolò, you ought to look in here. This 17th-century building seems a little gloomy and neglected, but brightness shines from the five charming scenes of "Tobias and the Angel" painted on the organ by Gianantonio Guardi (1750–53), possibly with the help of his more famous brother Francesco. **A** Map p. 172   ✉ Campo Angelo Raffaele   ☎ 041 522 8548   🕑 Closed Wed.   🚤 61, 62, 82 to San Basilio

SAN BARNABA & CAMPO

Movie buffs will recognize this campo and gaunt facade (an 18th-century echo of the Gesuati, by Lorenzo Boschetti) from two different films, *Summertime* and *Indiana Jones and the Last Crusade*. The interior is now only open for special events. Its simple brick

Street signs reveal there were once many *squeros*, or gondola yards, in Venice. This one at San Trovaso is one of two still active.

campanile dates from the year 1000, and is one of the oldest in Venice, though the conical spire and pinnacles were added in the 14th century. It is now occasionally used as exhibition space. **A** Map p. 172   ✉ Campo San Barnaba   ☎ 041 275 0462   🚤 51, 52, 61, 62, 82 to Zattere, or 1 to Ca' Rezzonico

SAN TROVASO

The name is a Venetian amalgam of its two obscure patron saints, San Gervasio and San Protasio. The church, dating from the ninth century, was rebuilt in 1584 by Francesco Smeraldi, a follower of Palladio, and it has two equally beautiful facades. One faces its raised campo—one of many in Venice—a feature that always indicates a former parish graveyard.

Inside the church are several paintings by Tintoretto and his sons, though the real treasures are in the Clary chapel: a group of white marble angels on the altarpiece (1470) thought to be from the school of Donatello, and the painting of "St. Chrysogonus on Horseback" by Michele Giambono (active 1420–1462). This glowing mythic vision in the International Gothic style suddenly makes everything else look muddy and cluttered. The altar on the right as you enter from the raised campo is still dedicated to the guild of the *squeraroli*, or boatmakers. **A** Map p. 172   ✉ Campo San Trovaso   ☎ 041 522 2133   🚤 1, 81 to Accademia; all lines to Zattere

SQUERO DI SAN TROVASO

A glance at the many streets named "Calle del Squero" confirms that Venice used to be full of these traditional gondola-making yards. This is one of only two that are still active in Venice itself, and is best seen from the fondamenta on the opposite side of the canal of San Trovaso. No two gondolas are perfectly identical, though experts can make a good guess as to who made them. It usually takes some three months to build a new one, with its eight types of wood and ten coats of black paint, and can cost as much as a good car (and last as long, or longer, with care). The adjoining wooden house is, as is customary, built in the style of a mountain chalet, reflecting the fact that many of these workers in wood came from the nearby Alps. The working area is still fairly traditional, complete with the battered wooden frame on which the gondola is constructed. Visits are not welcome, but you can watch all you like from across the canal. **A** Map p. 172   ☎ 041 522 9146   🚤 51, 52, 61, 62, 82 to Zattere, 1 to Accademia ■

The Lagoon is dotted with islands, some famous, some forgotten. The fact that some, especially Torcello and Mazzorbo, were once more important than Venice deepens their evocative beauty and the history of this watery realm.

The Islands

Murano's famous glass still fascinates.

Glass shops and *fornaci*, or furnaces, line Murano's canals.

The Islands

ALL SORTS OF LANDFORMS PUNCTUATE THE LAGOON. IN ADDITION TO the islands, there are countless sandbanks often dramatically laid bare at low tide, and the grassy, muddy islets called *barene* that just break the surface, the haunt of wildflower and waterbird. Almost all of the islands visible from Venice were once flourishing, though most have been abandoned over time, and now most bear the sad silhouette of ruins.

The better known islands have their own complicated histories, and even now are only imperfectly allied with Venice—a Venetian would never call someone from Burano, or even the Giudecca, a Venetian, no matter what the municipal map may say. Most of them, even those that are closest to Venice, are still distinctly individual, and a Venetian could immediately identify their natives by the subtle differences in their accents. And don't expect to apply logic to their names, either— the people from Murano are known as Muranesi, but those from Burano are called Buranelli. That's just the way it is. Murano is probably the best known island, famous worldwide since the medieval epoch for the production of glass. Burano is the home of hand-made lace, a craft which has had a harder struggle to survive.

In the past the islands were used mostly for monasteries or hospitals: San Servolo (now restored and active as the European University of Economics) was the male hospital for the mentally ill; San Clemente was its female counterpart; Sacca Sessola was a tuberculosis sanatorium; and La Grazia, which closed in 1999, was used for the treatment of infectious diseases, from smallpox to AIDS. Slightly farther out, Poveglia was most recently the site of a home for the elderly, and Santo Spirito boasted a church famed for its superb paintings by Titian and Veronese.

Toward the mainland, San Giorgio in Alga also had a little church, and San Giovanni in Polvere was an Austrian powder magazine. Northward toward Torcello are the ruined islets of San Giacomo in Palude and San Angelo della Madonna del Monte, both of

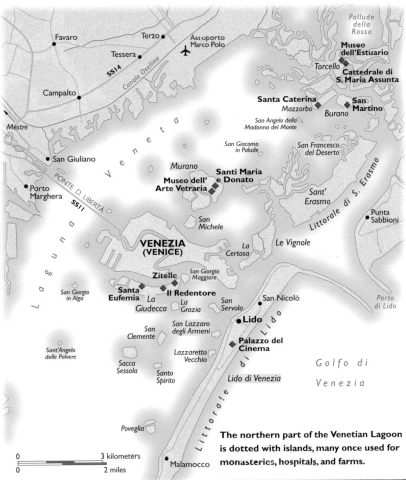

Pallude
della
Rossa

Favaro
Terzo
Aeroporto
Marco Polo
Museo
dell'Estuario
Tessera
Torcello
Cattedrale di
S. Maria Assunta
SS14
Canale Osellino
Campalto
Santa Caterina
San
Mazzorbo   Martino
Burano
San Angelo della
Madonna del Monte
Mestre
V   e   n   e   t   a
San Giuliano
San Giacomo
in Palude
San Francesco
del Deserto
Porto
Marghera
PONTE D. LIBERTÀ
Murano
Santi Maria
e Donato
Museo dell'
Arte Vetraria
Sant'
Erasmo
Littorale di S. Erasmo
Punta
Sabbioni
SS11
San
Michele
L   a   g   u   n   a
VENEZIA
(VENICE)
La
Certosa
Le Vignole
San Giorgio
in Alga
Zitelle
San Giorgio
Maggiore
Santa
Eufemia   Il Redentore
La
Giudecca   La
Grazia
San
Servolo
San Nicolò
Porto
di Lido
San
Clemente
San Lazzaro
degli Armeni
Lido
L   i   d   o
Sant'Angelo
delle Polvere
Lazzaretto
Vecchio
Palazzo del
Cinema
Golfo di
Sacca
Sessola
Santo
Spirito
Lido di Venezia
Venezia
Littorale di
Poveglia

0   3 kilometers
0   2 miles

Malamocco

**The northern part of the Venetian Lagoon
is dotted with islands, many once used for
monasteries, hospitals, and farms.**

which had their own church and monastery
(or convent).

In many cases malaria eventually forced
the abandonment of these islets, but the tides
rise and fall, and so do the fortunes of
mankind. Proposals for the resuscitation of
these islands is brought up from time to time,
with various possibilities being considered
(Poveglia was mooted as a youth hostel or
even a Club Med). San Clemente has been
bought by the Benetton group for conversion
to a luxury hotel, though an opening date has
not yet been set. In contrast, the 15th-century
Lazzaretto Vecchio, with its low brick walls—
Venice's earliest quarantine station—is
currently used as the stray dog refuge. ∎

La Giudecca

VIEWED FROM THE ZATTERE, THE GIUDECCA APPEARS uncannily like a stage set (the inescapable simile), made more dramatic by the majestic marble facades of no fewer than three churches designed by Palladio. Few sites in Venice could have afforded him such a setting for these neoclassic masterworks, and one can almost appreciate them more from afar than up close. They alone would be worth the voyage across the canal, with the added incentive of the earnest little 11th-century church of Santa Eufemia.

There are conflicting theories about how this island group got its curious name. In very ancient times it was called *spina longa*—perhaps because it resembles a fishbone—and its broad canal was named Canale Vigano. Some scholars contend that Giudecca derives from Giudei, or Jews, who once settled here. Others, however, maintain that it developed from *giudicati* (in Venetian, *zudegà*), the rebellious patricians who were "judged" and banished here in the ninth century. In any case, the residents are called Giudecchini, and would probably only refer to themselves as Venetian when talking to a non-Venetian.

During the medieval and Renaissance eras, when it still seemed distant and tranquil, there were as many as seven monasteries here; now only the Capuchin Franciscan friars of the Redentore and the Canossiane nuns still carry on (Michelangelo, also seeking solitude, lived here during his exile from Florence in 1529). Before the shores of the Brenta became fashionable as a summer retreat, the Giudecca was a favorite spot for Venetian nobles to build country villas. As recently as the turn of the 20th century, American novelist Edith Wharton, in *The Glimpses of the Moon*, set one of her wealthy

The Fondamenta Santa Eufemia, the street bordering the Canale della Giudecca, stretches toward the now derelict pasta factory, the massive Molino Stucky.

La Giudecca
Map p. 193

Church of the Zitelle
Map p. 193
Fondamenta delle Zitelle
041 523 1415
Open only Sun. for Mass at 11 a.m.
41, 42, 82 to Zitelle

expatriate Americans in a romantic palace on the Giudecca. In those days the island was still mostly gardens; in the 18th century some gardens were available for rent by the day for alfresco trysts and, as one source bluntly puts it, "orgies and bacchanales." The only remnant of this verdant luxury today is the multi-star Hotel Cipriani, with its beautiful oasis facing the Lagoon. As to trysts…who is to say?

As for the rest of the Giudecca, it has long since become thoroughly working class; as late as the 1960s there were houses without indoor plumbing. Many families worked in the numerous industries that took over the once idyllic gardens and suppressed monasteries: In the 19th and 20th centuries there were, among other things, the Molino Stucky (a flour mill and pasta factory), and factories producing pianos, watches, fireworks, and beer.

Today the only major activity is seen in several boatyards and the female prison. Some artists, in the time-honored way, have their studios in this down-market neighborhood, but it's not an artist's colony.

In case you wonder, as you step ashore at the vaporetto stop called Palanca, what this word could possibly mean, it recalls the years up to the sixties when there was still a *traghetto,* like the gondolas that cross the Grand Canal but in this case more often a boat called a *battello,* which rowed passengers between the Zattere and the Giudecca. The fee was a small coin, now extinct, called a *palanca.*

The church of the **Zitelle** is one of the Palladian wonders that have enhanced the Giudecca skyline. Its formal name is Santa Maria della Presentazione, but it's always been referred to as "the spinsters" because of the poor young women whom its convent was dedicated to helping—primarily by teaching lacemaking. Though the Zitelle was designed by Andrea Palladio, it wasn't actually built until after his death (1580). Jacopo Bozzetto carried out the work between 1582 and 1586, and the church is now administered by the friars of the Redentore.

With its simple Doric portico (1596) and squat campanile on the

Boats of every sort heading toward the Lido often take a short-cut through the Giudecca by means of the Rio del Ponte Lungo.

"Christic in the Garden of Gethsemane," by Palma Giovanni (1544–1628), hangs between marble columns in the Zitelle.

Santa Eufemia

- 🅐 Map p. 193
- ✉ Fondamenta Santa Eufemia
- ☎ 041 522 5848
- 🕐 Open only for Sun. Mass, & p.m.
- 🚤 41, 42, 82 to Palanca (or Santa Eufemia, when the stop is reinstated).

fondamenta facing the Giudecca Canal, the church of **Santa Eufemia** gives an appealing sense of the proportions of life here before Palladian grandeur struck. The church was founded in the ninth century, making it a slightly younger sibling to San Nicolò dei Mendicoli and San Giacometto in Venice proper, to which its outlines, though 11th century, bear a clear Veneto-Byzantine resemblance.

Inside, the nave and side aisles are from the original design, and a few of the 11th-century columns and capitals are still in place. The stuccowork and many of the paintings date from the 18th century, which gives the interior what may be a now familiar air of historical confusion, something many come to find attractive. The first altar on

the right aisle (facing the high altar) contains a triptych altarpiece of "San Rocco and the Angel," and a lunette painting above it showing "The Virgin and Child," by Bartolomeo Vivarini (1480). Other paintings are more often by followers of the great than the great themselves. For some reason this church possesses no Tintorettos.

One of Palladio's masterpieces, and still a landmark of Venetian religious and festive life, the church of the Most Holy Redeemer, or **Il Redentore,** dominates the Giudecca. It was the first of the two great churches (the other is Santa Maria della Salute) built in thanksgiving for deliverance from a plague, in this case the devastating epidemic of 1575–77 that killed 50,000 people, or one-third of the

population. The site was chosen partly because of its spectacular location, and partly to allow for a votive bridge to be built for the crucial religious procession. The church was completed in 1592, under the direction of Antonio Da Ponte (of Rialto Bridge fame).

This church is one of the touchstone Palladian creations: the soaring dome, the stately staircase leading to the entrance, the elegant but restrained proportions. The interior reflects all that Palladio learned in Rome, down to the "thermal" windows in the vaulting like those in the classic Roman baths. The white Istrian stone and white stucco may seem almost too stark, but Palladio was trying to mollify the Franciscan monks, who, mindful of their vows of poverty,

thought his design too grandiose. The statues flanking both the entrance and the high altar are of St. Mark and St. Francis. From its founding the church has lived its moment of glory on the third Sunday of July (see pp. 198–99).

An entrancing historical footnote is carved on the stone base of the flagpole outside. It commemorates the World War I exploit, the "Beffa (joke) di Buccari." From here on February 10, 1918, a small group led by poet Gabriele d'Annunzio slipped by night into the harbor of Buccari, where they torpedoed three Austrian ships and left blithe messages in bottles for the fleet command, boasting that "the seamen of Italy laugh at every sort of obstacle and are always ready to risk the unriskable." ■

The church of the Redentore is unquestionably the Giudecca's greatest attraction. There are conflicting theories about the two small towers that resemble minarets.

Festival of the Redentore

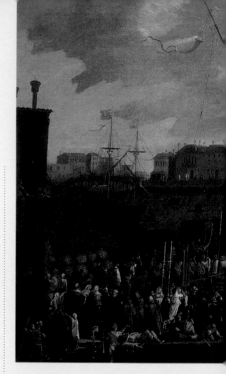

For centuries the Venetian year was studded with festivals that blended the sacred and profane with a splendor and passion almost impossible for us now to conceive. The feast of the Redeemer, or Redentore, is one of the few that remain, at least in its broad outlines.

During the Venetian empire, the doge solemnized the most important religious events by leading a ceremonial procession to the particular church, thus symbolically representing the power of the state rendering homage to the relevant saint. This state procession was a fantastic spectacle, in which the doge was sheltered by a huge umbrella made of cloth of gold, and followed by the Senate, chancellors, councilors, and every component of the government, plus the papal nuncio, ambassadors, legates, and Venetian aristocrats, accompanied by squires and pages bearing silken banners of white, red, blue, and green, all to the music of six silver trumpets.

But in the case of the Redentore, the procession faced the logistical problem of the water separating the Palazzo Ducale from the church. Hence a floating bridge—originally built on boats—would be constructed across the Giudecca Canal, stretching from the Zattere right to the foot of the church on the other side. Today, for at least two weeks before the feast day, military bridge engineers assemble a sturdy, olive-drab pontoon bridge.

The church itself (see pp. 196–97) was built in fulfillment of the vow that the Senate had made to the Redeemer in praying for deliverance from the catastrophic plague of 1575–77. With the church came the feast day (always the third Sunday in July), and with a feast day there always comes a celebration. Nowadays, early on that Saturday evening the Patriarch of Venice formally opens the festivities by walking across the bridge, followed by the mayor, various ministers, and an assortment of military officers.

If a few hundred have made the first walk across, thousands have spent the day preparing their boats, and endless amounts of food and drink, for the real event that evening. As sunset approaches, the Bacino di San Marco and the Giudecca Canal gradually fill up with boats that slip quietly across the still water (the bridge has blocked traffic for a blessed day and a half) to anchor and watch the fireworks. Until only a few years ago people still traditionally decorated their boats with homemade leafy arbors strung with paper lanterns—some paintings from the 18th century show how enchanting the scene was. Today, almost all of the boats are motorized, and decoration is becoming a lost art. But those who persevere are, perhaps without realizing it, continuing the Venetian tradition known over centuries of summer festivals on the water when hundreds of decorated boats would glide slowly along the Giudecca Canal, gleaming with lanterns, while their passengers sang and enjoyed the cool breeze after the heat of the day.

The fireworks and the food, though, haven't changed. Out come the traditional homemade Venetian dishes: *sarde in saor, bigoi in salsa, pasta e fasioi,* and *bovoleti,* the little

snails cooked with oil and garlic. And everyone seems to have at least one watermelon.
And so families and friends eat and drink and
occasionally sing and sometimes even swim
until darkness falls and midnight approaches
and then suddenly the sky explodes. Almost 45
minutes of nonstop fireworks flare over the
Bacino di San Marco, illuminating thousands
of entranced faces staring skyward from hundreds of boats and all along the shoreline.

When the last rocket flares, the boats disperse and the watchers ashore begin to trek
homeward. There are some who will still be
singing the rollicking old songs: "Viva viva
Redentore, here we sing and here we play,
here we eat and here we drink, sit down here,
come with me...Viva l'amor!" or the lilting
invitation that describes how the singer has
decorated his boat "with balloons and fes-
toons" and the only thing missing is the
singer's lady love—"I want you too, Ninetta,
to be there with me."

Some things have obviously changed over
the years, but the boats and the joy are still
central to what the Venetians call "the most
famous night." And whether or not they make
it to church the next day, it has still to be one
of the sacred moments of Venetian life. ■

**The votive bridge across the Giudecca
Canal was the scene of one of Venice's
most magnificent processions, as shown
above in a painting by J. Heinz. Today the
bridge and the boats are much less
elaborate, but the fireworks are thrilling.**

Lido di Venezia

VENETIANS SAY THAT THIS IS THE LEAST "VENETIAN" island in the Lagoon, and it's easy to see why. Before the 19th century the Lido di Venezia was just a strip of brushy dunes, another of those rustic spots favored for alfresco parties in warm weather, especially when the moon was full. Now it's where Venetians and vacationers alike come to enjoy the sun and fun of the city's beach resort.

The name is generic: *lido* simply means "beach," and at the beginning of the 20th century this was one of the most elegant sea-bathing resorts in Europe. The Lido di Venezia, generally just called "The Lido," was once an appealing blend of innocent charm—bicycles, horse-drawn carriages, and more artichoke farms than vacationers— and luxurious grandeur: the Hotel des Bains, the Hotel Excelsior, the summer Casino, and the decadent last days of the two main characters in *Death in Venice*. But this 7½-mile-long (12 km) island strip has been steadily built up in the past few decades, and far from being the tranquil seaside retreat of yore it now has much more the character

of a mainland suburb. The horses are gone, and the bicycles struggle to coexist with the ever heavier traffic; it is estimated that there are two motor vehicles (car or motorcycle) for each of the 25,000 inhabitants.

Nevertheless, having a resort so close to the city is a great thing, and many Venetian families make a lifelong tradition of renting a beach cabana for the season. The beaches in front of the big hotels are private, but by law the 30-foot (9 m) strip of sand bordering the water has to remain open to the public. If you plan a day at the beach—or have come to play golf, tennis, or ride horseback—you may want to consider heading home either by 5 or after 8 p.m.; the

Lido

 Map p. 193

I, 41, 42, 51, 52, 82 to Lido

vaporettos during the three hours in between are going to be full of hot, tired, exasperated people.

There are few sights of pressing import on the Lido—you really don't come here for history or art—but if you want a break from the beach, the 14th-century **Jewish cemetery** on Via Cipro can be visited, and the 17th-century **church of San Nicolò,** though not very conveniently located at the far northern end of the waterfront, has some carved choir stalls (1635) and two Veneto-Byzantine capitals from the original 11th-century church.

Clearly visible across the narrow strait from San Nicolò is the **Fort of Sant' Andrea.** It was designed by Michele Sanmichele in the 16th century, and at one time Casanova was incarcerated here. ■

Venice Film Festival

This was the first film festival as we know them—it was launched in 1932—and it remains one of the most famous, the Golden Lion award still carrying considerable prestige. For 12 days beginning on the last Thursday in August, parts of the Lido are as warm with movie stars, movie press, and movie faithful, who come to the Palazzo del Cinema and a few ancillary screening rooms to see both the occasional blockbuster and the plentiful art-house enigmas. The newspaper carries a full list of the screenings and notes the arrivals and departures of the actors, but, except for making it difficult to find hotel space, the city (unlike Cannes) actually remains fairly oblivious to the glamour. In fact, Venice has no film culture to speak of, and here, as elsewhere in Italy, almost all foreign films are dubbed into Italian.

Season tickets and individual tickets are on sale in the Palazzetto Selva near the Giardinetti Reali at San Marco (*Tel 041 521 2512*) or an hour before the screening at the PalaGalileo on the Lido, near the Palazzo del Cinema (*tel 041 272 6629*). ■

Tom Cruise, one of many stars who attend

A market boat sets up for business in a quiet canal on the island of Murano.

Murano, Burano, & Torcello

THIS TRINITY OF ISLANDS, EACH WITH ITS OWN UNIQUE appeal, is de rigueur for a leisurely day out in the Lagoon. Murano is famous for glass, Burano for lace, and Torcello for a cathedral that is also the oldest building in the Lagoon. Organized tours exist, but the islands are easy to reach on the frequent boats leaving from the Fondamenta Nuove, and it's far more pleasant to make your own plans.

MURANO

Murano is now so much a part of the typical Venetian visit that its former semi-independent status is easily forgotten. Because of the importance of the glass industry, Murano had its own council and mayor from 1272 until 1797, when Venice fell to Napoleon, as well as its own *Libro d'Oro* listing the ancient original families. This meant that a Venetian noble could marry the daughter of a glass master without losing any of his status. Murano was also permitted to coin the annual golden medal bearing the doge's crest. In case you're wondering what a lighthouse might be doing on Murano, strange as it may seem, its beam shines

Flourishing paint strokes on a teacup and saucer represent Murano's fine glass legacy.

more dependably on mundane items such as doorknobs and glass blocks used in building than on either the one-of-a-kind fine art sculptures at Venini or Seguso, or the ubiquitous little glass candies. At one time as many as 30,000 people lived on Murano; now there are about 5,000, and more than a few workers even commute here.

In 1291 the Venetian government, which always lived in dread of fire, decided to settle the glassmakers and their fiery furnaces on Murano. This was also a convenient way to maintain strict surveillance, as the industry even then was guarded as something akin to a state secret (as was Venetian scarlet, a particularly prized color devised by Venetian dyers). In the 16th

straight out into the Adriatic, an important beacon to the ships entering the Lagoon at San Nicolò.

This island may be almost as famous as Venice itself, having given its name to some of the most admired glass in the world. It still survives on glassmaking, though

Murano Regatta

Murano is the site, on the first Sunday in July, of the ultimate test of the ancient skill of rowing *a un remo*, or singly, with one oar. To win the Regata Storica as one of a pair is a very big deal, it's true, but doesn't require any solo rowing ability. Propelling a gondola in any circumstances calls for exceptional skill—and a hotly contested race

over 3 miles (5 km) at a top speed of 7 mph (11 kph) is quite a challenge. Sergio Tagliapietra ("Ciaci") won it 14 consecutive years, after which other racers refused to participate unless he withdrew. The vividly colored gondolas make a spectacular sight, and the finish is one of the most thrilling moments of the Venetian sporting year. ■

Above: Women at the Scuola di Merletti's lace museum create classic Burano lace by tying different knots according to a paper pattern.

Right: View overlooking Burano, with the church of San Martino rising above the houses

Murano
 Map p. 193

Museo dell'Arte Vetraria
 Map p. 193
✉ Fondamenta Giustinian
☎ 041 739 586
🕐 Closed Wed., Fri., Sat.
⚓ 41, 42 to Murano Museo

Burano
 Map p. 193

century Murano, like the Giudecca, became a favorite place for Venetian summer villas.

Murano's main sights today are the two main streets lined with glass shops—the **Fondamenta dei Vetrai** and the **Fondamenta Cavour**—the **Museo dell'Arte Vetraria,** with the largest collection of Venetian glass in the world; and the exquisite church of **Santi Maria e Donato,** a seventh-century Veneto-Byzantine jewel rebuilt in the 12th century with mosaic flooring from 1149, a 15th-century "ship's-keel" ceiling, and an imposing 13th-century mosaic of the Virgin in the apse.

BURANO
Like Murano, Burano has its own long history independent from that of Venice, and its natives would be most unlikely to call themselves Venetians. In its early centuries, it fell under the authority of Torcello, and was called Boreana, perhaps for the powerful "bora" northeast winds that bear down on it from the Gulf of Trieste. Though most of its people survived mainly on

fishing, for centuries Burano enjoyed international fame as the source of some of the most exquisite lace in Europe (in 1566, Philip II of Spain commissioned Mary Tudor's wedding trousseau from Burano). While many Buranelli, like their ancestors, still fish for a living, it's clearly tourism that has finally brought prosperity to this outpost, and, also like Murano, it subsists on the shadow of its past glory.

The lace so copiously on offer is almost always made elsewhere. Authentic Burano lace is available only in certain stores, or directly from the lacemaker herself, if you see one at work. Be aware that the dwindling number of women who make these intricately knotted wonders charge what they must for pieces that can represent hundreds

Burano lace

You may hear it said that lace-making developed in the Lagoon from the techniques of mending fishing nets. While there is a striking similarity between the two activities, lacemaking was originally an activity of nuns and noblewomen; later women of more humble status used it to beautify their linens and, if possible, augment their income.

Burano first became known for its lace in the 16th century, and its craftswomen used many different techniques, including the *punto Buranese,* or Burano point, a knotting method (each lacemaker on Burano specializes in one type of knot); drawn-thread work; *a reticello* (mesh); and the exclusively Venetian *punto in aria* (point-in-air), so called because it was done without being attached to any pattern. *Punto Buranese*, on the contrary, is worked following the design on a piece of paper. When all the knots are finished, the paper is simply pulled away, leaving the lace.

In 1872 the Countess Adriana Marcello established the Scuola di Merletti, which is still active, though struggling, and its building also houses a lace museum *(closed Tues.)*. Students are not plentiful; some believe it's an art that can be learned only when young, because of the physical (on the eyes and back) and mental exertion it needs. ∎

A different style of Venetian lace calls for bobbins.

Lagoon landmark, contains the island's only major artwork, a "Calvary" (ca 1725), an early work by Giambattista Tiepolo.

The little island of **Mazzorbo** is connected to Burano by an arching wooden bridge; it consists mostly of vineyards and farmland these days, and provides a peaceful haven where you can wander, away from the crowds in Piazza Galuppi. There are a few trattorias where you may be able to sample the local wine. The little 14th-century church of **Santa Caterina** is still active, though its Benedictine convent is long since demolished.

TORCELLO

Torcello is the sleeping beauty of the Lagoon. Its Byzantine cathedral and atmosphere of tranquil isolation can both calm and disturb the sensitive soul inclined to meditate too deeply on lost grandeur. The island of the "small tower" was once the most important island, and it still boasts the oldest church in the Lagoon. It also has a haunting beauty, enhanced by its sense of remoteness—English art historian John Ruskin characterized it as "widowhood"—that belies the fact that it takes only five minutes to get here from Burano.

The refugees from Altinum on the mainland made their first settlement here in the fifth century, and after the sack of Altinum in 639 their bishop transferred his seat to Torcello. The island prospered on farming, fishing, and trade, and at its peak numbered as many as 20,000 inhabitants. But with the decisive rise of Venice's power in the 14th century, and the constant problem of malaria, Torcello was eventually abandoned. Today only 30 or so people live here. A morning can hardly be better spent anywhere, with a leisurely look at its two churches, a hike to the top of

Torcello has only three restaurants, one of which is the tranquil Al Ponte del Diavolo.

Torcello
Map p. 193

of hours of work, prices that mass tourism isn't usually willing to pay.

The vividly colored houses are Burano's other claim to fame (colors that the owners aren't allowed to change any more), and may even be more beautiful on a foggy winter evening than a postcard-bright summer afternoon.

Composer Baldassare Galuppi (1706–1785) is Burano's only celebrity, having written some 112 "theatrical" operas, some of them to plays by his contemporary, Carlo Goldoni. Galuppi has given his name both to a street and Burano's main square, where an awkward statue has been erected. Robert Browning wrote a poem entitled "A Toccata of Galuppi's."

The 16th-century church of **San Martino**, whose leaning tower is a

the restored campanile (which has ramps, rather than stairs) to savor the panorama of the northern Lagoon, a visit to the modest **Museo dell'Estuario,** and lunch at one of the restaurants, perhaps the justifiably famous Locanda Cipriani (see p. 252).

The **Cattedrale di Santa Maria e Assunta** was founded in 639 by order of Isaac, the Exarch of Ravenna (the original inscription can be see to the left of high altar). It boasts the remains of an outdoor baptistery, while the interior, despite several restorations, retains its Byzantine solemnity. The austere beauty of the 13th-century mosaic of the Virgin in the apse presides over the original 7th-century altar. The far wall facing her is covered by a vast 12th- to 13th-century mosaic depicting the Last Judgment, whose tormented sinners seem much more alive than the saints.

The little church of **Santa Fosca,** next door, was built in the 11th century by the Greek workmen who built the cathedral. Obviously but beautifully restored, its simple interior is a fine example of the Greek cross plan.

Near the pathway leading to both churches is the so-called Throne of Attila, a massive stone hewn into the rough shape of a chair. It has no reliable connection whatever to the "Scourge of God," but it may once have served as a seat for Torcello's judges. Tradition holds that if you sit on it, you will marry within a year. The fate of a married person who sits on it has never been specified. ■

The Throne of Attila, in the background under the tree, recalls the islanders' memory of the barbarian hordes, but it was more likely the seat of early Torcello judges.

Museo dell'Estuario

🅰 Map p. 193

✉ Palazzo del Consiglio, Piazza di Torcello

☎ 041 730 761

🕐 Closed Mon. & lunchtime

💲 $

Glassmaking

The Venetians were not, obviously, the first or the only people to make glass. But canny merchants that they were, they discovered how to make the most of their limited resources by producing luxury goods of many types, and fine glass (though not lead crystal) has long been associated with Murano.

It isn't known exactly when glassmaking began in the Lagoon, but it may well have improved and developed in the 11th and 12th centuries after Venice had established stronger ties with the Middle East, particularly Syria.

In the early Middle Ages glass furnaces operated in Venice itself, but in 1291 the Senate decreed they should all be limited to Murano, for fear of fire. It is also likely that the government wanted to keep the glassworkers under surveillance, and this valuable commodity something akin to a state monopoly.

Murano glass reached its peak of glory between the 15th and 16th centuries, and some pieces from that period still survive in private collections and museums. If you look closely at the paintings of Titian and Veronese, you will often discover Murano mirrors, goblets, or chandeliers. Every technique has been used here: blown; diamond-engraved; gilt; frosted and "milk" glass; something called *lattisuol,* or fake porcelain; and filigree glass. One of Murano's more ingenious inventions was the "Venetian stiletto," a delicate knife made of glass so fine that an assassin could stab his victim with it and then break off the handle; the wound would close without a trace, leaving the victim's death a mystery.

At the end of the 16th century, the industry was in crisis as taste shifted to heavy cut glass, but its fortunes revived after an enterprising glassmaker named Antonio Briati in 1730 took the unprecedented step of going abroad—he went to Bohemia—to learn a new technique, for which he was first reviled by the Muranese, and later copied. After the fall of the Venetian empire in 1797 the craft went into decline, until Antonio Salviati, in the second half of the 19th century, helped restore it.

One aspect of historic Venetian glass artistry that often goes unnoticed or

Above: Glassmaking is a craft passed from father to son; women are only slowly making their way into the workshop.

unappreciated are the "pearls," or beads, that are used for making jewelry and even flowers. Within living memory there were still many Venetian women, called *impira perle,* who made money by stringing glass beads, sometimes extremely small ones, onto wires. You no longer see these women sitting in the campos with their aprons full of beads, but certain shops sell flowers whose petals are made of innumerable tiny glass beads.

Visits to glass furnaces are generally possible only if you come on an arranged visit with a tour leader; not surprisingly, the demonstration is brief, and the following visit to the showroom rather long. The prices on Murano may or may not be less than those you see in Venice; searching for a real bargain will probably be fruitless. ∎

Below: Blowing glass is still the ultimate expression of the glassmaker's art, and simple blobs of material take on every conceivable form. The furnaces, run by gas, never close except—understandably—for the month of August.

More islands to visit

SANT' ERASMO

This large, long island is called the "garden of Venice," since it is devoted to market gardens and most of its produce is sold by Venetian fruit and vegetable stands—the word *nostrani* indicates that it's "ours," or local. There is little to see here, but without much effort you can indulge yourself in what will feel like a trip to Indiana with its cornfields and flickering fireflies. The summer sunset views over the northern Lagoon are wonderfully beautiful, and there is a good restaurant, the Ca' Vignotto (see p. 252). The first Sunday in June is the patron saint's feast day, celebrated in typical island fashion with stands selling fresh vegetables by the crate, freshly barbecued ribs, dancing to a live band, and two passionately contested Venetian rowing races.

🗺 Map p. 193   🚤 13 to Sant' Erasmo Chiesa

San Giorgio Maggiore is admired as one of Palladio's greatest designs.

SAN FRANCESCO DEL DESERTO

Legend holds that St. Francis stopped at this cypress-covered islet between Burano and Sant' Erasmo on his way home from the Holy Land in 1220. It is now the site of a Franciscan monastery, where a monk gives conducted tours. Rooms are available for those who want to stay overnight, but you

need to make a reservation.

🗺 Map p. 193   ☎ 041 528 6863   🕐 Tour each a.m. & p.m.   💲 Donation   🚤 6, 12, 14 to Burano then take a water taxi

SAN GIORGIO MAGGIORE

Majestically presiding over the Bacino di San Marco is the elegant classical facade of the church of San Giorgio Maggiore, on the island of the same name. Although the blue-gray floodlight at night gives it a ghastly pallor, architect Andrea Palladio maintained that white was the color "particularly satisfying to God" (how did he know this?). Here, in 1576, Palladio built his first complete church according to classical principles (the facade was added in 1611 by Simone Sorella). The campanile was built in 1791, and some maintain that the view from the top is more striking than that from its counterpart at San Marco. Certainly the lines are shorter. There are often temporary exhibitions of high quality in the adjoining monastery, sponsored by the Cini Foundation. The monastery itself contains numerous treasures, as well as the refectory (Palladio's first work in Venice, 1560) and the double staircase by Baldassare Longhena (1641–47) leading to the library.

🗺 Map p. 193   ☎ 041 522 7827   💲 $ (campanile)   🚤 82 to San Giorgio

SAN LAZZARO DEGLI ARMENI

The Armenian community was a flourishing presence in Venice beginning in the 13th century, but it wasn't until the 18th century that they were given their own island. This is the site of the church, monastery, library, and printing press of the Mechitaristic friars, who follow the Catholic Armenian rite. The island is open for the tour, conducted by one of the monks, of its wildly eclectic collection of artworks and artifacts, including a mummy. Lord Byron spent a great deal of time here in 1818–19 studying Armenian, though his exact purpose for doing so is not clear. After a recent extensive renovation, guest rooms are now available; you'll need to make a reservation.

🗺 Map p. 193   ☎ 041 526 0104   🕐 Closed a.m.   💲 $$ 🚤 20 to San Lazzaro, leaving San Zaccaria at 3:10 p.m. ■

Seemingly remote and self-contained, Venice is also blessed with being in easy reach of plenty of other interesting places—alpine villages, historic cities, Palladian villas, and the Lagoon itself are all easy options for a day out.

Excursions

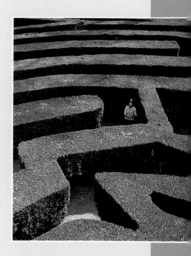

The maze at the Villa Pisani, Strà

Excursions

VENICE WAS FOUNDED FROM THE OUTSIDE IN, BY PEOPLE ALONG THE encircling shoreline who migrated into the Lagoon. But almost everyone has experienced a moment when the city's nautilus-shell character suddenly becomes oppressive. That's the time to take a break and venture outward for a day to the neighboring islands, the beach, or even the mainland.

You may be surprised to discover how many Venetians have had the same idea. Summer weekends mean trips to the countryside or the ocean for them, too, and the long holiday weekends at Easter, Pentecost, and Ferragosto (August 15) lure many Europeans to the Veneto as well. German families in campers virtually colonize the Adriatic beaches from Punta Sabbioni to Jesolo.

Any place you can reach on a day trip will at some point have belonged, willingly or not, to the Venetian empire, a fact that is constantly recalled by sightings of the winged lion of San Marco in spots where you might well have forgotten about Venice. Yet most of these towns have their own fascinating history, their variations on the dialect, and their typical dishes, and while the residents are proud of being

from the Veneto, they would never think of themselves as Venetian.

Along the nearby coastline, either the stretch edging the Lagoon or the seashore, there are distinctive fishing villages such as Pellestrina and Caorle whose popular annual festivals always draw large numbers of visitors. The town of Chioggia dates from Roman times, and, despite the gentle fun that the playwright Carlo Goldoni made of its volatile people in his comedy *The Chioggia Quarrels*, it is both a burgeoning beach resort as well as the "big city" to people near the southern part of the Lagoon.

The Venetian nobility loved country houses as much as anyone today, and in the 15th century began to build villas along the Brenta River for summer vacations that lasted for

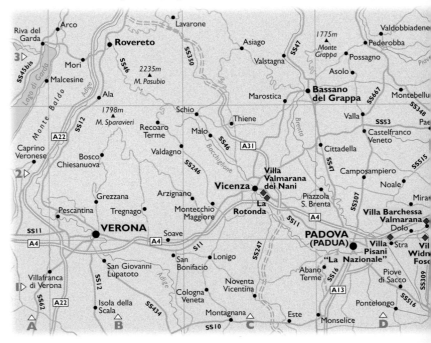

months. The program of activities here were equally as hectic as the winter social season in town, and the properties ranged from comparatively simple farmhouses that a succession of families rebuilt over the years, to virtual palaces thinly disguised as rustic retreats. The villas of the Brenta give an unforgettable glimpse of the astonishing amounts of wealth and imagination that the patrician class could devote to its personal pleasure.

Some of the Veneto's most historic towns are within easy reach of Venice. Ever since the medieval era, Padova (Padua) has both attracted artists to embellish its churches and palaces, and scholars to its university, one of Europe's earliest and best. The frescoes painted by Giotto in the Scrovegni Chapel are acknowledged as being among the greatest works of Renaissance art anywhere. And the Basilica of St. Anthony, a magnificent baroque structure, draws thousands of the faithful year-round, many of whom leave thank-offerings for prayers answered.

Vicenza, famous for textiles and jewelry (its artisans use 200 tons of gold each year), also boasts some of the most important buildings

The balcony of "Juliet's House" in Verona attracts lovers from around the world, although the house has no relation to Shakespeare's tragedy.

ever designed by Andrea di Pietro della Gondola, better known as Palladio, the Renaissance architect who rediscovered the classic style of Greece and Rome.

"Fair Verona" is destined to be forever associated with the story of Romeo and Juliet (the earliest version of the legend, by Luigi da Porto, was first published in Venice in 1530). But Verona began as a thriving Roman colony and has retained a number of monuments from that period, foremost among them being the Arena, the third largest Roman amphitheater in the world, where operas are performed every summer. The imposing castle and austere tombs of its medieval rulers, the Della Scala dynasty, recall the sterner days when patrons of the arts were also despots. ■

Jesolo is one of the largest and best known of the Adriatic resorts near Venice that draw tourists from across Europe.

The Littoral

THE SHORES THAT ENCLOSE AND FORM THE VENETIAN Lagoon also have history and monuments, and although many have developed into beach and camping centers, they have their own appeal. The long peninsula that arcs southward from the mainland was once primarily farmland, but today its bumper crop is vacationers, mostly Venetian and German. Discotheques, pizzerias, all-night bars, parks for campers, and the other accoutrements of youth- and family-oriented seaside resorts continue to flourish, with the concomitant occasional drug arrest and fatal motorcycle accident.

The Littoral
213 E1 & E2

Jesolo (pronounced YEZ-olo) is the better-known town, thanks to more aggressive development and a truly audacious advertising campaign showing a tanned, swan-diving man that promises the "sea all year long." (It remains a mystery how this squares with the climate it shares with Venice, which can be bitterly and foggily cold in winter.) There is a bus from Piazzale Roma to the Lido di Jesolo, but you can also take boat No. 12—a big double-decker—to Treporti, departing from San Zaccaria, and then take a bus to Jesolo or Cavallino.

Caorle, a placid fishing village and tourist haunt, is famous for its sanctuary of the Madonna dell' Angelo, perched at the harbor's point.

Punta Sabbioni, with its own *motonave* stop, is closer and more convenient to reach for just the day. This is a smaller, somewhat quieter locale, favored more by families than by the gilded youth.

The Lagoon (see pp. 218–19) is created by the long, narrow string of the **Barrier Islands,** which separate it from the Adriatic. The islands are dotted with small fishing villages that seem amazingly remote and detached from Venice, not to mention the rest of the world. Buses leaving from near the boat stop at Santa Maria Elisabetta on the Lido will trundle you all the way down to Chioggia, if you want. Even better, rent a bicycle and make a whole day (or two) of it.

Malamocco was one of the earliest Lagoon settlements, being founded in A.D. 568 (along with Torcello and Caorle) by refugees escaping the Lombard incursions on the mainland. For years, "Metamauco," as it was called, belonged to that early collection of coastal settlements stretching from Chioggia to Eraclea that formed a remote colony of the Byzantine Empire. In 742 this colony's seat of government was transferred from Eraclea to Malamocco, where it remained until 812. Malamocco's other claim to fame was as the home of "Buono of Malamocco," one of the two daring Venetians who stole the body of St. Mark and brought it to Venice (see p. 79). Today the village is a bit lost in the backwash, as it no longer survives on fishing and most of its inhabitants work elsewhere on the Lido, or even farther afield. Still, it's an attractive place for a wander, with small streets, promenades along either the Lagoon or the ocean, two good fish restaurants, and the chance occasionally to discover a woman outside her doorway making lace in the traditional way on a pillow, with bobbins. The second Sunday in July is the festival of the Madonna di Marina, complete with religious procession and boys trying to climb a greased pole over the Lagoon to snatch the flag from the end.

Pellestrina seems cast adrift in the farthest reaches of the watery world, suspended between sea and Lagoon. The village still relies heavily on fishing, and not only maintains its pastel houses but also has

A fisherman anchored at Caorle proclaims his boat, or perhaps himself, "indomitable."

its own distinctive version of the Venetian dialect. Everyone here has the same last name—or rather, one of four—which also define the four districts into which this tight-knit village long ago divided itself (Zennaro, Scarpa, Vianello, and Busetto). Pellestrina comes alive on the first Sunday in August, which is the feast day of the Madonna dell' Apparizione. The Virgin Mary reputedly appeared to a poor fisherman here in 1726, during one of Venice's countless wars against the Turks, and each year the locals commemorate the event with mountains of steamed local mussels, music, dancing, and two of the most fiercely contested Venetian rowing races in the entire calendar, easily visible from the street flanking the Lagoon. The

church of **Santa Maria di San Vito** was built to commemorate the miraculous apparition, and rebuilt in 1728 on a polygonal plan by the architect A. Tirali.

While you're here, take a walk along the elevated sea wall to see the *murazzi,* or sea defenses, that were built in 1744–1782. This 2½-mile (4 km) stretch of battlemented Istrian stone has been reinforced since the high tide of 1966, and recently a portion of sandy beach has been created in the hope of attracting tourists.

THE MAINLAND COAST
This fringe was the last bit of the old world for those who fled into the Lagoon for safety, but during the later days of the Roman Empire it was a flourishing trade route.

At **Altino** (the Roman Altinum, 700 B.C.–A.D. 400), just outside Venice on the road toward Trieste, a long-term archaeological dig of the settlement can be visited, as well as the small but attractive **Museum of Altino** displaying the finds. Many of these items are funerary fragments, resulting from the Roman practice of placing tombs alongside the road, in this case a road that connected with the Via Annia that went east to Aquileia. Two pathways have been marked; in the eastern portion of the dig you can walk along a part of one of the principal streets and see some mosaics that once decorated a house near by, as well as a metal smelting installation. In the northern portion, you can see a few remains of the city gate, which has

been dated to the first century B.C. It can be reached either by car or by bus.

On the very edge of the Lagoon is the town of **Caorle,** off the beaten track today but in a prime location in the days when boats were the faster means of transportation. This is the town, incidentally, that gave its name to the *caorlina*, the six-oar Venetian boat (see p. 62). Its charming small port is full of fishing boats, but the beaches have been discovered by sun-seeking vacationers. It still retains some of its original character, though the main streets have become a little more prettified than a hardy fishing village might warrant. The small church halfway along the sandy beach is a landmark, and the 11th-century duomo has some lovely frescoes. ■

Fish and mollusk "farming" are major Lagoon enterprises. Here, near Pellestrina, clam fishermen work near the mussel frames.

Altino

🅰 213 E2

Museum of Altino

✉ Via San Eliodoro 17

☎ 041 282 9008

💲 $

🚌 ATVO blue bus for Jesolo or San Donà di Piave stops outside the museum

Laguna Veneta

The Venetian Lagoon is one of the largest and most important wetland areas in Europe. A shallow sheet of water covering 210 square miles (259 sq km), it was formed some 6,000 years ago between the mainland and a long narrow strip of barrier islands. Here the waters of the rivers Po, Brenta, and Sile mingle with the tidal flux of the Adriatic, which passes through the three "mouths of the port" at Chioggia, Malamocco, and San Nicolò di Lido.

This complex ecosystem has supported Venice from its earliest days. With neither farming nor industry available to them, the early Venetians had a profound understanding of their dependence on the Lagoon. Their once extensive salt pans are gone, but fishing and fish farming are still major sources of income (see p. 22), with *capparossoli* (small clams) being the most important catch—some 40,000 tons a year are taken, though not always legally. Some areas have been totally overfished.

The centuries have seen a great deal of tinkering with the Lagoon, from the deepening of some canals to the diverting of the Brenta and Po Rivers, which otherwise by now would have completely silted up the entire area.

The 20th century saw other changes, which have not all been positive. Tidal flow patterns were altered, with various effects on birds, plants, and fish, due to several factors: the extension of the shoreline with landfill, and the disappearance of many of the *barene*, or marshy islets, due to erosion by waves from motorboats. (A few barene have been reconstructed, others temporarily defended.) The deep "Petroleum Canal" that enables tankers to cross the Lagoon from Malamocco to Porto Marghera has also affected tidal flows, not to mention the potential for an environmental disaster. The Italian government is currently considering forbidding tankers without a double hull from entering the Lagoon. Pollution from the industrial zone on the shoreline, though now much diminished, has left deposits of heavy metals in the sediments; those zones are now off-limits to clam fishing, though some fishermen illegally go there.

Septic tanks are now required in public buildings, and are being installed in private homes.

To the naturalist, the Venetian Lagoon is a remarkably rich wetland environment; not only the largest lagoon in the Mediterranean, but, as classified by the World Wildlife Fund, one of the primary migratory bird refuges in Europe, home, temporary or otherwise, to almost every species of waterfowl. Up to 40,000 birds winter here—widgeon, goldeneye, merganser, coot, pochard, cormorant, several types of herons, swans, and rare species such as marsh falcons and eagles. It is included in Project MAR, a United Nations program that lists wetlands of international importance. One study has shown that the Lagoon's biomass, or total of living forms, is more than ten times greater than in a forest.

After 20 years of seemingly endless studies, no agreement has been reached on the subject of high tides. Exceptional tides of varying depth have always been a fact of life in Venice, and Venetians regard them more as a nuisance than a threat. After all, a tidal cycle is only six hours long, which means at the most you'll be sloshing around in boots for only two hours. Since the catastrophic inundation of 1966 (due to a rare combination of weather events that has not been repeated), first-floor apartments have been banned and almost no one uses kerosene fuel anymore, which in 1966, mixed with the seawater, caused more damage to the city's stones than the salt water alone. Deep concern the long-term effect of any project that would interrupt the natural flow of the tide keeps the debate going.

Of much more drastic and immediate danger than the tide are the waves inflicted on the city (and the barene) by the ever increasing motorboat traffic. Recent studies have shown that in the Grand Canal, a wave strikes a building every second and a half (see pp. 15–16). There is no canal in Venice that does not demonstrate damage to foundations, and the corners of some buildings are already clamped from water level to the roof to keep them from collapsing completely. In the Lagoon itself, a census of traffic on a summer Sunday revealed two motorboats a minute

The Lagoon is a complex environment, always full of activity. Clockwise: Amateur rowers on their *caorlina*; a kingfisher; container winches

passed by, and many wetlands have now been surrounded by palisades of wooden pilings to protect them from the ceaseless surf. The various commercial interests (transportation companies, water taxis, sight-seeing launches) so far have frustrated most attempts to regulate the traffic. Venetians watch in speechless amazement as their brilliantly designed city, which survived more than a thousand years intact, has been driven to its knees in a mere thirty. ■

The Basilica di San Domenico was founded in 1200, although the current building reflects many renovations.

Chioggia

THIS CANAL-LACED CITY AT THE LAGOON'S SOUTHERN edge is proud of its history as a formerly independent town, and it would never admit to any inferiority in regard to its more famous neighbor, which dominated it after the War of Chioggia (1380).

Chioggia

🅰 213 E1

Tourist Office

✉ Lungomare
 Adriatico, 101
 (Sottomarina)

☎ 041 401 068

Founded by the Romans, who called it Fossa Clodia, Chioggia (pronounced KEY-od-gi-a) was once important enough to merit its own bishop and its own autonomous government. However, it found itself the excuse for another conflict between Venice and Genoa, and the so-called War of Chioggia (1378–1380) reduced the city to rubble, and gave it a future as a Venetian vassal. Venetian playwright Carlo Goldoni lived in Chioggia for five years, and *Le*

Baruffe Chiozzotte (The Chioggia Quarrels, 1760) is one of his more raucous comedies, an undoubtedly accurate if affectionate transcription of the impetuous locals that still inspires laughter.

Today Chioggia depends largely on fishing, either in the Lagoon or the sea, although tourism is steadily growing. The newer half of town, **Sottomarina,** has 73 hotels, many of them on the beach, while the older half seems eerily reminiscent of Venice, except for the traffic.

The **Corso del Popolo** divides the city and is just long enough for a reasonable stroll. (Oddly, the locals refer to this street as "the piazza.") At the end of the Corso where the ferry stops is the **Piazzetta Vigo,** with its 12th-century Greek marble column bearing the lion of San Marco (erected in 1786). The Venetians seem to think that this rather diminutive feline isn't much of a lion; they occasionally refer to it disparagingly as the "cat of Chioggia." For some reason this infuriates the locals.

The church of **San Domenico** *(Fondamenta San Domenico, tel 041 403 526)* near the Piazzetta Vigo boasts the last known painting by Vittore Carpaccio, of St. Paul (1520). A small chapel on the side contains a number of primitive paintings of sea disasters, given as offerings of thanks by the fishermen who survived.

The morning wholesale fish market *(closed Mon.)* is everything it ought to be: loud and busy. In its canal, and others, you can still see some examples of the heavy, stubby *bragozzo,* the typical Chioggia sea-fishing boat, though nowadays they're powered by motors rather than sail.

In front of the fish market you can see the former *granaio,* or grain warehouse. It was built in 1322 by the Chioggia architect Matteo Caime. A few original parts remain (the capitals, pillars, and arches) but it was modernized in 1864. The facade bears a small Gothic shrine containing a "Madonna and Child" in papier-mâché by Jacopo Sansovino (16th century).

Facing the church of San Giacomo is the **house of Rosalba Carriera,** the noted 18th-century painter of delicately colored portraits, who moved to Venice and eventually died insane; this was also

Right: Chioggia is among the top fishing centers of the Adriatic, and its fishermen have always been known for their courage and enterprise.

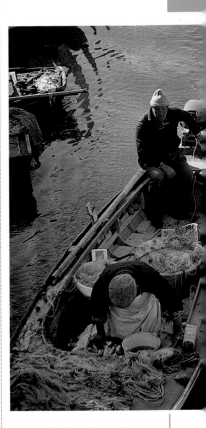

Carlo Goldoni's residence during the years he spent in Chioggia. The house is not open to the public, but bears a commemorative plaque.

There are two ways to get to Chioggia: The longer but more picturesque way is by the No. 11 bus that starts out from Santa Maria Elisabetta on the Lido and journeys down the entire stretch of the barrier islands, crossing the mouth of the port at Malamocco on a motor ferry. The end of the route is at Pellestrina, where you take the vaporetto across the channel to Chioggia, debarking at Piazza Vigo. The faster but less evocative option is the mainland bus marked "Chioggia" that departs from Piazzale Roma; the end of the line is in the center of Chioggia close to the duomo. ∎

Villas of the Brenta

VENETIANS, LIKE CITY-DWELLERS EVERYWHERE, HAVE always been keen to leave town in the summer. In the 15th and 16th centuries they built pleasure villas on the then leafy islands of Murano and the Giudecca, but in the following two centuries they headed for the mainland. The villas they built along the sylvan shores of what appears to be a placid little canal—really an offshoot of the Brenta River—are among the loveliest in the world, designed by some of the greatest names in architecture, and give a glimpse of the leisured life during the June through November *villeggiatura* (country holiday) of the last days of the republic.

The stretch of land between the Lagoon and Padua was once marshy and prone to floods (the Brenta also threatened to silt up the Lagoon). Between the 13th and 15th centuries it was the scene of fierce battles between the Venetians and the Paduans. None of it very conducive to expensive settlement. But when the fighting stopped and Venice diverted much of the river southward toward Chioggia, the area became much more attractive for building.

In 1770 a collection of engravings of these villas was published under the quaint title, "Brenta, almost a suburb of Venice," and its pages contained more than 70 villas belonging to the greatest patrician families of La Serenissima. Entire patrimonies were lavished on these estates, and the social life here, despite its tranquil setting, was scarcely less hectic than back in town. Guests such as Giacomo Casanova would come for weeks at a time, and were expected to participate in all sort of outings, picnics, gambling, concerts, fortune-telling seances, and balls.

With the fall of the empire many of the families were ruined, or at least drastically reduced in circumstances, and not a few of the palaces were sold or left to decay. A devoted student of the era could plan an interesting itinerary of the ruined or converted villas, but anyone looking mainly for charm will probably stop only at the main villas listed below. You can get there aboard the *Burchiello*, the boat that goes from Venice up the Brenta to Padova (Padua) and stops (possibly not long enough to suit you) at a few of the most important mansions. It takes its name from the heavy padded barge that in the 18th century carried the patrician families' best furniture to their summerhouses. There is also a highway: The SS11 clings to the riverbank, adding unromantic traffic to the scenery but making it convenient for you to plan your own itinerary by means of the public buses from Piazzale Roma.

The 15th-century Villa Widmann Foscari, after much alteration and decoration, now bursts with ornate French rococo style.

Villa Widmann Foscari

🅐 212 D1 & D2

✉ Via Nazionale 420, Mira Porte

☎ 041 424 156

🕐 Closed Mon.

💲 $$

🚌 ATVO blue bus No. 53 to Padova, or orange ACTV bus marked "Padova"

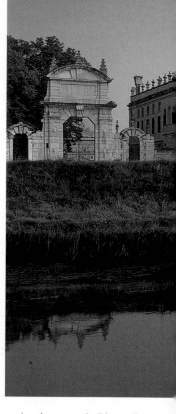

Mira Tourist Office

✉ Villa Widmann Foscari, via Nazionale, Mira

☎ 041 424 973

Not all of the villas are still inhabited, and even fewer are open to the public. If villas are your passion, the tourist office in Mira can provide all the information you might need.

Villa Foscari, more commonly called La Malcontenta, is a classical temple transposed to the riverbanks. It is one of the best known and most admired buildings by Andrea Palladio, the preeminent Veneto architect of the 16th century

In one of Villa Pisani's ornate rooms, centaurs and nymphs frolic in the classical landscape favored for elegant country houses.

Villa Barchessa Valmarana

🅰 212 D2

✉ Via Nazionale, Mira Porte

☎ 041 510 2341 or 041 426 6387

🕐 Closed Mon.

💲 $$

🚌 ATVO blue bus No. 53 to Padova, or orange ACTV bus marked "Padova"

and one of the greatest in the history of Western architecture. Some have even called it the most beautiful house in the world. It was built in 1559 for the brothers Alvise and Nicolò Foscari, and is supposedly named for one of the melancholy Foscari ladies who was banished here for adultery. The story seems pretty unlikely, considering the high level of tolerance Venetians had for the most outrageous behavior; actually, the area had long borne this name, possibly referring to the political exiles who used to hide in the marshes.

Palladio drew his strongest influences from Roman buildings; in this case, the main hall recalls the design of the thermal baths of the classical epoch, complete with the arched window in three

sections known as the "thermal" window. The frescoes are by Battista Franco and Giovanni Battista Zelotti, and depict a wide variety of mythological scenes. The frescoes in the central hall represent scenes from Ovid's *Metamorphosis,* an odd choice for this idyllic setting, considering that they illustrate the divine disgust at humanity's wickedness.

The **Villa Widmann Foscari** is an attractive, compact villa whose current form reflects numerous additions and subtractions to the original one-story palazzo of 1550 made by a series of patrician owners up until 1759. The cruciform top floor with the barrel roof, the last addition, was very unusual for Venice. Inside there is a very high-ceilinged ballroom with a

balustrade of wrought iron and brass, and the gold and white stucco decoration favored during the 18th-century rococo period.

At the **Villa Barchessa Valmarana,** the actual villa is no longer there —it was demolished by the family in the 19th century to avoid paying taxes. What can be visited is one of the two *barchesse* that formerly served as granary and boathouse for the villa and later, during the 17th century, were converted into guest quarters. The furniture is original, and the dining room's ceiling fresco, somewhat ironically now, shows the apotheosis of the Valmarana family. The other barchessa has been converted into private residences. **Villa Pisani "La Nazionale"** is an immense, ornate palace evoking memories more of Versailles than simple pastoral diversions—something Napoleon appreciated when he bought it from the Pisani family in 1807. It was here that Mussolini and Hitler first met in 1939.

The unfathomably wealthy Pisanis commissioned the house from architect Girolamo Frigimelica of Padova in 1735, when Alvise Pisani was elected doge, and it was completed in 1760. The luxurious furnishings are long gone, which gives the rooms an even chillier aspect, but the frescoes still glow, particularly Giambattista Tiepolo's "Glorification of the Pisani Family" in the ballroom, his last work in the Veneto, which he painted in 1762 when he was 73. The vast park contains a maze and the stables. ∎

With 114 rooms, the Villa Pisani at Strà is the queen of the Brenta. Formerly owned by various royals, it is now a national monument.

Villa Pisani "La Nazionale"

🅰 212 D1 & D2

✉ Via Doge Pisani 7, Strà

☎ 049 502 074

💲 $$

🚌 ATVO blue bus No. 53 to Padova, or orange ACTV bus marked "Padova"

Padova

ONCE ALMOST AN ISLAND, ENCIRCLED BY THE BRENTA River, Padova (Padua) was already a prosperous town under the Roman Empire. It is famed as the home of one of Europe's oldest and most respected universities (founded in 1222), the Scrovegni Chapel, containing one of the greatest fresco cycles in the world, and the basilica dedicated to one of the best-loved saints, Anthony.

"Il Santo" in Padova is Antonio, and his splendid basilica was begun soon after the monk's death in 1231.

Padova (Padua)
🅰 212 D1

Scrovegni Chapel
✉ Piazza Eremitani 9
☎ 049 820 4550
🕐 Reservations required
💲 $$

Basilica
✉ Piazza del Santo
☎ 049 824 2811

Said to have been founded in 1186 B.C., Padova became a Roman *municipium* in 45 B.C. Once a powerful opponent to Venetian expansion, in 1406 it finally submitted to the "Dominante"—politically, but never in spirit. Even today the doggerel that characterizes each important town in the Veneto labels the Paduans *"gran dottori,"* great scholars.

Both the university and the town's importance as a commercial center attracted a substantial Jewish population—the university was the first in Europe to accept Jewish students, who came to study medicine. Like Venice, Padova required its Jews to inhabit a ghetto, of which few traces remain.

The city drew the most brilliant names of their day: Dante, Petrarch,

Giotto, Donatello, and Mantegna were often in Padova, and Galileo conducted a number of important experiments here.

An easy half hour from Venice by train, Padova is well worth at least half a day's exploration, and the principal sights are all within walking distance of the station.

The **Scrovegni Chapel** is one of the great monuments of Western art, in which the Byzantine-Gothic tradition of painting first began to warm under Giotto's humanizing hand. The series of frescoes (1303–1305) with which he illuminated the walls of the Scrovegni family's private chapel (the palace was demolished in 1827) show the sequence of events in the life of the Virgin Mary, and later, Jesus; even more clearly, they show Giotto's

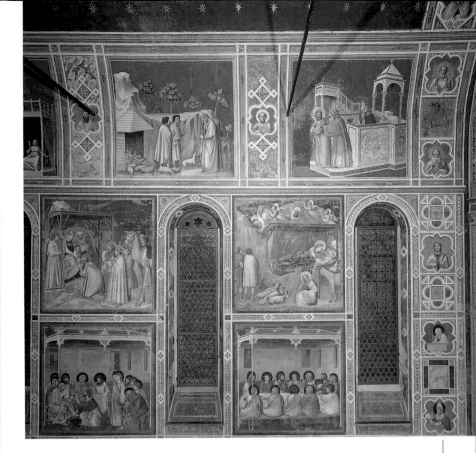

revolutionary step toward a more naturalistic depiction of both people and their behavior. Emotion had suddenly become paintable, and even after 700 years the works provoke a response.

Amid the splendor of blue and gold, look for the many moments of human encounter—Anne and Joachim, Mary's parents, embracing at the city gate; Judas reaching forward to kiss Jesus and betray him; the assorted characters in the backgrounds; and the distraught angels above the Crucifixion, rending their garments and clutching their faces. None of this had ever been thought of before Giotto, much less depicted.

The increasing number of visitors—up to 250,000 a year now—has presented severe challenges to

this delicate environment. The entrance (from the side, its original connection to the palace) is now a sort of purifying passageway to prevent dust and drastic changes in temperature from damaging the chapel; there is also a limit to the number of people allowed in at once, and the length of time they may stay. These regulations, along with special "cold" halogen lights, have already been greatly beneficial to the frescoes.

St. Anthony of Padova—with his symbol, the lily—is one of Italy's, if not the world's, best loved saints; helper in locating lost objects, and a host of other specialties, too, as the innumerable votive offerings and letters attest. The **Basilica di Sant' Antonio** (popularly known as the Basilica del Santo, or just Il

Giotto's cycle of frescoes in the Scrovegni family chapel retells the lives of the Virgin and Jesus in a style that revolutionized Western art.

The Prato della Valle was once the field for periodic animal fairs. Now circled by a wall topped by statues, it is a huge and shady public park.

Orto Botanico (Botanical Garden)

✉ Via Orto Botanico 15

☎ 049 656 614

🕐 Closed Nov.–March

masterpiece of High Renaissance sculpture." The seventh panel, the poignantly named "Miracle of the Miser's Heart," is one of Lombardo's most powerful works. The ceiling is decorated with stucco work by Giovanni Maria Falconetto (1533) and is considered among the Veneto's finest.

In the piazza outside is Donatello's bronze equestrian statue (1443–1453) of the mercenary captain Erasmo da Narni, called **"Gattamelata."** This is one of Italy's two most important Renaissance equestrian statues—the other is Verrocchio's statue of Colleoni in the Campo Santi Giovanni e Paolo in Venice (see p. 105), though "Gattamelata" was made first.

Not all monuments are created by artists: The **Orto Botanico** (Botanical Garden), established by order of the Venetian government in 1540, was the first botanical garden in Europe and now represents some 400 years of care and study. It still regularly receives and sends horticultural specimens around the world.

The medical faculty of the university was the first to benefit from the garden's array of medicinal plants, which are mostly arranged according to the original design of a circle within a square—just like a classical temple. The palm tree, which was planted in 1585, is standing just as it was in 1786 when it inspired German writer Johann Wolfgang Goethe to pen his reflections on the metamorphosis of plants.

There are a number of other notable sights in Padova, among them the **Prato della Valle.** At 107,640 square yards (90,000 sq m), it's considered the largest 18th-century piazza in Europe, although it's more of a park than the usual sort of piazza. ■

Santo) remains, as it has always been, one of the great pilgrimage sites of the world.

This Franciscan friar was born in Lisbon in 1195, but it was in Padova that he died, in 1231. Already loved and greatly admired for his powerful preaching against usury—and with several miracles to his name—he was canonized just a year after his death, and it wasn't long before work began on his church. This fabulously ornate basilica, now more baroque than Gothic, is full of art and relics; the saint's body is in the Cappella dell'Arca, while fragments of others are in the Cappella del Tesoro.

The **Cappella dell'Arca,** through which the faithful stream every day, is full of touching testimonies to the saint's influence and requests for his help. Note also the nine superb marble bas-reliefs showing events from Anthony's life sculpted by such Renaissance masters as Tullio Lombardo and Jacopo Sansovino. The fourth panel, Sansovino's "Miracle of the Maiden Carilla" (1562), has been called "the unchallenged

Vicenza

FAMED NOT ONLY FOR ITS MOST ILLUSTRIOUS SON, THE Renaissance architect Andrea Palladio, but also for a long tradition of exquisite goldsmithing, this historic city about 30 miles (48 km) beyond Venice enjoys a striking setting between its two rivers and the Berici hills.

Like Padova (Padua), Vicenza was once a Roman town, and like Padova it was conquered by Venice in 1404, though it did not accept this event with much grace, having been sacked both by its adversaries and its former ally, the Holy Roman Emperor. This may account for the curious Venetian characterization: "*Vicentini, mangia gatti*—the people of Vicenza eat cats"—though its most famous dish is unquestionably the succulent salt cod recipe known as *baccalà alla Vicentina*.

Long wealthy as a textile center, the proud Vicentine aristocracy could boast of having a hundred palaces, almost as many as Venice. Stylish Vicenza is still wealthy—among the top six wealthiest cities in Italy— thanks as always to its textiles, as well as a slew of high-tech companies.

Palladio isn't Vicenza's only famous name: The Gothic **house of Antonio Pigafetta,** one of 21 survivors of Magellan's voyage around the world (1519–1522), can be seen at via Pigafetta 5 *(closed to public),* just behind the Piazza delle Erbe.

Access to cars has been severely restricted in Vicenza's historic center, which adds to the enjoyment of a walk among its principal sights: the **Piazza dei Signori,** the Gothic **Duomo** (reconstructed after almost complete destruction during World War II), and the Dominican church of the **Santa Corona** (1261) with "The Adoration of the Magi" by Veronese (1573) and "The Baptism of Christ" by Giovanni Bellini (1501). The other sights all are connected to Palladio, an inescapable architectural presence in the city.

An artisan's draft demonstration draws onlookers in the **Piazza dei Signori,** under the watchful gaze of a lion of **San Marco.**

Vicenza
🔼 212 C2

Basilica
✉ Piazza dei Signori
☎ 044 432 3681
🕐 Closed Mon.
💲 Free. Fee for specific exhibitions

The canal entrance to the *barchessa* (boat-house) at the Villa Valmarana

Museo Civico

✉ Palazzo Chiericati, Piazza Matteotti 37–39

☎ 044 432 1384 or 044 432 5071

🕐 Closed Mon.

💲 $$

Palladio designed 11 palaces and public buildings in Vicenza, and many more villas in the surrounding countryside, and even more throughout the Veneto. Foremost among his works to be seen here is the so-called **Basilica,** which some consider his masterpiece; it was his first public commission, and his only work to be constructed completely of stone. Not actually a building, it is a wall surrounding the 15th-century Palazzo della Ragione.

Other buildings include his unfinished **Loggia del Capitaniato** (1571–72) in the Piazza dei Signori; the **Casa Civena** (1540–46) on Viale Eretenio; the **Palazzo Chiericati** (begun in 1551), now housing the **Museo Civico,** which comprises painting by local artists as well as works by Tintoretto, Tiepolo, Veronese, and Giovanni Bellini; and the **Teatro Olimpico,** his last and in some ways most interesting building, designed for the Vicentine Academy. The street named Contrà Porti contains three Palladian palaces: No. 11, No. 12, and No. 21.

Just barely outside the city are two sights you can reach on foot. One is the **Villa Valmarana dai Nani** ("of the dwarves"), so called for its statues of the same. It is a sober 18th-century villa, but the

decoration of its rooms is superb, ranging from mythological scenes of heroes and gods by Giambattista Tiepolo to more domestic vignettes of country life by his son, Giandomenico. The other is **La Rotonda,** Palladio's most famous villa (1566) and the inspiration for many buildings in England and France. Unlike the rest, which retained some function as working farmhouses, this was designed solely for entertaining—its circle-within-a-square design is the bane of architecture students.

When planning a trip to Vicenza, bear in mind the fact that every September the city is full for conferences and an international jewelers' fair. If you enjoy markets, visit on a Tuesday, when stands line the streets around the Duomo. ■

Palladio's design for "La Rotonda" epitomized the Renaissance ideal. It was originally intended to be a city palace.

Teatro Olimpico
- ✉ Piazza Matteotti
- ☎ 044 422 2800
- 🕐 Closed Mon.
- 💲 $

Villa Valmarana dai Nani
- 🅰 212 C2
- ✉ Via dei Nani 2–8
- ☎ 044 454 3868
- 💲 $$

La Rotonda
- 🅰 212 C2
- ✉ Via della Rotonda 2
- ☎ 044 432 1793
- 🕐 Closed except Wed.; grounds closed every day except Tues., Wed., & Thurs.

Palladio & his villas

There is little debate that Andrea di Pietro della Gondola—Palladio—is one of architecture's greatest geniuses. With brilliant ingenuity and profound aesthetic sensitivity he adapted the classical forms he studied in Rome and reinterpreted them in palaces, villas, and churches that are still regarded as the perfection of their type. "Palladian" has come to describe not only a style, but also an almost sublime excellence.

Born in Padova in 1508, Palladio moved to Vicenza when he was 16 to work as an apprentice stone-cutter. When Count Giangiorgio Trissino befriended him 14 years later, he received his classical nickname and an education to match. Palladio's building experience and his own talent enabled him to interpret the classical forms in a way that became not only the dominant style of his epoch, but has made his name synonymous with restrained elegance. Palladio was no unsung hero; when he died in 1580 he left scores of enviable buildings, along with a number of designs and works in progress that were completed by his followers. ■

Verona

VERONA HAS ALWAYS BEEN RICH, FAMOUS, AND BEAUTIFUL, thanks to its location at the perfect geographical crossing on the routes from central Italy northward to Austria and Germany, and eastward to Venice and Trieste. A flourishing Roman settlement founded in the first century B.C., in the eighth century it became the seat of the Frankish ruler, Charlemagne's father Pepin the Short. Today it is the largest city in the Veneto.

Below: Verona is shaped by the curving Adige River, echoed by the long row of cafés lining the Piazza Bra.

Verona
🅼 212 B2

San Zeno Maggiore
✉ Piazza San Zeno 2
☎ 045 800 6120
💲 $

Giusti Gardens
✉ Via Giardini Giusti 2
☎ 045 803 4029
💲 $$

Opposite: The Teatro Romano is now used for plays, often those by Shakespeare.

In the 11th century this independent city-state was tormented by the internecine rivalries recounted much later in *Romeo and Juliet*, but with the rule of the Della Scala, or Scaliger, family (1262–1387) Verona enjoyed its greatest years. The Scaligeri were tyrants, but also patrons of the arts. Dante, in exile from Florence, was given refuge by Cangrande I, and the grateful poet dedicated the "Paradiso" of his *The Divine Comedy* to him.

In 1404 Verona, like its sister cities, fell to Venetian power (the Piazza delle Erbe bears the winged lion on its pedestal). Its fortunes then followed those of Venice, passing to the French, despite heroic resistance, in 1797, then to the Austrians, and finally unification with Italy in 1866.

It is not always possible to include all the interesting sights in a too-hurried visit, but among the choices you have, try not to miss the 12th-century church of **San Zeno Maggiore,** considered one of the most outstanding Romanesque churches in Europe. The triptych over the high altar by Andrea Mantegna (1457–59), still in its original frame, is the first major Renaissance painting done in Verona. Note also, in the chapel to the left of the high altar, the little painted marble statue of "San Zeno Laughing" (14th century). The **Giusti Gardens** are a lovely hidden retreat, not too big and everything you'd want a Renaissance garden to be, complete with moldy statues. And the first-century B.C. Teatro Romano stages theater, ballet, and jazz.

The immortal star-crossed lovers, Romeo and Juliet, are better appreciated in the theater than in Verona. This story was first penned in 1530 by one Luigi Da Porto, a nobleman from Vicenza. The Capulets and Montagues existed, but they lived (peacefully) near Vicenza. Verona's "House of Juliet" was probably an inn, and "Juliet's balcony" was added in 1928.

Near the heart of Verona's historic center is the spacious **Piazza Bra,** just inside the 16th-century city walls. From here the streets radiate out according to the plan laid out by the Romans under the decree of Emperor Augustus. On

Arena di Verona

✉ Piazza Bra

☎ 045 800 3204

🕒 Closed Mon.

💲 $

Castelvecchio

✉ Corso Castelvecchio 2

☎ 045 801 5435 or
045 592 985

🕒 Closed Mon.

💲 $$

Palazzo del Comune

🕒 Closed Mon.

the south and west sides are 19th-century municipal buildings, while the north side is filled by a row of restaurants and cafés, all lined up facing the Arena. The Via Mazzini is one of the main shopping streets, a pedestrian zone leading you to the Piazza delle Erbe (see below) and its neighboring monuments. The Via dei Alpini takes you directly to the Castelvecchio, the city's old castle (see below). A number of plaques on buildings in the piazza and near-by commemorate heroic moments in various wars of the last 200 years.

The **Arena di Verona,** finished in about A.D. 30, is one of the best preserved arenas extant, with 44 tiers seating 22,000 spectators. It has been used for gladiatorial contests, public executions, fairs, tournaments, and bull-baiting, but

The setting for summer opera productions, Verona's Arena is the third largest amphitheater in the world.

since 1913 it has hosted the well-respected summer opera festival, whose singers are first-rate even if the productions can occasionally be disappointing.

The **Castelvecchio** was built between 1345 and 1375 by Cangrande II, and was redesigned by Venetian architect Carlo Scarpa as a museum space. The works by Mantegna, Veronese, Tintoretto,

Canaletto, and many local artists are no less impressive than the castle itself. The bridge spanning the Adige River was reconstructed after German bombs destroyed it—like all of Verona's bridges—in World War II.

Originally the Forum of the Roman city, the attractive **Piazza delle Erbe** is still in some ways the center of town. The jumble of stalls in the middle may obscure certain views but also give it real life. The dignified statue of "Madonna Verona" was erected in 1368; the marble fountain basin at her feet is of the Roman period. The lion of San Marco atop its column is a reproduction of the original, destroyed during the Veronese resistance to Napoleon's advance in 1797.

Passing under the arch linking the Palazzo degli Scaligeri to the Palazzo del Capitano, you come to the **Arche Scaligeri,** the tombs of the Scaligeri rulers, among the most impressive and best preserved medieval funeral monuments in Italy. The little adjacent church of **Santa Maria Antica** (12th century) has been restored.

The **Piazza dei Signori** next to the Piazza delle Erbe was the civic center of the medieval city, formed by the 12th-century **Palazzo del Comune** (with the Torre dei Lamberti); the Palazzo dei Tribunali (or courts), with its gateway designed by Sanmicheli; the Renaissance Loggia del Consiglio, where the citizens' council met; and at the far end is the 13th-century Palazzo del Governo, once the Scaligeri family residence.

For all its modern importance as a regional center, Verona has carefully maintained its historic character. And it has the ability to surprise you, especially at odd hours, with its particular character, all warm brick and faded ocher, and its unmistakable pride. ■

Travelwise

**Young women on scooters
in Chioggia**

TRAVELWISE INFORMATION

Venice may, at first sight, give the impression that it is a vast museum or theme park. It is neither. It is a city that is still organized more for its residents than for visitors, and its overall appeal may well depend on how much you like the unpredictable. There are many things that will strike you as illogical but are perfectly acceptable to the Venetians, who, like most Italians, do not make a cult of efficiency. An anecdote, often recounted by Venetians, tells of a desperate lost tourist who finally asks a little old lady for directions. Her reply is *"sempre dritto"* ("just keep straight on"). The funny thing is, there is no "straight" in Venice, but you can still get from here to there, and if you take this as your guide to the Venetian universe, you'll have many happy surprises.

PLANNING YOUR TRIP

WHEN TO GO

At one time tourists came mainly in the summer, but now they come year-round, though there are relatively fewer in winter (Nov.–March). Having said that, many major cultural events tend to take place between October and April, including the Fenice and Teatro Goldoni seasons. There are times each year during which huge numbers of visitors are always expected, and hotels can get booked up months in advance. The biggest is Carnivale (Feb./March), but you should also book early if your visit is to coincide with the Biennale (begins June, odd-numbered years) or the Vogalonga weekend (variable dates in May). Late August/early September is very busy because of the Venice Film Festival, the Regata Storica, and the awarding of the "Campiello" literary prize. In October hotel space is tight due to commercial expositions.

Museums generally remain open all year, though you may find one shut for reasons of its own (renovation work, for instance). Some shorten their hours in winter, so it is always wise to check. Hotels occasionally shut for a winter break, sometimes reopening only for Carnivale.

Although the weather can be surprisingly good in August, this is by no means the best time to visit. It is the holiday month in Italy, and Venetians leave the city in droves and head for the mountains. As a result, the character of the city changes considerably, with the majority of people on the streets being tourists. The fact that many restaurants and shops close during August contributes to a strangely thinned-out feeling in the city, despite the crowds.

The "best" time to visit is therefore a matter of weighing up all the variables: the most beautiful months are May and September, but it's crowded; the number of visitors thin out in winter and there are events to be enjoyed, but there will be fog, rain, cold, and early nightfalls.

CLIMATE

Venice's weather is fairly comparable to New York City: It can be terrifically hot in the summer, bitterly cold in winter, and sublimely beautiful in spring and fall. Humidity can intensify the sensation of either heat or cold. It rarely snows, but there will be fog and rain. On the other hand, there can be bright, clear, and calm winter days, and summer days that are dry and breezy. Air-conditioning is not common. Mosquitoes can be.

The famous *acqua alta* (or high water, which technically is not flooding, but high tide) can happen between September and March. Some years it's frequent, other years it doesn't occur at all. Wooden walkways are placed above areas most likely to be under water; walk carefully, as they tend to get crowded. Better yet, a pair of lightweight plastic boots that reach to the knee should keep you moving without too much inconvenience; local hardware stores sell them. Plastic leaf and lawn bags also work, pulled up to your thighs. In any case, the tide turns every six hours, so it doesn't last all day.

The average temperatures for Venice are:
spring (March–May) 60°F (16°C)
summer (Jun.–Aug.) 80°F (26°C)
fall (Sept.–Nov.) 55°F (13°C)
winter (Dec.–Feb.) 35°F (2°C)

Weather patterns throughout Europe have been changing in the past few years, and this seems set to continue for some time. In general, winter tends to be wetter than summer in Venice, though the frequency and amount vary from year to year. It is best to come prepared for at least some precipitation.

WHAT TO TAKE

Venice is a casual yet elegant city, where attractive, even designer, sportswear is usually appropriate for all but the most formal occasions. Men will need a jacket and tie to dine at the best restaurants. A lightweight raincoat is useful in all but the coldest months, and a sweater or wrap to ward off evening breezes. Lightweight thermal underwear can be useful for the deep winter, and a suitable hat. Comfortable walking shoes are indispensable. Women are no longer required to cover their heads when they enter a church, but men are expected to doff their hats, and doorkeepers and clergy can be very strict about scanty garments and bare limbs. A large, lightweight scarf to swath you while you're inside is a very useful accessory to carry.

Summer can be hot, and cool clothing is sensible, but Venetians are intensely proud of their city and their history, and look with dismay and even repugnance on those visitors who appear to confuse the city of the doges with a beach resort and wander around barefoot and scantily clad. Comfort is understood, but so is respect, and the Venetians will notice it and appreciate it.

Don't forget the essentials: Passport, driver's license (if you intend to rent a car for excursions out of the city), insurance documentation, and traveler's checks.

INSURANCE

Make sure you have adequate coverage for medical treatment and expenses, including repatriation, and loss of baggage and money.

PASSPORTS

U.S. and Canadian citizens only need a passport to enter Italy for a stay of up to three months. No visa is required. Tourists must be registered with the local police on arrival. Your hotel will do this for you, and for this purpose the receptionist will ask for your passport when you check in. It will be returned to you after a few hours.

HOW TO GET TO VENICE

BY AIR

AIRLINES
Air France, tel 147 884 466
Alitalia, tel 147 865 542 (international reservations) or 147 865 641 (national reservations)
Delta, tel 800 864 114 (toll free)
KLM, tel 147 865 060
Lufthansa, tel 0280 663 025

At the time of writing, the only non-stop flight to Venice from the U.S. is operated by Delta Airlines from JFK airport, New York City. Otherwise, there are many options for connection services through major European cities: London, Paris, Amsterdam, Zurich, Frankfurt,

Munich, Brussels, and, of course, Rome and Milan. In addition to considerations of airfare and timetable, be aware that these connections may involve changing terminals and passing through passport control/immigration (though you will not have to collect your bags), which can be somewhat time consuming. Allow ample time—an hour is not enough, no matter what the regulations or your travel agent may claim.

AIRPORTS
Marco Polo Airport, Via Galilei, 30 Tessera, tel 041 260 6111. Venice's airport is the third busiest in Italy, with over a thousand flights a week. There are several ways to reach Venice from the airport:

By land: Meter taxis are lined up at the curb outside, and will take you to Piazzale Roma (average fare L40,000, depending on traffic). There are also two bus companies that run to Piazzale Roma. The blue ATVO buses cost L5,000 per passenger (pay the driver when you board). They run every 30 minutes, and the schedule is posted on the sign at the boarding point on the curb. The orange ACTV (city buses) run every 30 minutes, at 10 and 40 minutes past the hour. The cost is L1,500 per person, but the tickets are only on sale at the newsstand just inside the departures area by the bus stop.

On all orange buses you are required to validate your ticket on boarding by stamping it in the small yellow machines mounted on stanchions in the front and rear of the bus. Inspectors board at random and can ask to see your ticket. If you don't have one, or haven't stamped it, they will fine you on the spot.

The advantage of the land buses is that they are inexpensive and fast: You'll be in Piazzale Roma in 20 minutes. However, you will then have to either walk to your hotel or take a vaporetto, thus adding time and extra logistics to the arrival process.

By water: Private water taxis can be rented just outside the arrivals area (L150,000 for the trip, payable in cash only). If you are staying in a multi-star hotel, it may have its own launch; ask at the hotel's desk in the arrivals area. The cost will be added to your room bill.

There is also a large yellow launch operated by Alilaguna (tel 041 523 5775), which stops at the Zattere, San Marco, Arsenale, Lido, and Murano; another route stops at the Riva degli Schiavoni and the Fondamenta Nuove. It runs hourly at 6:15 a.m., 7:15 a.m., 8:10 a.m., 9:05 a.m., and thereafter at five minutes past every hour until 12:05 a.m. The cost is L17,000; ticket available at the desk in the arrivals area. The trip from the airport to San Marco takes an hour and ten minutes.

BY RAIL

Venice is very well served by trains from all over Italy and Europe. Be sure to note if the arrival is listed as "Venice S.L." for Santa Lucia station, in the city itself, as some trains officially categorized as being for Venice actually terminate at Mestre on the mainland, requiring you to change trains for the brief connection to Venice. The toll-free number in Italy for train information is 147 888 088; in Venice, tel 041 785 570. Both numbers are in service from 7 a.m. to 9 p.m. Check online at www.fs-on-line.it

The Eurailpass is valid for travel on Italy's thousand daily trains covering 3,750 miles (6,000 km), as well as trains connecting Italy with other European countries. There is also an Italian Railpass, but it cannot be purchased in Italy. You need to buy it in the U.S. before you leave. Information online at www.naplesinfo.com/dertravel/eurail_passes_multi_country_railpasses.htm.

BY BUS

Long-distance regular buses, similar to Greyhound, don't operate within Italy. Euroline, based in Florence, provides scheduled services between Italy and other European countries. For information, tel 055 357 110; fax 055 350 565.

GETTING AROUND

Venice is one of the few cities on Earth in which cars do not exist. Thus, the options for transportation are fairly few: a *vaporetto* or *motoscafo* (waterbus), the *gondola traghetto*, or ferry, that crosses the Grand Canal, a water taxi and, simply put, your feet.

BY PUBLIC TRANSPORTATION

Don't automatically assume that you need to take the vaporetto to get where you're going; in many cases your fastest and shortest route between two points may well be on foot. Otherwise, the ACTV "waterbuses" are in two forms: the vaporetto, which is big and clumpy and high in the water, and the motoscafo, which is smaller, sleeker and lower. There are many routes that circle the city and islands, and a few are designed with a minimum of stops to expedite travel between the major points of interest. Information on routes and printed timetables are available at the ACTV office at Piazzale Roma, the ACTV office near the Piazza San Marco at San Marco 1810 (Ponte dei Fuseri), and at the ticket booths at major landing stages such as San Zaccaria, Accademia, San Tomà, and Rialto. Timetables often list hours according to whether they are *festivo* (Sunday) or *feriale* (weekdays). Alternatively, tel 041 528 7886 for information.

You must have a validated ticket to ride the waterbuses. If the ticket booth is closed (or nonexistent), ask the *marinaio* (the uniformed person who ties up the boat at each stop) to sell you one as soon as you board. Your ticket isn't always checked, but inspectors board at random and if you don't have a ticket, you will be fined on the spot.

The normal one-way ticket costs L6,000. There is also a L10,000 round-trip ticket (which can be used for two consecutive rides, not necessarily a literal round-trip, within one day). There is also a variety of other one-way tickets at slight discounts: For a group of three, L15,000; four, L20,000; or five, L25,000. Dogs and cats and/or large bags are L6,000 extra. Unfortunately, there are no discounts for couples.

There are also "travel cards" for unlimited use as specified: 24 hours from the time it is stamped: for one person, L18,000; for a group of three, L45,000; for a group of four, L60,000; for a group of five, L75,000. For one person, 72 hours validity, L35,000; for seven days, L60,000.

If you are staying longer than a few days, you might want to apply for a "Carta Venezia," which enables you to buy one-way tickets for only L1,500 each. Apply by filling out a form at the ACTV office at Piazzale Roma, with passport photo and by paying a L10,000 fee.

The ACTV information office also provides a complimentary booklet of the timetables of all routes, including buses on the Lido, with a complete listing of ticket options and prices (in Italian and English). For further information, consult the ACTV websites: www.actv.it or www.velaspa.com.

It is specifically prohibited to board vaporettos in swimwear. Also note that space is obviously very limited aboard the vaporettos, so it will be appreciated if you do your best not to block traffic with your luggage. If you are carrying a backpack, take it off when you board and set it at your feet, so as to not to annoy those standing nearby or who need to pass.

Pickpockets take advantage of the crush onboard. Guard your possessions. If your wallet is taken, or you see it happen to someone else, notify the marinaio immediately; the captain will stop the boat until the police arrive.

To avoid possible misroutings, ask the marinaio before you board if the waterbus is in fact going where you want to go. In some cases waterbuses replicate route numbers but not the exact route, in others they vary the route according to the time of day, and it's not uncommon to see the route sign on the side of the bus (which is supposed to be switched at the end of the line) with the arrows pointing in the wrong direction. A simple question before you step aboard can save time and aggravation.

BY GONDOLA TRAGHETTOS

These are gondola "ferries" rowed by two gondoliers that cross the Grand Canal at established points. These points are clearly marked by a standard large wooden sign above the small wooden staircase leading to the water. These are: San Marcuola/Fontego dei Turchi, Santa Sofia/Pescheria (Rialto), Rialto (Riva del Vin/Riva del Carbon), San Tomà/Sant'Angelo, Ca' Rezzonico/San Samuele, Giglio/San Gregorio, and Salute/San Marco. This is a convenient, inexpensive, and very Venetian mode of transport. The cost per person is L700; you pay as you board or, if there is lots of confusion, as you disembark. Each traghetto keeps its own hours, some working all day, and some only in the morning. This isn't Switzerland. However, the hours are posted at the embarkation point.

GONDOLA RIDES

This remains the classic and unique way to experience Venice at its magical best. It is not unreasonable or uncommon to engage a gondolier for a whole day to transport you wherever you want to go. For example, if you have a list of churches you want to see, having a gondola at your disposal can actually be a very efficient way to get to them with a minimum of effort and maximum of charm. For those keen on photographing or even sketching the secret byways, there is no better way than by gondola, as views from the water are amazingly different from on shore. The cost depends primarily on the season—it costs much less in the winter than in the summer, naturally, but some winter days can be beautifully calm and mild. The cost also depends on the gondola "station" where you seek out a willing gondolier; the price will be agreed on by you and the gondolier (it won't be the usual per-hour price multiplied by the number of hours you request). It will be up to you to arrive at a fee that seems acceptable. To find a gondolier, talk to the *bancale,* the chief of each station, who will suggest some gondoliers who are scheduled to work on the day you request. All that said, it's not inconceivable that you could have a gondola for a full winter day for as little as L500,000. (Tips are welcome, but not required.) It is recommended that you go in person rather than telephone the various stations to arrange this service.

There are two ways to rent a gondola: One is to go to a *stazio* where the gondolas are grouped The Bacino Orseolo, Molo and Danieli are closest to San Marco, and there are two at the Rialto, one on each side of the Grand Canal. There is also one in front of the church of San Moisè. The others are at the train station, Piazzale Roma, Santa Sofia, Santa Maria del Giglio, Calle Vallaresso, and San Tomà. You will be given a boat in order, according to the gondoliers' rotation, or you can simply approach one of the gondoliers standing there saying "Gondola?" The other way is to accept the invitation of whatever

gondolier you encounter standing on a bridge in many places throughout the city—he is a regular gondolier working on his day off. There are no "gypsy" gondoliers; the number of licenses is exactly 405, and the gondoliers all know each other. An interloper would never be tolerated.

The cost for a ride has been established by the gondoliers' association, and is displayed in fantastically tiny print on the white card on the prow of the boat. The normal price is L120,000 for 50 minutes on a set route. The maximum number of passengers is six, and the price is for the ride (not per person). If you request a different route, or a longer ride, the price will vary, but you should agree on it before you start. Each additional 25 minutes is L60,000. Between 8:00 p.m. and 8:00 a.m. the cost is L150,000 for 50 minutes, and 75,000 for each additional 25 minutes. If you have any questions, you can contact the gondoliers' association, the Ente Gondola (tel 041 528 5075).

Gondoliers work for themselves (and are extremely proud of their independence), so they generally set their own schedules. You probably won't find a gondolier who is ready to take you out before 9:00 a.m. But in the summer many of them are still available at midnight, or even later.

The gondola is most easily distinguished by the large metal plate with comblike prongs on its prow, while the *sandolo* (see next column) has a little metal curlicue instead.

It is not customary to tip the gondolier, though you may if the spirit moves you. However, if a grizzled old boatman is there with a boathook to hold the gondola steady and to help you ashore, he will have placed a hat strategically nearby into which a tip would fit nicely. As with tips anywhere, it is at your discretion, but less than L5,000 would not be very appropriate.

One further note: The time

of day can have a powerful influence on your experience of Venice in a gondola. Mornings are when workaday Venice gets things done, and the Grand Canal and many side canals are roiling with motorboat traffic until around 1 p.m. Not very romantic. If you have the luxury of choosing your moment, the best time is toward the late afternoon or early evening, when the water is calm and the sunlight mellows and the city seems to breathe a deep and languorous sigh. This is the time when Venice will reveal herself to you in all her murmuring, unforgettable enchantment.

SANDOLOS

Shorter and smaller than a gondola, seating a maximum of four, the sandolo (rowed by a *sandolista*) is a traditional Venetian boat with a design that it still common as a private all-purpose vessel. However, the sandolos for rent have been painted black and furnished with all the gondola trimmings; the sandolistas even dress like gondoliers and stand on bridges saying "Gondola, gondola." You can have a perfectly nice ride in a sandolo, but you might as well go in a real gondola—the total price for the ride is the same, and, because they carry fewer passengers, the sandolos actually cost more per person.

ORGANIZED SIGHT-SEEING

An organized tour can be the most efficient way to see the major sites if your time is limited. Full- and half-day tours are offered by most large travel agencies (American Express, Thomas Cook, Bassani, Guetta, and Trident on the Lido); your hotel concierge will have details. There are also tours that offer a different eye on the city: **Itinerari Segreti, Palazzo Ducale.** This tour takes you behind the scenes in the Palazzo Ducale into rooms that aren't open to the general public. Also

GETTING AROUND/PRACTICAL ADVICE

conducted in English. Tours at 10 a.m. and noon; L24,000, by reservation, tel 041 522 4951.

Jewish Cemetery, Lido: A guided tour of this historic cemetery for those interested in Jewish history and culture. Sun. 2:30 p.m. (group tours other days by reservation); L12,000, tel 041 715 359.

Richard Wagner Hall, Calle Larga Vendramin. The Wagner Association offers a tour of the rooms occupied by the famous composer in this palace on the Grand Canal. Tours in English if there are enough English-speaking visitors to warrant it. Sat. a.m.; free, but by reservation, tel 041 523 2544.

For a boat tour out of the city to the villas of the Brenta, the *Burchiello* goes once a day between March and October from Venice to Strà along the Brenta River. Schedule varies seasonally; L114,000 one way (return by bus; fare not included in price); lunch (optional) L40,000, tel 049 660 944.

TOUR GUIDES
The Associazione Guide Turistiche can provide custom-made tours, or a qualified person to accompany you and simplify things for you. Advance booking is usually advisable, tel 041 520 9038, fax 041 521 0762.

BY CAR

The streets of Venice are no bigger than sidewalks, so driving is nonexistent here and cars can't come any farther than Piazzale Roma. If you arrive by car, there are three garages: the Autorimesso Comunale in Piazzale Roma (tel 041 523 7763; L30,000 per day), the Parcheggio Sant' Andrea i Piazzale Roma (tel 041 520 6235; L8,000 for two hours) and the Autorimessa at Tronchetto (tel 041 520 7555; L25,000 per day).

CAR RENTAL
It's possible that you might want to have a car for exploring the Veneto region, to roam the

countryside, where public transportation is rare or inconvenient. However, if your goal is a city, a car makes little practical sense. Most towns are easily accessible either by train or bus, either of which will deposit you virtually in the center. Trains and buses also spare you the often too intense excitement of driving in Italy, not to mention the adventure of finding a place to park.

If you decide to rent, all major companies have branches either at Marco Polo Airport or at Piazzale Roma, or both.
Hertz tel 041 528 3524
Avis tel 041 522 5825
Europcar tel 041 523 8616
Budget tel 041 541 5040 (at Mestre train station and airport)
Mattiazzo tel 041 522 0884 (chauffeur-driven limousines are also available)

DRIVING REGULATIONS
Seat belts are required for all passengers, even in the back seat; don't be influenced in any way by how many Italians you will see not using them. All other regulations are the generally standard ones you're already accustomed to. However, you should be aware that the Italian urge to be first applies on the road as well as at the bus stop, and Italian drivers speed at any opportunity. They often pass on blind curves and in tunnels. Late at night on a weekend, many young people may be driving home from the discos and this can be a dangerous time to be on the road. One rule Italians do observe is the opposite of the custom in the U.S.: at a traffic circle, the incoming traffic has the right of way and any vehicle already within the traffic circle has to yield.

CAR BREAKDOWNS
For rental cars, check the package of information in the glove compartment for the emergency number; the Automobile Club of Italy (ACI) can be reached at their emergency phone number: 116.

ADDRESSES

You will immediately notice that Venice has a rather odd system of numbering houses. The number goes with the name of the *sestiere* (Cannaregio 2956) and not with the street name. Street names have been listed here for individual places, but you could also purchase an inexpensive "Guida Anagrafica" available in most bookstores. This little paperback cross-references each street number with its corresponding street name. Be sure to note the sestiere when you start looking for a particular number; you could search fruitlessly for Cannaregio 2956 only to discover you really needed Castello instead. You may also become baffled by the number of streets that have the same name, for instance Calle del Forner (in Venetian, Calle del Pistor), but this is just another indication of how self-sufficient each little city neighborhood used to be (and how many bakers there were).

PRACTICAL ADVICE

COMMUNICATIONS

POST OFFICES
Main branch: Fondaco dei Tedeschi, at the Rialto Bridge, tel 041 271 7111, vaporetto: Rialto, Open Mon.–Sat. 8:15 a.m–7 p.m.
Local branches: Open Mon.–Fri. 8:10 a.m–1:30 a.m., Sat. 8:10 a.m.–12:30 p.m., and 8:10 a.m.–noon on the last working day of the month.

There seem to be fewer and fewer branch post offices throughout the city. Tobacco shops usually sell stamps, but aren't permitted to weigh mail.
Mailboxes: Red *cassette delle lettere* (mailboxes) are located outside every post office, as well as on walls near where there used to be a post office. They have separate compartments, one for the city of Venice *(per la città)*, the other for anywhere else in the world *(tutte le altre destinazioni)*.

TELEPHONES

To call Italy from the United States, dial 011-39 (the international code and the country code for Italy) and the ten-digit number (including the initial zero of the city prefix).

To make a domestic call from a telephone booth within Italy, it's most convenient to use a *scheda telefonica* (phone card) available from the post office or one of the many tabaccheria. It is sold in denominations of L5,000, L10,000, and L15,000. Be sure to tear the perforated corner off the card.

A local call costs only L200. Calls to cellular phones are more expensive.

Orange public phones are plentiful and can take coins (L200 or L500 coins), phone cards, or credit cards. Some take only credit cards (the words *solo c. di credito* will appear). If you use coins, the phone will not give any of them back to you once you start to talk.

The following instructions will appear on the telephone, on a small LED screen above the number keys: *Sganciare* (pick up the receiver); *inserire la carta* (insert your card); *attendere prego* (wait) and then you can dial. Cafés usually have coin-operated phones. For a call within Venice, L200 will probably be enough.

Every call within Italy requires the city prefix, including calls you make within the city itself. Within Italy, the prefix begins with 0. Hence a call to a number in Venice from a phone in Venice begins with 041.

To make an international call from Italy, dial 00, followed by the country code (1 for the U.S. and Canada), the area code, and the subscriber number. The toll-free access numbers for long-distance operators in North America include:

AT&T: 172 1011
MCI: 800 014 340
Sprint: 172 1877

ELECTRICITY

Italian circuits use 200 volts; a transformer and adapter plug are needed for American appliances that operate on 110 volts. Many appliances are equipped with switches that convert them from one voltage to another, but an adapter plug is still needed. Before you leave home, ask at an electrical supply store, or one that sells clocks and small electrical appliances.

LOCAL CUSTOMS

Despite the impact of millions of tourists a year, Venetians are still open to foreigners who are genuinely interested in their city, culture, and history, and they are partial to Americans. "Just be yourself" is the best rule of thumb, as long as you remember you're in a place that has more the character of a living room than a city—somebody else's, and not your own. It's considered polite to say *buon giorno* or (toward evening) *buona sera* and *arrivederci* when you enter and leave a restaurant, shop, or café, even if you don't immediately see anybody to say it to. *Scusi* means "excuse me" if you've stepped on someone's foot, or if you want to attract their attention. If you want to ask them to make room for you to pass, you say *Con permesso,* or simply *permesso.*

You're on vacation, so relaxing is important. But by now Venetians have seen so much appalling behavior from so many tourists that any indication of regard for public decorum is noticed and intensely appreciated. Tourists don't disappear into the crowd here—they *are* the crowd. Sitting on bridges, eating an impromptu picnic on the street, putting your feet up on your seat or the one ahead of you on the vaporetto are not interpreted as charming, casual joie-de-vivre, but will label you as ignorant and uncouth.

Venetians will take you to their hearts if you make even the most hesitant attempt to

speak a few words of Italian. They will also be quick to help you with directions, but may doubt that you can remember every right-and-left turn they describe; they may often explain to a certain point and then say "and then ask again."

If you are invited to dinner in a Venetian home, flowers, wine, or an assortment of fresh pastries are very welcome.

The days of bargaining are long past. The shop owner may spontaneously offer a token discount for his own reasons, but don't expect it or think you can wheedle him into it. Assume that prices are as marked.

MEDIA

NEWSPAPERS

A few kiosks, though not most, sell some English-language newspapers, including the *International Herald Tribune, U.S.A. Today, The Financial Times,* and a number of British dailies, as well as the international editions of *Time* and *Newsweek* magazines (out on Tuesday). The major Italian daily papers are the *Corriere della Sera, La Stampa,* and *La Repúbblica.* There are two local papers: *La Nuova Venezia,* a tabloid with short articles, and the *Gazzettino di Venezia.* Its first section is national and international news, the second section focuses on Venice and the nearby communities.

The *Gazzettino* always publishes a little list of useful local numbers, details of which pharmacies are open, and information on cultural events for the day (only good for last-minute decisions). They never list any ticket prices, though.

RADIO

Radio Venezia (101.1 and 92.4 FM) play easygoing pop music and occasional news (in Italian); Radio Venezia Sound (98.5 FM) offers up-to-the-minute pop, both Italian and American; Radio Base Network (93.7 FM) plays a wide variety of music, with the exception of classical.

TELEVISION

The national stations available on non-cable TVs are RAI1, RAI2, and RAI3; other channels are Canale 5, Italia 1, Rete 4, Telemontecarlo, and TMC2. Most programs are in Italian. American films or sitcoms are dubbed in Italian.

MONEY MATTERS

American Express, San Marco 1471 (Salizzada San Moisè), tel 041 520 0844, closed Sun., vaporetto: Giglio, Vallaresso.

In July 2001, one U.S. dollar equaled approximately L2,300. The lira comes in coins of 50, 100, 500, and 1,000. Note that the L50 coin comes in two different sizes (tiny and medium), and the L100 coin comes in three different sizes (tiny, medium, and large). As we go to print, the tiniest coins are being recalled by the banks.

Telephones and vending machines don't accept all sizes of coins. The L500 coin and the L1,000 coin are startlingly similar in appearance, being almost the same size, and with a border of contrasting metal (the L500 has a copper center, the L1,000 has a copper border). Note that the L200 and L500 coin are very useful for the machines in churches that automatically turn the lights onto works of art. The L100 coins can sometimes be used for this, too.

The lira also comes in bills of 1,000, 2,000, 5,000, 10,000, 50,000, 100,000 and (not often seen) 500,000.

On January 1, 1999, the euro became the official currency of Italy, and the Italian lira became a denomination of the euro. Lira notes and coins continue to be legal tender during a transitional period. Euro banknotes and coins are to be introduced by January 2002. (At the time of writing 1 euro = L2,300.)

Commercial currency exchanges are located in banks, at the airport and train station, and in travel agencies. Bank branches that exchange currency display a sign saying *Cambio*. A commission is usually charged. Rates can vary, but only slightly. Cash withdrawals against a credit card are possible at banks and currency exchanges, and with an ATM card at banks. The American Express office exchanges currency, offering special service to holders of an Amex card.

There are a large number of ATMs in the city, where you can make cash withdrawals with your credit card, but you will need to have an international PIN number to use this service. Check with your bank before leaving. Cash machines occasionally have problems with magnetic strips; try another one elsewhere. A fee is usually charged for credit card advances, but the exchange rate may be more advantageous than those offered by banks.

Many shops advertise that they accept credit cards, but sometimes prefer cash, and may even offer a slight discount for a cash purchase.

OPENING TIMES

Most banks are open Monday to Friday from 8:30 a.m.–12:30 p.m., and from 2:45–3:45 p.m. Some of the central offices keep longer hours. Boutiques open at 9 a.m. or even 10, and generally close at 7 or 7:30 p.m.; they are usually closed on Monday morning and at lunchtime (anywhere between 12:30 and 4 p.m.). The closer you are to the Piazza San Marco, the more likely the shops are to be open all day, even on Sunday. Shops on the Strada Nova are often open on Sunday, too. Most hair salons are closed on Monday. Dry cleaners are often closed on Saturday.

Cafés are generally open at 7 a.m. and may stay open until 8 p.m. or even until midnight, depending on the neighborhood and clientele (for instance, in the university area). Most restaurants are open noon–3 p.m. and 7:30–11 p.m. Many stores and restaurants are closed in August.

REST ROOMS

Most bars and cafés (though not all) have *toilette* (toilets) you can use, though it is expected that you will purchase something, if only a small glass of mineral water. Most large hotels have rest rooms on the first floor. There are also a few pay public toilets (Campo San Bartolomio, the Accademia Bridge on the Accademia side). The cost is either L500 or L1,000; to enter you purchase a plastic card from a vending machine at the entrance. The card is then inserted into the turnstile mechanism. These facilities also have a space for changing baby diapers, and are usually very clean. They are open from 8 a.m.–7 p.m. During Carnival portable toilets of the Port-o-San variety are set up in a few major campos.

All restaurants are required to have rest rooms, but they may not always be up to the highest standards of cleanliness. Don't be surprised to find a squat toilet, or one without a seat, and take the precaution of carrying a packet of Kleenex.

TIME DIFFERENCES

Venice is one hour ahead of Greenwich Mean Time. If it is midnight in Venice, it is 6 p.m. in New York, and 3 p.m. in California. Italy observes daylight saving time. The date when the clocks change in the fall *(ora solare)* is usually the same as in the U.S., though the spring date *(ora legale)* may vary by a week. Check with the tourist office before you go, or at your hotel once you are there.

TIPPING

Most restaurant bills include a service charge. This is generally indicated at the bottom of the menu. If in doubt, ask *"E' incluso il servizio?"* If you feel that you have had exceptional service, you can modestly round up. But don't feel awkward about leaving the exact amount, even if it's some strange number like L147,000. Venetians wait for their change, and waiters bring it. It is usual to give porters and doormen from L5,000–10,000. Tour guides would expect 5 to 10 percent of the total cost of their services. Hairdressers don't expect a tip, but sometimes there is a container at the desk for tips that are shared at the end of the day.

TOURIST OFFICE

Associazione di Promozione Turistica (APT)
San Marco 71/f Calle dell' Ascensione (entrance to Piazza San Marco)
Tel 041 529 8711
Fax 041 523 0399
 or 041 529 8730

The tourist office publishes *Leo* magazine every other month, with interesting articles on Venice in both Italian and English. It also includes a wealth of useful phone numbers and a map. Ask for your complimentary copy at the APT office at the entrance to the Piazza San Marco nearest to the San Marco vaporetto stop.

TRAVELERS WITH DISABILITIES

Venice presents considerable challenges to a person with a physical disability. Elevators are rare, and small; only a few buildings have installed entrance ramps, and although there are a few bridges with wheelchair elevators (not the Rialto Bridge, though), these can't be relied on to be functioning. Organized group tours, or with a professional private tour guide, are the best way to see the major sights, as the leader will have been able to arrange access in advance (though boarding and debarking from a water taxi is a formidable undertaking; it's somewhat less demanding from a waterbus).

For those trying to see the city on their own, it will be a Herculean task.
Escort services for travelers with disabilities
For information contact the Tour Guide Association, San Marco 750 (Calle Morosini della Regina gia' del Pignoli, near the church of San Zulian), tel 041 520 9038.

EMERGENCIES

CRIME

Venice has justifiably been proud of its reputation as a safe city, and it still has remarkably little violent crime. However, there has been an increase in recent years in incidences of pickpocketing and purse-snatching. Be prudent at all times, especially in crowded areas (of which there are many in this tiny city). Don't take too much cash with you at one time, keep your documents and credit cards separate from your cash, make a photocopy of your passport to expedite replacement if necessary. Needless to say, you cannot possibly win the "shell" games that are occasionally operated by Eastern Europeans in the street, and the minimum bet is a whopping L100,000 (about $43). There are emergency rooms (*Pronto Soccorso*) at the Ospedale Civile in Venice at Campo San Giovanni e Paolo, or at the Ospedale Umberto I in Mestre at via Circonvallazione, 50.

EMBASSIES & CONSULATES

Most embassies and consulates in Venice are honorary, and much of the real work is done in larger Italian cities. Their functions vary, depending on which country they represent, but in general they are on hand to help their nationals in distress in a temporary way (such as emergency identification documents) until the main

embassy can act. They are also involved in various matters involving commercial activity in the port and airport.
United States Largo Donegani, Milan, tel 02 29 03 51
Canada Riviera Ruzzante 25, Padova, tel 049 876 4833
Great Britain Dorsoduro 1051 (Accademia), tel 041 522 7207
For legal assistance in an emergency, contact your embassy or consulate for a list of English-speaking lawyers. Or you may request assistance from the Corpo Consulare, a consortium of consulates, at Campo Santa Sofia, Cannaregio 4201, tel 041 528 9875.

EMERGENCY TELEPHONE NUMBERS

Ambulance: 118
Fire: 115
Police: 112

LOST PROPERTY
ACTV: 041 272 2179
Airport: 041 260 6436
Train station: 041 785 238

LOST CREDIT CARDS
American Express: 800 872 000
Diners Club: 800 864 064
MasterCard: 800 870 866
Visa: 800 877 232

MEDICAL EMERGENCIES
For medical emergencies that don't warrant the calling of an ambulance (see above), you should call the Guardia Medica, which maintains a doctor on call at night (Mon.–Fri. 8 p.m.–8 a.m.) and from Saturday at 10 a.m. to Monday at 8 a.m. The number for Venice and the Giudecca is 041 529 4060. There is a pediatric doctor on call daily 8 a.m. to 8 p.m., tel 199 152 152. there is also an emergency dentist available Sunday 9 a.m. to noon and 3 to 6 p.m., tel 033 626 2418.

 Pharmacies take turns staying open all night; the name and address of the ones that are on duty at night is posted on every pharmacy door.

HOTELS & RESTAURANTS

Venice is the most expensive city in Italy. This doesn't mean that you need a bank loan to survive, but you could spoil your visit by constantly comparing prices with costs at home. And certain pleasures, like the fragrant espresso or the incredible ice cream, can be surprisingly modest. It all evens out.

HOTELS

Venetian hotels, listed here by price then in alphabetical order, are officially rated from no stars to five stars (see below). Even some of the more modest hotels will have an in-house restaurant. Value-added tax and service are included in the price.

Many hotels will include breakfast in the room cost, usually continental-style (bread, croissant, jam, and tea or coffee), but sometimes a more substantial buffet is provided.

Little has been done to make the city's hotels and restaurants accessible to disabled visitors. There are no specific facilities and buildings will almost certainly have steps to be navigated. Travelers with disabilities should check when making a reservation to ensure the hotel or restaurant meets their needs.

Space is at a premium in Venice, and except for the luxury hotels, your room—and especially the bathroom—may well be smaller than you're used to. Asking for a larger room may entail a higher cost, if such a room even exists in your hotel. If having a double bed is important, you should request a *letto matrimoniale* when booking, but this may well turn out to be simply the regular twin beds pushed together.

Disturbance from street traffic obviously isn't a big problem here, but there can be noise. If your room is facing a canal you may well hear the barge motors starting up in the morning, or even the roaring hydraulic winch of the garbage barge emptying the dumpsters. If your room faces a busy campo, especially one with outdoor tables or even live music in the summer, be prepared for

decibels. Proximity to the kitchen is also a factor. If a quiet room is crucial, you should ask about all this when making your reservation.

Check the address of your hotel: If the address has "Via" in it, it's not going to be in Venice. (Streets on the Lido are called "Via.") Some tour operators book package space in hotels on the mainland in Mestre and imply that you will be in Venice, saying that it is "ten minutes from San Marco." This means ten minutes by bus to Piazzale Roma. There are nice hotels in Mestre, reasonably priced and with car parking, but they're not in Venice.

Private bathrooms

Unless otherwise stated, all these hotels have at least some private bathrooms with shower and/or bathtub.

Many hotels, even the better ones, also have rooms without private bath, at a lower price. When booking, be sure to specify if you have a preference.

Credit cards

Many hotels and restaurants accept all major credit cards. Smaller ones may accept some, as indicated in their entry. Abbreviations used are:
AE American Express, **DC** Diners Club, **MC** MasterCard, **V** Visa.

Star ratings

The current system of price-to-star is currently under revision. The "high season" is considered to run from Easter through November. There may also be price spikes during holidays such as Christmas and New Year's. Some hotels close during the winter. There can be a wide range of cost-value within a star rating; some four-star hotels can

PRICES

HOTELS
Prices are given for guidance only and reflect the high season cost of a double room with private bath, breakfast, and taxes. Prices are indicated by $ signs.
$$$$$	Over $300
$$$$	$200–$400
$$$	$125–$250
$$	$115–$150
$	$75–$100

RESTAURANTS
An indication of the cost of a three-course dinner without drinks is given by $ signs.
$$$$$	Over $80
$$$$	$50–$80
$$$	$35–$50
$$	$20–$35
$	Under $20

have rooms that are more expensive than some in a five-star hotel, depending on many additional factors such as terrace, view, suites, and so on.

✪✪✪✪✪ Five-star hotels are luxury accommodations in every sense of the word, offering superb facilities and impeccable service, and usually including large rooms.

✪✪✪✪ Four stars indicate a hotel with a restaurant, and all rooms with private bath/shower rooms.

✪✪✪ Three-star hotels have at least 80 percent of the rooms with bath/shower, and offer breakfast in the room.

✪✪ Two-star establishments must have 40 percent of the rooms with bath/shower, and a telephone in each room.

✪ One-star hotels offer plain but adequate accommodations.

Other options

Besides hotels, there are also apartments available for rent through a number of agencies, some of them in refurbished palaces. Some convents and monasteries rent guest rooms, though they usually have curfews, and don't always accommodate couples. There are even a few bed-and-breakfasts in private homes. Details on these options are best requested directly from the tourist office, the Azienda di Promozione Turistica, tel 041 529 8711, fax 041 523 0399 or 041 529 8734, www.provincia.venezia.it/aptve, e-mail apt-06@mail.regione.veneto.it. There are also some sites on the Internet that offer apartments in Venice. Any search engine, such as www.google.com, searching "Venice, Italy, Rent, Apartment," will turn up hundreds of possibilities.

RESTAURANTS

Restaurants are listed by price, then in alphabetical order.

Italian cuisine is one of the most varied, healthy, and delectable in the world, with far more to recommend it than pizza and lasagna. If you are the slightest bit curious, you will almost certainly discover wonderful traditional dishes made with the freshest in-season ingredients.

The *menu turistico* (tourist menu) is usually reasonable, but rarely interesting. For a frugal lunch, it would probably make more sense to order a sandwich or a plate of *cichetti*, or snacks, from the bar. It's true that you won't be able to sit while you're eating, but it's fast, nourishing, and much more Venetian than a slice of cold pizza gnawed while sitting on a bridge. A plate of pasta and a salad won't set you back much, if dinner is to be your main meal of the day.

Don't be overwhelmed by everything that's listed on the menu; you're not expected to order every course if you don't feel like it. You can skip around.

Venetians never put grated cheese on any fish dish, with the exception of *seppie* (cuttlefish). But they firmly believe that a piece of cheese, usually Parmegiano (what they generically term *formaggio*

grana), is the best thing to eat after a plate of fish.

Venetians eat salad or cooked vegetables after the main course, not as an appetizer. You can order the house wine by the carafe (*caraffa*) of either a quarter-liter, half-liter, or one liter. Bottled mineral water is available either in nonsparkling (*non-gassata*) or sparkling (*gassata*, or con *gas*). Tap water is completely safe to drink. See also the menu reader on page 264.

Dining hours

Lunch usually begins at noon, though most bars offer snacks all morning long if you're getting hungry sooner. Lunch is usually over by 2 p.m., but a few places go till 3 p.m., and some self-service restaurants near the Piazza San Marco offer continuous service. Dinner is usually eaten at 8 p.m., but a few places may begin earlier. At the better places, a reservation is almost always wise.

Cafés

The Italian café can be either a place to linger indefinitely over one tiny, long-empty cup, or a place to order, drink, pay, and leave in mere seconds. There is an apparently infinite variety of ways to prepare coffee, from extra-strong espresso (*caffè ristretto*) to weaker espresso (*caffè lungo*). "American coffee" is often espresso that has been drastically diluted. Decaffeinated coffee has made inroads; it's easy to ask for a *caffè decaffeinato*. Or a decaffeinated cappuccino. In the morning there will be a warming rack containing croissants, usually containing marmalade, and other breakfast pastries. There is normally a surcharge for waiter service at tables. If no waiters are visible, you could order at the bar and then take your coffee to a table.

Smoking

Smoking is not permitted in many public places (it is absolutely forbidden on public

transportation), but you will notice that smokers are tolerated, if grudgingly. There are restaurants that hang signs on the wall asking diners not to smoke, yet put ashtrays on the tables. If smoke is an issue, ask before being seated if there are separate smoking and non-smoking sections.

Tipping

A service charge is usually included in the bill; this should be listed clearly on the menu. Make sure to review your bill. It's not considered rude, and you may discover an error. If a restaurant is reported to the Carabinieri (police) as having overcharged a customer, it is compelled not only to pay a fine, but to close for a period of time. Better to have settled matters peaceably first.

CANAL GRANDE

Hotels and restaurants along the Grand Canal are listed under their appropriate sestiere. See map on p. 49 for boundary information.

SAN MARCO

🏨 GRITTI PALACE
$$$$$ ○○○○○
SAN MARCO 2357, CAMPO SANTA MARIA DEL GIGLIO, 30124
TEL 041 794 611
FAX 041 520 0942
E-MAIL res073.grittipalace@luxurycollection.com
As the name states, this was once a palace belonging to one of Venice's greatest families, and it remains one of Venice's greatest hotels. The rooms are large and modern, but the public areas are Renaissance lavish. It's still famous as Ernest Hemingway's hotel, and his room can be rented, though one wonders how a man who liked to drink with the gondoliers would have picked such an elegant hotel.
🛈 93 🚇 Giglio 🔄 🅾
🏧 All major cards

HOTELS & RESTAURANTS

🏨 EUROPA-REGINA

$$$$ ○○○○

SAN MARCO 2159, CALLE
LARGA XXII MARZO, 30124
TEL 041 520 0477
FAX 041 523 1533
E-MAIL res075.europa&regina
@westin.com

You have to look hard to see
that one of these two ultra-
modern hotels, now part of
the Westin chain, was once
the palace of the Tiepolo
family. But the standard is
luxurious, if somewhat lacking
in character, and being one of
the few hotels on the Grand
Canal it has the advantage of
a marvelous waterside
terrace. Arriving by water
makes you feel like visiting
royalty; arriving from the
street makes you feel like a
cat burglar.

🛏 192 🚤 Vallaresso ⇄
♿ 💳 All major cards

🏨 BEL SITO

$$$$ ○○○

SAN MARCO 2517, CAMPO
SANTA MARIA DEL GIGLIO,
30124
TEL 041 522 3365
FAX 041 520 4083
E-MAIL belsito@iol.it

This is a real little jewel of a
hotel, and though its rooms
may be a bit on the small side,
they are all beautifully
decorated in pastel colors and
18th-century-style florals. The
service is faultless.

🛏 34 🚤 Giglio ♿ 💳 AE,
MC, V

🏨 FLORA

$$$ ○○○

SAN MARCO 2283/A, CALLE
LARGA XXII MARZO, 30124
TEL 041 520 5844
FAX 041 522 8217
E-MAIL info@hotelflora.it

In a secluded location at the
end of a narrow alley, just off
a bustling main street, the
Flora is charming, perhaps
even a little homey. It also has
a garden that is positively
irresistible in summer.

🛏 44 🚤 Giglio ⇄ ♿
💳 All major cards

🍽 CAFFÈ FLORIAN

Florian was one of the first
coffeehouses in Venice, and
being on the piazza meant it was
one of the most important in the
whole city. Its 17th-century
murals and huge mirrors make
the tiny rooms seem dreamlike
and wonderfully seductive. Don't
resist your urge to linger—for
the prices you pay, you should
make the most of the experience.
In summer, an orchestra plays a
selection of light classics, but a
surcharge for the concert is
added to your bill. Think of it as
a visit to a museum, with great
drinks. In the winter, try the hot
chocolate with whipped cream.

$$$$

PIAZZA SAN MARCO 56-59,
30124
TEL 041 520 5641

🍴 100 inside, 80 in the
outdoor gallery, 400 on the
piazza 🚤 San Zaccaria,
Vallaresso 🕐 Closed Wed.
in winter 💳 AE, MC, V

🍽 HARRY'S BAR

$$$$

SAN MARCO 1323, CALLE
VALLARESSO, 30124
TEL 041 528 5777

The tiny bar is too crowded
with rich foreigners showing
off, but the softly lit dining
room upstairs has an
intelligent menu and flawless
service. For a place that could
have become just another
tourist stop, it has first-rate
cuisine and many Venetian
specialties. Try the cocktail
"Bellini," invented by the
founder and made of peach
juice and sparkling white wine.
Reservations required.

🍴 80 🚤 Vallaresso ♿
💳 All major cards

🍽 PIETRO PANIZZOLO "DA CARLA"

$$

SAN MARCO 1535, CORTE
CONTARINI, 30124
TEL 041 523 7855

If you turn off the Frezzeria

and pass under the
sotoportego Contarini, you'll
find this tiny treasure. With
only seven tables, you'll
probably have to share space,
but ordering the daily specials
arrayed on the bar will give
you one of the most reasonable meals in Venice. A choice
of good pastas, some Venetian
dishes such as sarde in saor,
and lots of cooked fresh
vegetables. Open all day until
11 p.m., so you can have
decent food at odd hours.
Good selection of wines.

🍴 22 🚤 Vallaresso
🕐 Closed Sun. ♿ Cash only

🍽 ENOTECA AL VOLTO

Down a completely
unremarkable street
flanking Ca' Farsetti, this very
remarkable wine bar is tucked
inside a vaulted space that
almost certainly would have
been a warehouse in an earlier
life. Dark and inviting, it offers a
selection of more than a
thousand Italian and foreign
wines plus a very satisfying
choice of Venetian cichetti to
snack on. The taped music may
be anything from blues to jazz.
Open until 10:30 p.m.

$

SAN MARCO 4081, CALLE
CAVALLI, 30124
TEL 041 522 8945

🍴 25 🚤 Rialto 🕐 Closed
Sun. ♿ Cash only

🏨 CASA FONTANA

$$$ ○○

CASTELLO 4701, CAMPO SAN
PROVOLO, 30122
TEL 041 522 0579
FAX 041 523 1040
E-MAIL htlcasa@gpnet.it

A somewhat cramped family-
run hotel, but reasonable
considering its location so
near to San Marco. It has very
helpful staff.

🛏 16 🚤 San Zaccaria
💳 All major cards

SOMETHING SPECIAL

🏨 METROPOLE

In what was once the orphanage connected with Vivaldi's church, the Metropole combines intimacy with a sort of faded elegance. The small restaurant offers a lavish buffet at lunch and dinner at a fixed price. The garden in summer or the cozy front parlor in winter are especially appealing havens from the bustle outside.
$$$$ ○○○○
CASTELLO 4149, RIVA DEGLI
SCHIAVONI, 30122
TEL 041 520 5044
FAX 041 522 3679
E-MAIL venice@hotelmetropole
.com
🛏 72 🚏 San Zaccaria 🚭
🅰 🅰 🅰 All major cards

🏨 BISANZIO
$$ ○○○
CASTELLO 3651, SAN
ZACCARIA, 30122
TEL 041 520 3100
FAX 041 520 4114
E-MAIL email@bisanzio.com
Hidden on a side street just behind San Zaccaria, the Bisanzio is part of the Best Western chain. It has modern, if not particularly memorable rooms, an excellent location, and very efficient service.
🛏 39 🚏 San Zaccaria 🚭
🅰 🅰 AE, MC, V

🏨 HOTEL SANTA MARINA
$$ ○○○
CASTELLO 6068, CAMPO
SANTA MARINA, 30122
TEL 041 523 9202
FAX 041 520 0907
E-MAIL info@hotelsantamarina.it
Recently renovated, this small hotel on a charming small campo, seems off the beaten track but is actually convenient to most major sights and transportation. One of the best pastry shops, Didovich, is just facing the front door.
🛏 16 🚏 Rialto, Fondamenta
Nuove 🅰 🅰 All major
cards

🏨 SCANDINAVIA
$$ ○○○
CASTELLO 5240, CAMPO
SANTA MARIA FORMOSA,
30122
TEL 041 522 3507
FAX 041 523 5232
E-MAIL info@scandinaviahotel
.com
The Scandinavia was once in vogue with younger travelers, but after a recent renovation it seems more grown up. It's right on one of the busiest campos, and it's only five minutes to almost anywhere.
🛏 34 🚏 San Zaccaria 🅰
🅰 AE, MC, V

🏨 PENSIONE WILDNER
$$ ○○
CASTELLO 4161, RIVA DEGLI
SCHIAVONI, 30122
TEL 041 522 7463
FAX 041 526 5615
E-MAIL wildner@veneziahotels
.com
The Wildner, though modest, has amassed a loyal following over the years, in part because of its front-row-center location facing the Lagoon.
🛏 16 🚏 San Zaccaria 🅰
🅰 All major cards

🍴 AL COVO
$$$$
CASTELLO 3968, CAMPIELLO
DELLA PESCARIA, 30122
TEL 041 522 3812
Open since 1986, the Al Covo has passed from being one of the fashionable new places to one of Venice's most reliably innovative restaurants, renowned for its "interpretations" of Venetian dishes. The focus is on fish—sea bass ravioli is especially good, as well as tiny soft-shell crabs in *saor*, pasta with oysters or with bass roe—but there is also game in season, and the vegetables are all from the owner's own garden. Diane, the American wife of the owner, can explain everything.
🍽 47 🚏 San Zaccaria,
Arsenale 🕐 Closed Wed.,
Thurs. 🅰 🅰 Cash only

🍴 CORTE SCONTA
$$$$
CASTELLO 3886, CALLE DEL
PESTRIN, 30122
TEL 041 522 7024
Part of the appeal of the "hidden court" is the fact that it is indeed a little hard to find. The Corte Sconta has grown from a small family-run restaurant, and now probably more foreigners than Venetians come to enjoy its homemade pasta and fresh fish in unusual concoctions, such as gnocchi with calamari, fried soft-shell crabs and sautéed eel. The restaurant can get very loud when crowded, though, so this may not be the place for that romantic interlude. The garden is open in summer.
🍽 70 🚏 Arsenale
🕐 Closed Sun., Mon. 🅰 All
major cards

🍴 AL GALEON
$$
CASTELLO 1308, VIA
GARIBALDI, 30122
TEL 041 520 4656
A real neighborhood place, with small noisy rooms full of Venetians. The fish menu is good value.
🍽 43 🚏 Arsenale, Giardini
🕐 Closed Tues. 🅰 All
major cards

CANNAREGIO

🏨 GRAND HOTEL
🍴 PALAZZO DEI DOGI
$$$$ ○○○○○
CANNAREGIO 3500,
FONDAMENTA MADONNA
DELL' ORTO, 30121
TEL 041 220 8181
FAX 041 722 278
E-MAIL hotels@boscolo.com
Once a convent, then an embassy, this 18th-century palace in a serene, remote corner of Venice has been transformed into a luxury hotel, complete with extensive garden and rooms with views over the canal at the front or the Lagoon behind. Two-level suites are also available, and a private

HOTELS & RESTAURANTS

launch offers hourly shuttle service to Rialto and San Marco. The restaurant is elegant and offers a range of imaginative dishes, such as scallops with rice pilaf and asparagus, ricotta tortelli with rucola pesto sauce, sauteed beef carpaccio and duck with balsamic vinegar.

🛏 70 🚤 Madonna dell'Orto 🛗 🚹 🅰 AE, MC, V

🏨 GIORGIONE
$$$ ✪✪✪✪
CANNAREGIO 4587, CALLE LARGA DEI PROVERBI, 30121
TEL 041 522 5810
FAX 041 523 9092
E-MAIL giorgione@hotelgiorgione.com

Little remains to convey its origins as a 15th-century palace, but this well-located hotel near Rialto has been welcoming guests for a hundred years. The 1995 renovation has spruced up its public areas, and the rooms, though smallish, have every modern convenience and are attractively decorated. The games room includes a computer with free Internet access. The small garden has a fountain to soothe the weary senses. There is also a room completely designed for wheelchair access.

🛏 72 🚤 Fondamenta Nuove, Ca' d'Oro 🛗 🚹 🅂 Some rooms 🅰 All major cards

🏨 ABBAZIA
$$ ✪✪✪
CANNAREGIO 68, CALLE PRIULI, 30121
TEL 041 717 333
FAX 041 717 949
E-MAIL Abbazia@iol.it

Behind the train station isn't usually the spot to find a charming hotel, but the Abbazia is more correctly behind the church of the Scalzi, and it was originally the abbey of the Barefoot Carmelite Friars. The renovation has left intact the Gothic

outline of its refectory (now the main salon), complete with the raised wooden pulpit for Scripture reading during meals. The rooms are modern if a bit austere, but the gorgeous garden is a real touch of luxury.

🛏 40 🚤 Ferrovia 🅂 🅰 AE, MC, V

🏨 HESPERIA
$$ ✪✪
CANNAREGIO 459, CAMPIELLO RIELLO, 30121
TEL 041 715 251
FAX 041 715 112
E-MAIL hesperia@shineline.it

A sturdy, homey hotel that has stood the test of time. The rooms are spacious and the bathrooms fine. Some rooms still have Murano glass chandeliers. The restaurant **Melograno** offers an attractive, reasonable menu with some surprises: risotto with scampi and champagne, sole with walnuts, and seasonal dishes such as pumpkin ravioli.

🛏 16 🚤 Ferrovia, Guglie 🅰 AE, MC, V

🍴 FIASCHETTERIA TOSCANA
$$$$
CANNAREGIO 5719, CAMPO SAN GIOVANNI CRISOSTOMO, 30121
TEL 041 528 5281

Even though it's named for a Tuscan wine shop, the menu is strictly Venetian. Classic specialties such as *bigoi in salsa* and *sarde in saor* are first rate, and the fresh fish entrees are superb. The decor is somewhat austere, but the service is faultless. In summer an appealing small terrace is set up in the courtyard.

🍽 80 🚤 Rialto 🕐 Closed Mon. lunch, Tues. 🅂 🅰 All major cards

🍴 AI 40 LADRONI
$$
CANNAREGIO 3253, FONDAMENTA DELLA SENSA, 30121
TEL 041 715 736

This family operation (brother and sister) used to be way off the beaten track, but has been discovered by a wildly varied but extremely loyal local clientele. The fish is absolutely fresh, and to spend a summer evening at a table by the canal can be a memorable experience. The mixed fish appetizer is a meal in itself.

🚤 San Marcuola, Sant Alvise 🕐 Closed Mon. 🅰 DC, MC, V

🍴 ANTICA MOLA
$$
CANNAREGIO 2800, FONDAMENTA DEI ORMESINI, 30121
TEL 041 717 492

Just on the other side of the canal behind the Ghetto, this fish restaurant manages to maintain the atmosphere of a strictly local joint, even when there are obviously tourists around. The typical menu might include spaghetti with clams or pasta with *seppie* in their ink, and all the dishes are very well prepared.

🍽 70 🚤 San Marcuola, Sant Alvise 🕐 Closed Sat., 3 weeks in Aug. 🅰 All major cards

SOMETHING SPECIAL

🍴 CAFFÈ COSTARICA

One of the best cups of espresso in Venice is made in this very old-fashioned café, but don't expect to enjoy it at a table—the little space that might have been given to perhaps three tables at most is devoted instead to huge sacks of coffee beans waiting to be roasted. This is also one of the best places in the city to mingle with the locals, or to buy roasted coffee beans.

$
CANNAREGIO 1337, RIO TERRÀ SAN LEONARDO, 30121
TEL 041 716 371
🍽 None 🚤 Guglie, San Marcuola 🕐 Closed Sun. 🅰 Cash only

KEY 🏨 Hotel 🍴 Restaurant 🛏 No. of bedrooms 🍽 No. of places 🚤 Vaporetto/motoscafo 🕐 Closed 🛗 Elevato

🍴 BREK
$
CANNAREGIO 124, LISTA DI
SPAGNA, 30121
TEL 041 244 0158
There may be no Venetian
character whatsoever at this
branch of a small Italian chain,
but it offers very acceptable
food at very reasonable
prices. Arranged as a sort of
cafeteria, you can carry your
tray from station to station,
picking out pasta, meat, salads,
and dessert with a minimum
of fuss and confusion.
Excellent value.
🛏 130 🚇 Ferrovia
🕐 Closed Mon. 🚫 All
major cards

SAN POLO & SANTA CROCE

🏨 SANTA CHIARA
$$$ 🔴🔴🔴
SANTA CROCE 548,
FONDAMENTA SANTA CHIARA
(PIAZZALE ROMA), 30125
TEL 041 520 6955
FAX 041 522 8799
E-MAIL conalve@doge.it
Hotels near the bus depot
(which is what the Piazzale
Roma basically is) aren't
usually very attractive, but this
small hotel offers charm as
well as convenience. For all
the boat and bus traffic
outside, it's surprisingly quiet,
too. Just a short walk to the
Frari, San Rocco, and Campo
Santa Margherita.
🛏 28 🚇 Piazzale Roma 🔁
🚭 🚫 AE, MC, V

🏨 AL SOLE
$$ 🔴🔴🔴
SANTA CROCE 136,
FONDAMENTA MINOTTO
(TOLENTINI), 30125
TEL 041 710 844
FAX 041 714 398
E-MAIL info@corihotels.it
Here is yet another palace—
the 16th-century Ca'
Marcello—that has become a
hotel. The Al Sole has a
wonderful facade, foyer, and
garden, not to mention a
position on one of Venice's
more charming stretches of

canal. The rooms have been
completely modernized and
are a little sterile, but they do
have some charming period
touches, such as the carved
wooden headboards on the
beds; a few rooms are more
spacious than is often the case
in Venice. The location is very
convenient to Piazzale Roma
and Campo Santa Margherita.
The service can be a bit on
the brusque side.
🛏 62 🚇 Piazzale Roma 🔁
🚭 🚫 All major cards

🏨 LOCANDA STURION
$$ 🔴🔴🔴
SAN POLO 679, RIVA DEL VIN,
30125
TEL 041 523 6243
FAX 041 522 8378
If you look at Bellini's 15th-
century painting of this area in
his "Miracle of the Holy
Cross," you'll see that this
hotel was already in business.
The Sturion ("sturgeon" in the
Venetian dialect) is still going
strong, has recently been
renovated and is still one step
from the Rialto, with a
marvelous view over the
Grand Canal. Make a
reservation well in advance.
🛏 11 🚭 🚫 AE, V

🏨 SAN CASSIANO/CA' FAVRETTO
$$ 🔴🔴🔴
SANTA CROCE 2232, CALLE DE
LE ROSE, 30125
TEL 041 524 1768
FAX 041 721 033
E-MAIL cassiano@sancassiano.it
You will already have admired
this exquisite little red palace
as you passed in the
vaporetto—one of the few
hotels right on the Grand
Canal. The public rooms, and
the second-floor balcony
facing the canal, will make you
feel like at least a visiting
ambassador. The rooms are
small and simple, but perfectly
adequate, and the service is
first rate.
🛏 35 🚇 San Stae 🚭
🚫 Some rooms 🚫 AE,
MC, V

🍴 OSTERIA DA FIORE
$$$
SAN POLO 2202/A, CALLE DEL
SCALETER, 30125
TEL 041 721 308
Not to be confused with the
Trattoria da Fiore at Santo
Stefano, this establishment not
far from San Giacomo dell'
Orio is the only restaurant in
Venice to have earned a place
in the Michelin guide, with
two stars, no less. Imaginative
fish dishes such as fried soft-
shell crabs with polenta are
perfectly prepared and
presented. There is an
impressive wine list and an
interesting choice of Veneto
cheese. Reservations required.
🛏 80 🚇 San Silvestro, San
Stae 🕐 Closed Sun., Mon.
🚭 🚫 All major cards

🍴 OSTERIA SORA AL PONTE
$$
SAN POLO 1588, RIALTO, 30125
TEL 041 718 208
As the name states, this
typically Venetian wine
bar/restaurant is indeed atop
a bridge, just behind the fish
market at Rialto. The bar
offers lots of typical Venetian
ciccheti to munch with
your wine, and a sturdy menu
of excellent fish served on
heavy wooden tables with
brown-paper place mats. All it
lacks is sawdust on the floor.
A real find.
🛏 40 🚇 San Silvestro, San
Stae 🚭 🚫 All major cards

🍴 TRATTORIA NOVA
$$
SANTA CROCE 1252, LISTA DEI
BARI, 30125
TEL 041 524 1353
This tiny, sometimes noisy
family-run restaurant offers
home cooking that's better
than most, and it comes in
generous portions. In the fall
game, including venison and
mountain goat, is sometimes
on the menu.
🛏 20 🚇 Riva di Biasio
🕐 Closed Sun. 🚭 🚫 All
major cards

HOTELS & RESTAURANTS

DORSODURO

🏨 AMERICAN
$$ ❍❍❍
DORSODURO 628,
FONDAMENTA BRAGADIN
(SAN VIO), 30123
TEL 041 520 4733
FAX 041 520 4080
E-MAIL reception@hotelamerican
.com
In one of the city's loveliest
spots, right on a canal and
two steps from the Grand
Canal and the Accademia
Gallery, the American has
lovely public rooms decorated
in the Renaissance manner
using brocades and low
lighting. The rooms are
completely modern.
🛏 28 ⛴ Accademia 🅂
🅂 AE, MC, V

🏨 PAUSANIA
$$ ❍❍❍
DORSODURO 2824,
FONDAMENTA GHERARDINI
(SAN BARNABA), 30123
TEL 041 522 2083
FAX 041 522 2989
Once a private palace on a
tranquil side canal, its
entryway still boasts the
original marble wellhead and
exterior staircase. An ideal
location for a spot that seems
so secluded, just between
Campo Santa Margherita and
Campo San Barnaba. The
rooms are somewhat less
elegant than the palace seems
to promise, but are perfectly
clean and serviceable. Ask
about their special taxi service
to and from the airport.
🛏 24 🅂 🅂 All major cards

🏨 PENSIONE LA
CALCINA
$$ ❍❍❍
DORSODURO 780, ZATTERE,
30123
TEL 041 520 6466
FAX 041 522 7045
E-MAIL la.calcina@libero.it
Space is always hard to book
in this small hotel with a
fiercely loyal following. Famous
as 19th-century English art
historian John Ruskin's

lodgings, it has recently been
renovated yet again. With its
first-rate location on the
Zattere, you can enjoy the
views over the Giudecca
Canal from the roof terrace
or the terrace with tables
built over the water.
🛏 29 ⛴ Zattere,
Accademia 🅂 🅂 All major
cards

🏨 LOCANDA SAN
BARNABA
$$ ❍❍❍
DORSODURO 2785-2786,
CALLE DEL TRAGHETTO (SAN
BARNABA), 30123
TEL 041 241 1233
FAX 041 241 1233
E-MAIL info@locanda-
sanbarnaba.com
This 16th-century palace has
only recently been converted
to a hotel, and the elegant
main salon still conceals
doorways in each corner
behind the original curious
curved wooden screens. The
rooms are rather small and
completely modern, but the
ceilings of several still boast
their lovely Renaissance
frescoes. A courtyard garden
for summer breakfasts and a
small terrace for sunning are
lovely touches. The location is
one of the best in the city.
🛏 14 ⛴ Ca' Rezzonico 🅂
🅂 V

🏨 PENSIONE ALLA
SALUTE DA CICI
$ ❍❍
DORSODURO 222,
FONDAMENTA CA' BALA,
30123
TEL 041 523 5404
FAX 041 522 2271
E-MAIL hotel.salute.dacici@iol.it
One of the city's best budget
hotels, the Cici has clean
rooms, some with private bath,
and a friendly, helpful staff. Very
close to the Accademia and
Guggenheim galleries and the
church of the Salute.
🛏 50 ⛴ Salute 🕘 Closed
Nov.–mid-March, but open
during Carnival 🅂
🅂 Cash only

🍴 AI GONDOLIERI
A rarity in Venice, the menu
offers no fish at all, but
concentrates on meat, as well as
delectable dishes using local
seasonal ingredients such as
risotto with *castraure* (small
early artichokes), risotto with
quail and *bruscandoli* (a wild
green plant), as well as veal,
duck, and venison. In the fall the
menu brims with dishes
featuring the heavenly truffles
from Alba in Piedmont. There
are two small but beautiful
dining rooms and service is
impeccable.
$$$
DORSODURO 366, PONTE DEL
FORMAGER, 30123
TEL 041 528 6396
🍽 50 ⛴ Accademia
🕘 Closed Tues. 🅂 🅂 All
major cards

🍴 L'INCONTRO
$$
DORSODURO 3062, RIO TERRÀ
CANAL (CAMPO SANTA
MARGHERITA), 30123
TEL 041 522 2404
The owner is from Sardinia, so
the menu leans toward
ingredients from the
mountainous island including
the distinctive pecorino
(sheep's cheese) and Sardinian
wines. A favorite with locals,
its small, low rooms are
especially inviting in winter.
Some tables are set outside in
the summer.
🍽 60 ⛴ Ca' Rezzonico
🕘 Closed Mon. 🅂 All
major cards

🍴 RANDON ENOTECA
$$
DORSODURO 2850, CAMPO
SAN BARNABA, 30123
TEL 041 522 4410
Right on Campo San Barnaba,
this tiny spot used to be a
wine shop and before that, a
little store that sold spices and
herbs. They still sell wine, but
offer a small but varied menu
as well with a few first and

second courses that change daily. An appealing spot to pause for a satisfying uncomplicated meal at reasonable cost.

🏠 30 🔲 Ca' Rezzonico ⊕ Closed Sun. 💷 AE, V

🍴 RIVIERA
$$
DORSODURO 1473, ZATTERE (SAN BASILIO), 30123
TEL 041 522 7621
Located in what was once the building belonging to the sausagemakers' guild, the Riviera offers a select menu of fish dishes in either its attractive small dining room or outside on the Zattere. The view is mostly occupied by a large abandoned landing dock, but summer sunsets and breezes make this an ideal spot just the same.

🏠 60 🔲 San Basilio, Zattere ⊕ Closed Mon. 🈺 💷 AE, MC, V

🍴 TRATTORIA CA'FOSCARI AL CANTON
$$
DORSODURO 3854, CROSERA SAN PANTALON, 30123
TEL 041 522 9216
At a busy intersection near the university and the fire station, this trattoria has a good variety of seasonal dishes at reasonable cost. If you sit at an outside table you'll probably want to linger.

🏠 45 inside, 35 outside 🔲 San Tomà ⊕ Closed Sun. 🈺 💷 MC, V

THE ISLANDS

BURANO

🍴 DA ROMANO
$$$
VIA GALUPPI 221, 30012
TEL 041 730 030
This is Burano's most famous restaurant, and the walls of its several dining rooms are covered with art by generations of gratified

visitors, some of them more famous than the restaurant. The menu is ample, offering some traditional Venetian dishes no longer offered by most restaurants (such as the risotto di gò, or rice with gobies). Don't assume that the cuisine is Roman; Romano was the name of the founder.

🏠 100 🔲 Burano ⊕ Closed Tues. 🈺 💷 All major cards

🍴 AI PESCATORI
$$
VIA GALUPPI 371, 30012
TEL 041 730 650
Not as famous as its neighbor, Romano, but the food is fine and the people-watching from its tables outside on the main street is just as good.

🏠 160 🔲 Burano ⊕ Closed Wed. 🈺 💷 All major cards

LIDO

🏨 EXCELSIOR
$$$$$ ⭕⭕⭕⭕⭕
LUNGOMARE MARCONI 41, 30126
TEL 041 526 0201
FAX 041 526 7276
At the turn of the 20th century, the Excelsior was among the first European hotels to make a month (or entire summer) at the sea a fashionable holiday alternative. It is still huge, glamorous, and offers virtually everything you could want. In early September it becomes base camp for the hordes of press and movie stars who flock here for the film festival.

🛏 207 🔲 Lido ⊕ Closed mid-Nov–mid-March 🈺 🈺 Some rooms 🈺 💷 All major cards

🏨 DES BAINS
$$$$ ⭕⭕⭕⭕
LUNGOMARE MARCONI 17, 30126
TEL 041 526 5921
FAX 041 526 0113
Now part of the Sheraton chain, this fabulous relic of the

great late-Victorian age was the setting of the final moments of Death in Venice, but certainly suggests nothing at all of melancholy. On the contrary, it is grand and proud, and the veranda with its vast wicker chairs will give you some sense of what relaxing at the beach used to mean in a less frenetic era.

🛏 181 🔲 Lido 🈺 🈺 Some rooms 🈺 🈺 🈺 💷 All major cards

🏨 VILLA PANNONIA
$$ ⭕⭕⭕
VIA DOGE D. MICHIEL 48, 30126
TEL 041 526 0162
FAX 041 526 5277
E-MAIL hotel-pannonia@libero.it
This is a smallish hotel that caters mainly to European travelers who like the option of half-board (breakfast and dinner), which makes budgeting the trip more reliable. The food is good, though not especially imaginative. The tranquil little garden in the back is a lovely spot for an afternoon retreat or drink before dinner.

🛏 32 🔲 Lido 💷 All major cards

🍴 TRATTORIA DA ANDRI
$$$
VIA LEPANTO 21, 30126
TEL 041 526 5482
The young owner quickly made his name with this upscale restaurant, which has simple decoration and absolutely perfect fish dishes. The mixed grilled fish is consistently excellent. Attractive small shaded terrace in summer. Reservations advisable.

🏠 60 🔲 Lido ⊕ Closed Mon., Tues. 💷 All major cards

🍴 "161"
$$
VIA SANDRO GALLO 161, 30126
TEL 041 526 7256
This neighborhood trattoria and pizzeria has reliable

HOTELS & RESTAURANTS

Venetian home cooking such as *bigoi in salsa* and pasta with *fasioi* (beans). Service is brisk and friendly. Pizza is only available in the evening.

🏨 65 🚤 Lido 🕐 Closed Wed. 🔲 🚗 AE, DC, V

MURANO

🍴 BUSA ALLA TORRE

If you find yourself on Murano at lunchtime, you could hardly do better than to come here to see what Lele, the genial, Falstaffian owner and guiding spirit, has whipped up for your delight. Notable are the delicate fish ravioli with crab sauce, and a glorious assortment of fried seafood, including sole, cuttlefish, and soft-shell crabs. There are also some tables outside in the small campo under the bell tower.

$$$

CAMPO SANTO STEFANO 3, 30121

TEL 041 739 662

🏨 50 🚤 Colonna 🕐 Closed evenings 🔲 🚗 All major cards

🍴 AL CORALLO

$$

FONDAMENTA DEI VETRAI 73, 30121

TEL 041 739 636

This is a well-known trattoria on the main route from the vaporetto stop toward Murano's Grand Canal. It offers the usual assortment of fish and pasta, including the classic spaghetti with such accompaniments as *capparossoli*, local clams, the ink of the *seppie*, or with *ragù*, the ground-meat and tomato sauce. You can follow this with grilled or fried fish—as well as less Venetian but equally good dishes such as lasagna, but the quality is reliable and there are some tables by the canal.

🏨 80 🚤 Colonna 🕐 Closed Tues. 🔲 🚗 All major cards

SANT' ERASMO

🍴 CA' VIGNOTTO

Sant' Erasmo is Venice's farmland, a longish island virtually covered with market gardens. Vignotto's menu concentrates on local ingredients, some from its own farm, and the portions are generous and well prepared. It's a ten-minute walk from the stop down a country road that is reminiscent of Indiana, especially on a summer evening when the fireflies are flickering amid the corn. There are no menus; they bring whatever is on that day, from gnocchi with rabbit, risotto with grapes, above-average mixed fried fish, and always the freshest vegetables. Reservations strongly advised on weekends.

$$$

VIA FORTE 71, 30141

TEL 041 244 4000 OR 041 528 5329

🏨 90 🚤 13 from Fond-amente Nove to Chiesa 🕐 Closed Tues. 🚗 Cash only

TORCELLO

🏨 LOCANDA CIPRIANI

$$$$ ○○○

TORCELLO 29, 30012

TEL 041 730 150

FAX 041 735 433

E-MAIL info@locandacipriani.com

The only hotel on Torcello in living memory. Rustic yet elegant, it has welcomed virtually every famous visitor to Venice in the past hundred years, from Hemingway to Queen Elizabeth II. The rooms are not large, but are perfectly appointed, and in the winter a fire blazes in the foyer as the perfect welcome. Torcello's air of magical, remote tranquility is perfectly mirrored by this small hotel.

🛏 6 🚤 Torcello or private launch 🔲 🚗 All major cards

🍴 OSTERIA AL PONTE DEL DIAVOLO

$$$

TORCELLO 29, 30012

TEL 041 730 401

A group of former employees of the Locanda Cipriani decided to strike out on their own, and opened this attractive, spacious restaurant right on the path from the vaporetto to the cathedral. It has made its name as a reasonable alternative to its more famous neighbor. The fish risotto is very good, as is the grilled fresh fish, which might include John Dory and gilthead. There is a lovely shady terrace that may induce you to linger.

🏨 70 🚤 12 from Fond-amenta Nuove 🕐 Closed Wed. 🔲 🚗 All major cards

VIGNOLE

🍴 TRATTORIA ALLE VIGNOLE

$$

ISOLA DELLE VIGNOLE, 30141

TEL 041 528 9707

If you should want to spend a summer afternoon (or evening) on a little island once covered with vineyards in the company almost exclusively of Venetians, this is the place. It all started when the farmer next door started offering some wine and his own salami, and, though the menu has grown, it is still a rustic favorite. You choose from the array on the steam table inside, which may include spaghetti with clams, or with tomato sauce, and a daily special, as well as fried fish and lots of seasonal vegetables, such as spinach, green beans, and artichokes, then carry your tray to one of the tables either inside or outside under the trees. Be sure to bring mosquito repellent.

🏨 150 🚤 No. 13 from Fondamente Nove to *Vignole* 🕐 Closed Mon. 🚗 AE, MC, V

GIUDECCA

CIPRIANI
$$$$$ ✪✪✪✪
GIUDECCA 10, 30123
TEL 041 520 7744
FAX 041 520 3930

This luxury hotel is so complete that you could stay here for days and never even feel the need to visit San Marco—which may well be what many guests choose to do. The Cipriani is utterly beautiful, especially in summer when its stretches of greensward overlooking the Lagoon could make you decide to stay indefinitely. A meal on the terrace in summer can be close to a perfect experience, but it's not for the budget-conscious, and for those who are not staying in the hotel the service can sometimes be rather lacking in charm.

🛏 92 🚊 Zitelle or private launch 🔁 🅢 Some rooms 🅢 🌊 🍸 🅢 All major cards

🍽 ALTANELLA
$$$
GIUDECCA 268, CALLE DE LE ERBE, 30123
TEL 041 522 7780

The main attraction of this restaurant is the wonderful wooden terrace over the canal, where you will surely be tempted to stay for hours. The fish dishes are very good and the front room will be full of locals—a sure sign of a decent place to eat.

🍴 40 🚊 Giudecca 🕐 Closed Mon., Tues. 🅢 Cash only

🍽 DO MORI
$$
GIUDECCA 588, SANTA EUFEMIA, 30123
TEL 041 522 5452

Founded by some former Harry's Bar employees, the "Two Moors" soon gained a reputation for providing good food at reasonable prices. The traditional Venetian fish specialties—spaghetti with clams, or *alla busera*, *baccalà*, mixed fried fish—are especially good and the experience is enhanced by the fact that you can also watch the summer sunset from your table on the *fondamenta* overlooking the Giudecca Canal.

🍴 50 🚊 Giudecca 🕐 Closed Sun. 🅢 🅢 All major cards

🍽 HARRY'S DOLCI
$$
GIUDECCA 773, SANTA EUFEMIA, 30123
TEL 041 522 4844

This is a summertime "annex" to Harry's Bar (see p. 246) that has now blossomed into a modest but excellent restaurant in its own right. Chic but casual, the menu features light dishes that are more suited to warm weather, such as tuna tartare, cold marinated salmon, salad of *seppie*, veal with tuna sauce, and cold tomato soup. There is not a huge choice of desserts, but they are perfect, including Harry's trademark *crespelle*, or crepes, with cream. The tables set up on the *fondamenta* by the Giudecca Canal are almost irresistible, especially on a summer evening under their twinkling strings of lights.

🍴 50 🚊 Giudecca 🕐 Closed Tues., Nov.–April. 🅢 🅢 All major cards

see p. 246

EXCURSIONS

THE LITTORAL

🍽 TRATTORIA AL PONTE DI BORGO
$$
CALLE DELLE MERCERIA, MALAMOCCO 27, 30126
TEL 041 770 090

This is one of Malamocco's two restaurants (the other is Scarso), and it's easily found straight down the main street from the main square and church. The front room and the bar are usually crowded with locals, but the dining room in the back has plenty of room and the menu is first rate. Fresh local fish, such as gilthead and sea bass, or perhaps small sole, is reliably prepared, and the service is always excellent.

🍴 80 🚊 Lido, then bus B to Malamocco 🕐 Closed Mon. 🅢 Cash only

SOMETHING SPECIAL

🏨 CA' DEL BORGO
Having served most of its existence as a fishing village, Malamocco wouldn't seem to be the place to find a hotel in a small 15th-century palace. Nevertheless, Ca' del Borgo has been beautifully restored and retains all the charm of an elegant country villa. The grassy garden is a perfect spot to take an alfresco breakfast, and the Lido's beaches, tennis and golf courses are not far away. To witness the sunset over the Lagoon can be an unforgettable experience.

$$$ ✪✪✪✪
PIAZZA DE LE ERBE, MALAMOCCO 1, 30126
TEL 041 770 749
FAX 041 526 9441

🛏 8 🚊 Lido, then bus B to Malamocco 🅢 🅢 All major cards

🍽 TRATTORIA SCARSO
$$
5 PIAZZA MALAMOCCO, 30010
TEL 041 770 834

This trattoria has been here forever, and is one of only two still flourishing in the village. The fish is always good, and the vegetables are often local (try the famous artichokes in the spring). Service can be erratic, but the garden in the summer is a real oasis.

🍴 50 🚊 Lido, then bus B to Malamocco 🕐 Closed Tues. 🅢 Cash only

SHOPPING IN VENICE

Your first wander through town may give you the impression that there is nothing on sale here but Carnival masks, Murano glass, and incredibly expensive jewelry. This isn't true. Beyond the predictable purchases, you can actually find a variety of surprisingly original items, many locally made, that are as Venetian as you could wish.

OPENING HOURS & SERVICE

Shop opening hours and days can vary, but stores in Venice tend to open later than in other Italian cities, a fact some attribute to its Byzantine-Levantine orientation. More shops are beginning to stay open all day and also on Sunday, especially ones near San Marco (though occasionally for shorter hours). The farther you go from the Piazza, however, the less likely it is you will find a shop open on Sunday, with the exception of the Strada Nova. If it's really important, call first to make sure.

As for service, it can range from the tireless and amazingly thoughtful to, well, the opposite. On the whole, Venetians (possibly another sign of their long connection with the eastern Mediterranean) tend to regard the shopping experience as a more leisurely encounter than the get-it-done approach Americans are more accustomed to. It's possible that a shopkeeper who appears brusque may actually be reflecting more your attitude than his or her own. Most shopkeepers are accustomed virtually from birth to foreign customers, and will almost certainly speak some English. They will do their best to help you, but may not always appear to be exerting themselves tremendously to induce you to buy. Try not to give this undue weight when shopping.

Two curious facts that you will notice almost immediately: One is that although every shop has a name, often it isn't anywhere to be seen on a sign outside. Therefore, obviously, to find a shop listed here you need to go by the street address almost more than the name. The other is that when stores close up at night, many completely cover their doors and windows with super-secure metal shutters. This fact makes after-dinner window-shopping somewhat less diverting (and useful) than it could be, as you often have no clue even as to the type of merchandise the store is selling.

Shops that accept credit cards sometimes offer a small discount if you decide to pay cash instead. There may be several options on shipping your purchase, if you decide not to carry it home yourself, and the cost isn't usually exceptionally high. There is also a Federal Express office at the mouth of the Piazza San Marco, across from the Hotel Luna Baglioni, if you decide to send your things home by courier yourself.

There is a refund on the Value Added Tax which is valid for purchases over L300,000. This can be obtained at the specially designated window at the airport before you depart; it can also be obtained at the office of Global Refund Contact Point at the mouth of the Piazza San Marco (San Marco 72/b, Calle de l'Ascensione). Bring your passport, your credit card, and your receipts. Sometimes the shopkeeper will deduct the tax refund immediately from the price in the store. This amounts to an instant discount even if you pay by credit card (which means that you've got your tax deducted even before the bill arrives.)

You will see stores that sell cameras and photographic equipment, film, and even develop film quickly. But there is no place in Venice that repairs cameras. If you have camera troubles, you will have to go to the mainland.

DEPARTMENT STORES

Limited space, high rents, and a tradition much more rooted in the individual shop make Venice an unpromising environment for department stores. In fact, there is only one: **Coin** (pronounced Co-een), Cannaregio 5787, Ponte del Olio, 30121, tel 041 520 3581, vaporetto 1, 82 to Rialto. The variety and quality of merchandise here is good, if unimaginative, but the selection in each department is necessarily fairly limited and the prices are not appreciably lower than in the smaller boutiques.

ANTIQUE SHOPS & FLEA MARKETS

Numerous antique shops sell paintings, furniture, silverware, and glass. Flea markets are more rare, and mainly sprout up around Christmas. The two main ones are set up in Campo San Bartolomeo and Campo San Luca.

ANTIQUE SHOPS

You'll come across antique shops almost everywhere, but there is a concentration of them in Dorsoduro and in the area between San Samuele and San Marco; the Calle delle Botteghe is lined with them. Between the Rialto and the Piazza San Marco is another prime neighborhood. **Antiquus**, San Marco 3131 (Calle delle Botteghe, San Samuele), 30124, tel 041 520 6395, vaporetto 82 to San Samuele, 1 to Sant'Angelo. Small but clearly world-class assortment of paintings, silverware, and furniture. Also has some antique jewelry.
Dolcetta Arredimenti, Castello 5672 (Salizzada San Lio), 30122, tel 041 522 6923, vaporetto 1, 82 to Rialto. Chess sets with clever pieces (Romans and Barbarians, Camelot, Napoleonic troops, etc.), reproduction period pistols, walking sticks, and a large selection of attractive prints of Venetian scenes, all on sale at very reasonable prices.

La Luna nel Pozzo, Dorsoduro 2860 (Calle Lunga San Barnaba), 30123, tel 041 523 7072, vaporetto 1 to Ca' Rezzonico. Attractive variety, from mirrors to old silverware, glass, and even costume jewelry.

Luciano Zardin, Dorsoduro 2899 (Campo Santa Margherita) 30123, tel 041 523 4307, vaporetto 1 to Ca' Rezzonico. Small shop, but interesting variety, especially the old engravings of Venetian events such as Carnival.

Michele Cicogna, San Polo 2867 (Campo San Tomà), 30125, tel 041 522 7678, vaporetto 1, 82 to San Tomà. Michael is the third generation of a family that opened its workshop at the end of the 19th century to decorate wooden antique furniture. He reproduces Venetian paintings to any dimension on wooden panels or furniture, and the delicately painted wooden boxes are especially beautiful. Frames are made to order, with lacquer or gold leaf.

BOOKS & MUSIC

With two universities, there's no lack of bookstores here. But many specialize and don't always offer books in English. Remember that *libreria* means bookstore; library is *biblioteca*.

Ariel, Dorsoduro 2946 (Campo Santa Margherita), 30123, tel 041 523 6570, vaporetto 1 to Ca' Rezzonico. Lots of illustrated books for children, mostly in Italian. If you should need a gift for an Italian child, there's a good choice here.

Einaudi, San Polo 2598 (Rio Terrà, Frari), 30125, tel 041 714 035, vaporetto 1, 82 to San Tomà. Shop by Bacino Orseolo, vaporetto 1 to Vallaresso, 82 to San Marco. This fine-art publisher offers a full line of guidebooks to palaces and other sights, and other lavishly illustrated Venetian themes.

Libreria Cafoscarina, Dorsoduro 3259 (Calle Foscari), 30123, tel 041 522 9502. Two steps from the University of Venice, with an excellent variety of books on art; also has some books in English.

Libreria di Demetra, San Polo 1228 (Campo San Aponal), 30125, tel 041 520 8760, vaporetto 1, 82 to San Tomà, 1 to San Silvestro. Also: Cannaregio 282 (Campo San Geremia), 30121, tel 041 275 0152, vaporetto 1, 82, 41, 42, 51, 52 to Ferrovia. Also: Departure Hall, Marco Polo airport. This huge store is utterly without character, but has almost everything, from calendars to the classics and a good section of English-language paperbacks, guidebooks, and even Venetian cookbooks.

Libreria Goldoni, San Marco 4742 (Calle dei Fabbri), 30124, tel 041 522 2384, vaporetto 1, 82 to Rialto. Outstanding collection of books about Venice, art books, and guidebooks to other regions of Italy and the world.

Libreria al Ponte, San Marco 3717/d (Calle de la Mandola), 30124, tel 041 522 4030, vaporetto 1, 82 to Rialto. Good selection of art books and calendars; also some posters.

Libreria Sansovino, San Marco 84 (Bacino Orseolo), 30124, tel 041 522 2653, vaporetto 1 to Vallaresso, 81 to San Marco, 41, 42, 51, 52 to San Zaccaria. Small, but packed with irresistible art books, calendars, guidebooks, and maps, and in a convenient location at the Piazza San Marco.

Libreria Studium, San Marco 337 (Calle de la Canonica, behind Palazzo Patriarcale), 30124, tel 041 522 2382, vaporetto 1, 41, 42, 51, 52 to San Zaccaria. Densely supplied with art books, calendars, and guidebooks, along with popular paperbacks in English and also Catholic publications, including Bibles (in Italian).

Libreria alla Toletta, Dorsoduro 1214 (Calle de la Toletta), 30123, tel 041 523 2034, vaporetto 1 to Ca' Rezzonico, 82 to Accademia. Excellent range of paperbacks, and lots of coffee-table art books, too, always at a discount.

Nalesso, San Marco 2765 (Calle del Spezier, Santo Stefano), 30124, tel 041 520 3329, vaporetto 1 to Santa Maria del Giglio. Venice's premier music shop, selling CDs of Venetian composers played on original instruments in Venetian churches, most other classical artists, as well as instruments and sheet music.

Il Tempio della Musica, San Marco 5358 (Calle Ramo Fontego dei Tedeschi), 30124, tel 041 523 4552, vaporetto 1, 82 to Rialto. A bit of everything, from classical to jazz and rock.

CARNIVAL MASKS

There are so many mask shops it's become a bitter Venetian remark; whenever some neighborhood shop closes, everyone assumes the next tenant will be selling masks. Still, if you look close you'll discover there is a surprising variety.

L'Arlecchino, San Polo 789 (Ruga Vecchia San Giovanni, Rialto), 30125, tel 041 520 8220, vaporetto 1 to San Silvestro. Exquisitely made masks in classic and modern designs.

Il Canovaccio, Castello 5369-70 (Calle al Ponte della Guerra), 30122, tel 041 521 0393, vaporetto 41, 42, 51, 52 to San Zaccaria. First-rate designs made with flair and skill; especially unusual animal masks.

Creazioni Marega, San Polo 3046/a (Campo San Rocco), 30125, tel 041 522 1634. Varied selection of well-made masks, sized to wear as well as larger, more elaborate masks to hang on your wall.

CHILDREN'S CLOTHES & TOYS

The number of tempting shops for infants and small children is remarkable; considering the falling Italian birthrate and the prices, most of these must be aimed at doting grandparents of every nationality.

CLOTHES

Annelie, Dorsoduro 2748 (Calle Lunga San Barnaba), 30123, tel 041 520 3277, vaporetto 1 to Ca' Rezzonico. Exquisite white cotton dresses and bibs, hand-embroidered or with handmade lace.

Cacao, Cannaregio 5583-86 (Campo Corner) 30121, tel 041 522 9946, vaporetto 1, 82 to Rialto. Lots of casual clothes in this Benetton 012 look-alike.

Mammolo, San Marco 4461 (Calle dei Fuseri), 30124, tel 041 522 6328. Designer names such as DKNY for children from the cradle to about eight years old.

Il Nido delle Cicogne, San Polo 2806 (Campo San Tomà), 30125, tel 041 528 7497, vaporetto 1, 82 to San Tomà. The "storks' nest" has a selection of beautiful clothes for children from newborn to past kindergarten age.

TOYS

Beatrice Perini, San Polo 1462 (Calle della Madonetta, San Polo), 30125, tel 041 520 7502, vaporetto 1, 82 to San Tomà. Dolls, doll clothes, and stuffed animals. There are also hats for real children.

Carta & Penna, San Marco 4340 (Calle dei Fuseri), 30124, tel 041 522 6225, vaporetto 1, 82 to Rialto, 1 to Vallaresso, 81 to San Marco. Sells school supplies for children, including backpacks, but also has a good selection of stuffed animals and other toys.

C'era una Volta, Dorsoduro 3753 (San Pantalon), 30123, tel 041 718 899, vaporetto 1, 82 to San Tomà, 1 to Ca' Rezzonico. The name means "Once upon a time," and here you'll find not only dolls and teddy bears, but also stencils, rubber stamps, and other small diversions.

Città del Sole, Castello 5379 (Calle delle Bande), 30122, tel 041 528 1902, vaporetto 1, 82 to Rialto, 41, 42, 51, 52 to San Zaccaria. Toys of a more scientific or educational nature than the usual.

Molin, Cannaregio 5899 (Ponte San Giovanni Crisostomo) 30121, tel 041 523 5285. Toy soldiers, jigsaw puzzles, kits, Lego sets, dolls, all in a store that has been here since 1865. Locals ignore the nearby bridge's official name and universally refer to it as the "bridge of the toys."

Pettenello, Dorsoduro 2978 (Campo Santa Margherita), 30123, tel 041 523 1167, vaporetto 1 to Ca' Rezzonico. Generations of Venetian children have tormented their parents for something from this Aladdin's cave of games, crafts, stuffed animals, and gadgets. Not inexpensive, but good variety.

CLOTHING

Venice, like most important Italian cities, is full of the great designer names, though depending on the exchange rate the prices may or may not be much lower than you would pay in the United States. The greatest concentration of luxury shops is in or around the Piazza San Marco and radiates outward from there. However, fashion fans will notice that it's not only the famous names that have interesting clothes, but the wealth of local boutiques that offer original designs.

For many reasons, Italian women, especially in the north, are still passionately devoted to fur, and if you are here in the winter you'll see more fur coats than you could imagine. Visitors who find this offensive should at least be aware that this is simply a fact of life here. Almost all clothing stores are closed on Monday mornings.

Blumarine, San Marco 1674 (Frezzaria), 30124, tel 041 520 6063, vaporetto 1 to Vallaresso, 82 to San Marco. An array of original designs for women, from woolen coats to gorgeous beaded evening dresses.

Al Duca d'Aosta, San Marco 4946 (Marzaria del Capitello), 30124, tel 041 522 0733, vaporetto 1, 41, 42, 51, 52 to San Zaccaria. High-end menswear,

with Burberry, Zegna, and other world-class names. The women's shop is just a few doors away.

Emporio Armani, San Marco 989 (Calle dei Fabbri), 30124, tel 041 523 7808, vaporetto 1, 41, 42, 51, 52 to San Zaccaria. The classic style of Armani aimed at the younger market.

Giorgio Armani, San Marco 4412 (Calle Carlo Goldoni), 30124, tel 041 523 4758, vaporetto 1, 41, 42, 51, 52 to San Zaccaria. Absolute perfection in women's fashion.

Giuliana Longo, San Marco 4813 (Calle del Lovo, San Salvador), 30124, tel 041 522 6454. Handmade hats for women, from casual to lushly elegant, as well as genuine Panama hats.

Gucci, San Marco 258 (Marzaria deli Orologio), 30124, tel 041 522 9119, vaporetto 1, 41, 42, 51, 52 to San Zaccaria. Also San Marco 1317 (Calle Vallaresso), 30124, vaporetto 1 to Calle Vallaresso, 82 to San Marco, tel 041 520 7484. Everything for which Gucci is famous: leather goods, silk scarves, ties, and updated design in women's wear.

Karin, San Marco 5332 (Rialto Bridge), 30124, tel 041 528 6905, vaporetto 1, 82 to Rialto. Wide selection of silk scarves and ties (some with Venetian motifs), cashmere and camel-hair mufflers, pashminas, as well as some leather goods. The perfectly fashioned little leather "suitcases" are perfect for cigarettes or lipstick.

Krizia, San Marco 4948/4949 (Marzaria del Capitello), 30124, tel 041 521 2762, vaporetto 1, 82 to Rialto. More youthful casual wear, but clearly designer.

Luisa Spagnoli, San Marco 740 (Marzaria San Zulian), 30124, tel 041 523 7728, vaporetto 1, 41, 42, 51, 52 to San Zaccaria. Also San Marco 5533 (Campo San Bartolomeo), 30124, vaporetto 1, 82 to Rialto, tel 041 523 4378. With shops throughout Italy, it's clear that Luisa Spagnoli's day and evening wear always hits the right note: conservative but never stuffy, and always

with beautiful fabrics.
Maneki Neko, San Marco 3820 (Campo Sant'Angelo), 30124, tel 041 520 3340, vaporetto 1 to Sant'Angelo, 82 to San Samuele. Great collection of women's shirts, classic designs using the highest quality cotton.
Max Mara, San Marco 268-270 (Marzaria del'Orologio), 30124, tel 041 522 6688, vaporetto 1, 41, 42, 51, 52 to San Zaccaria. Elegance with an edge from the great Parma design house.
La Perla, San Marco 4828 (Campo San Salvador), 30124, tel 041 522 6459, vaporetto 1, 82 to Rialto. This renowned name is justly famous for exquisite lingerie and underwear for men and women.
Prada, San Marco 1464-69 (Salizzada San Moisè), 30124, tel 041 528 3966, vaporetto 1 to Vallaresso. Those unmistakable bags as well as clothes that are just as distinctive, though possibly more avant-garde than most people over 20 will want to consider buying.
Valentino, San Marco 1473 (Salizzada San Moisè), 30124, tel 041 520 5733, vaporetto 1 to Vallaresso. This Roman couturier offers a variety of ready-to-wear separates that always look good.
Valeria Bellinaso, San Polo 1226 (Campo San Aponal), 30125, tel 041 522 3351. Original creations, with sumptuous shirts and evening jackets in silk and velvet; velvet slippers, bags and gloves, and a few hats, too.
Versace, San Marco 1462 (Campo San Moisè), 30124, tel 041 520 0057/0176, vaporetto 1 to Vallaresso. Definitely for those with attitude and money in equal quantities.
Versace Versus, San Marco 1722-25 (Frezzaria), 30124, tel 041 528 9319, vaporetto 1 to Vallaresso, 82 to San Marco. This is Versace for the younger, sportier faction.
Yachting Club, San Marco 5097/b (San Bortolomio), 30124, tel 041 521 0020. Elegant men's sweaters, trousers, jackets, and windbreakers. Best of all, the

gondolier's classic white-and-blue striped wool pullover, with its quilted lining.

FOOD & WINE

Mascari, San Polo 381 (Ruga degli Speziali), 30125, tel 041 522 9762. The ultimate in gourmet treats, from coffees and herbal teas to candies, dried mushrooms, dried and candied fruits, and balsamic vinegars. Near Christmas they also sell jars of *mostarda*, the favorite Venetian after-dinner nibble (think applesauce mixed with hot mustard). They say it settles the digestion.
Pantagruelica, Dorsoduro 2844 (Campo San Barnaba), 30123, tel 041 523 6766, vaporetto 1 to Ca' Rezzonico. Also: Giudecca 461, Tel 041 523 1809, vaporetto 41, 82 to Giudecca. Balsamic vinegar, truffles, Italian rice, oil-cured olives, plus cheeses, prosciutto, and smoked salmon.
Pasticceria Marchini, San Marco 2769 (Calle del Spezier, Santo Stefano), 30124, tel 041 522 9109. A tempting range of wonderful pastries and cookies, cakes of all sizes, and boxes of chocolates. Some Venetian specialties in tins or boxes.
Pasticceria Rosa Salva, San Marco 951 (Calle Fiubera), 30124, tel 041 521 0544, vaporetto 1 to Vallaresso, 82 to San Marco. Also: San Marco 4589 (Campo San Luca), 30124, tel 041 522 5385, vaporetto 1, 82 to Rialto. Also: Castello 6779 (Campo Sts. Giovanni e Paolo), 30122, tel 041 522 7949. Possibly the foremost name in Venice for pastry, ice cream, and other sweets, as well as catering.
G. Rizzo, Cannaregio 5778 (Calle San Giovanni Crisostomo), 30121, tel 041 522 2824, vaporetto 1, 82 to Rialto. This shop sells bread, polenta, rice, and other starchy specialties, but is probably best known for its pasta in every color of the rainbow. If you feel the need for turquoise linguine,

this is your place.
Rizzo, San Marco 933/a-938 (Calle Fiubera), 30124, tel 041 522 3388, vaporetto 1 to Vallaresso, 82 to San Marco. One of a chain of bakeries that offers all sorts of bread, cookies, and pastas, but here with the added benefit of some prepared dishes to take out (cooked artichokes, vegetable lasagna, salads). Olive oil, vinegar, and also wine.

GIFTS & SOUVENIRS

Atelier Laura Scocco, San Marco 3654/a (Calle de la Mandola), 30124, tel 041 523 1747, vaporetto 1, 82 to Rialto, 82 to San Samuele. Interesting mirrors with mosaic frames, as well as custom mosaic work. Also sells the mosaic *tesserae* by weight for do-it-yourselfers.
Capriccio, Dorsoduro 880/a (Rio Terrà Foscarini, behind the Accademia), 30123, tel 041 520 9097, vaporetto 1, 82 to Accademia. Classic and modern designs in small dishes, vases, and handblown drinking glasses, with an especially interesting assortment of jewelry including glass link bracelets and rings.
Claudia Zaggia, Dorsoduro 1195-97/a (Calle de la Toletta) 30123, tel 041 522 3159, vaporetto 1 to Accademia or Ca' Rezzonico. Lovely jewelry and flowers made of Murano glass beads, many of them antique. Loose antique beads are also for sale.
Giovanni Moro, Dorsoduro 1193 (Calle de la Toletta), 30123, tel 041 521 1399, vaporetto 1 to Ca' Rezzonico or Accademia. This little shop is devoted solely to small hand-painted replicas of Venetian buildings: palaces, churches, some complete with courtyards and bridges. Outstanding selection.
Maria-Grazia Moroni, San Polo 1863 (Campo San Tomà), 30125, tel 041 520 3399. Silver boxes and all sorts of little silver doodads. Most original desk-size picture frames, with a silver border in the shape of a Venetian window.

Paolo Brandolisio, Castello 4725, (Ponte del Diavolo), 30122, tel 041 522 4155, vaporetto 1, 41, 42, 51, 52 to San Zaccaria. One of the few craftsmen still making forcolas and oars for every kind of Venetian boat, he also makes forcolas for display in varying sizes. The workshop alone, which is several hundred years old, is worth a visit.

A. Santi, Castello 5276 (Calle delle Bande), 30121, tel 041 522 7222, vaporetto 1, 82 to Rialto, or 41, 42, 51, 52 to San Zaccaria. Pens and desk accessories, but the best items are the brass doorknockers and doorbells in the shape of lions' heads. Brass keychains also with Venetian pendants (forcola, gondola, carnival mask).

La Scialuppa, San Polo 2680 (Calle Secondo dei Saoneri), 30125, tel 041 719 372, vaporetto 1, 82 to San Tomà. Owner and craftsman Gilberto Penzo sells Venetian boat models, boat-model kits, Venetian boat plans, reproductions of sailors' ex-votos, and small forcolas. Some books on Venetian boats.

Spazio Legno, Castello 3865 (Fondamenta dei Penini, San Martino), 30122, tel 041 522 5699, vaporetto 1 to Arsenale. Two steps from the Arsenal is this oar and forcola workshop, where Saverio Pastor makes the tools of the trade for gondoliers and Venetian rowing racers. Small forcolas and wooden bookmarks shaped like forcolas make unusual mementos.

Venanzio Temporin, Castello 6360/a (Barbaria de le Tole, in front of the Ospedaletto), 30122, tel 041 528 6818, 041 520 8367, vaporetto 41, 42, 51, 52 to Fondamente Nuove. This artist will paint a ceramic tile of various sizes with any name you wish in the style of the distinctive Venetian street signs, or *nizioleti*. After 20 years here, he's still one of a kind.

GLASS

Cenedese, Piazza San Marco 40/41, 30124, tel 041 522 5487, vaporetto 1, 41, 42, 51, 52 to San Zaccaria. 1 to Vallaresso, 82 to San Marco. Also Murano: Fondamenta Venier 48, 30121, tel 041 739 101, vaporetto 41, 42 to Murano "Colonna." The finest art glass, from relatively small to overwhelming, by one of Murano's premier names.

Guglielmo Sent, Fondamenta dei Vetrai 8/a, Murano, tel 041 739 100, vaporetto 41, 42 to Murano "Colonna." Best of all are the delicate glass flowers, either singly in a small bud vase or combined as small bouquets, perfect for place settings and party favors.

Leonardo Tiberio, San Marco 941/a (Calle Fiubera), 30124, tel 041 523 2250, vaporetto 1 to Vallaresso, 82 to San Marco, 41, 42, 51, 52 to San Zaccaria. Assorted pieces of excellent glass, from the modern to the antique; many of the older pieces are signed by the owner's late father-in-law.

Il Mercante di Sabbia, San Polo 2600/a (near the Frari), 30125, tel 041 713 494. Simple modern designs for the home, in the style of Crate and Barrel.

Rose Douce, Cannaregio 5782 (Salizzada San Giovanni Crisostomo), 30121, vaporetto 1, 82 to Rialto. Charming and imaginative bowls, lamps, paperweights, and bibelots, not unreasonably priced.

La Trottola di Barbara, Castello 6468 (Barbaria de le Tole, near Sts. Giovanni e Paolo), 30122, tel 041 520 0204, vaporetto 41, 42, 51, 52 to Fondamente Nuove. Original items with Murano-glass beads. Most unusual are the small weeping willows, and a few oval boxes, made of incredibly tiny beads. Carnival masks, too.

VeniceShop, San Marco 1278 (Bocca di Piazza, Piazza San Marco), 30124, tel 041 528 5899, vaporetto 1 to Vallaresso, 82 to San Marco. This is the place for glass angels and other Christmas ornaments, silver boxes and keychains with Murano glass "murrina" decoration.

Venini, San Marco 314 (Piazzetta dei Leoncini), 30124, tel 041 522 4045, vaporetto 1, 41, 42, 51, 52 to San Zaccaria. One of Murano's greatest glassmakers, always surprising in the originality and restrained good taste of their designs.

FOR THE HOME

When you start thinking of designer glass vases and lamps, you're in the perfect city, and there are beautiful fabrics here that are also justly famous.

Bevilacqua, San Marco 337/b (Fondamenta Canonica) 30124, tel 041 528 7581, vaporetto 1, 41, 42, 51, 52 to San Zaccaria. Also San Marco 2520 (Campo Santa Maria del Giglio) 30124, tel 041 241 0662, vaporetto 1 to Santa Maria del Giglio. The Bevilacqua family has been weaving brocades and tapestries since 1800 in their workshop on the Grand Canal, and they still produce historic patterns with the old looms. Fabric also for cushions, and silk braiding and tassels. The napkin rings are *elegantissimo*. Shop in Calle Fiubera, vaporetto 1, 41, 42, 51, 52 to San Zaccaria.

Bottega dell'Acciaio, San Marco 791 (Calle Fiubera), 30124, tel 041 522 8509, vaporetto 1 to Vallaresso, 82 to San Marco. This is just the place for knives, pepper grinders, Parmesan-cheese knives, cheese graters, and other kitchen accoutrements.

ColorCasa, San Polo 1989-1991 (Campo San Polo), 30125, tel 041 523 6071, vaporetto 1, 82 to San Tomà. Also: Castello 5640 (Campo San Lio), 30122, tel 041 521 2640, vaporetto 1, 82 to Rialto, or 41, 42, 51, 52 to Fondamente Nuove. A wide selection of sumptuous silk, brocade, and velvet fabrics for drapes, slipcovers, cushions, and other decorating touches (wonderful silk tassels). The shop in Castello concentrates primarily on draperies, but the shop at San Polo has a fantastic assortment of handbags and

totebags made of leftover bits of the rich fabric; consequently, each piece is individual.
Domus, San Marco 4746 (Calle dei Fabbri), 30124, tel 041 522 6259, vaporetto 1, 82 to Rialto. All the glass, china, and cookware you could hope for, some rather expensive.
Epicentro, San Marco 932 (Calle dei Fabbri), 30124, tel 041 522 6864, vaporetto 1 to Vallaresso, 82 to San Marco. Witty, high-design kitchen and table accessories, bottle openers, potholders, many designed by Alessio.
Frette, San Marco 2070/a (Calle Larga XXII Marzo), 30124, tel 041 522 4914, vaporetto 1 to Vallaresso, 82 to San Marco. One of the greatest names for household linens, especially sheets that literally last a lifetime.
Jesurum, San Marco 4857 (Marzaria del Capitello), 30124, tel 041 520 6177, vaporetto 1, 82 to Rialto, 1, 41, 42, 51, 52 to San Zaccaria. Also: San Marco 60-61 (Piazza San Marco), 30124, tel 041 522 9864, vaporetto 1, 41, 42, 51, 52 to San Zaccaria, 1 to Vallaresso. This Venetian family has been producing linens for generations; their richly colored tablecloths and napkins look like heirlooms even when they are new.
Norilene, Dorsoduro 727 (Calle della Chiesa, San Vio), 30123, tel 041 523 7605. Hand-stamped fabrics, a Venetian tradition reinterpreted by Helene and Nora Ferruzzi. Wall hangings, cushion covers (even scarves and soft hats) made either of silk or "velvetized cotton" in subtle abstract patterns and with the most sensuous muted colors and textures. No two pieces are alike, so you can be sure of getting an individual item.

JEWELRY

Italy's grand tradition of fine work in gold and precious stones is well represented here. In the most expensive shops, you may

notice a particularly Venetian creation: a brooch of a black man with turban and earrings, usually set with diamonds and rubies. He represents a *moretto*, or Moor, and most great families had at least one among their servants, who often began their careers as petted little boys who ran simple errands.
Aldo Ottochian, Cannaregio 6064 (Campo Santa Maria Nova) 30121, tel 041 528 9807, vaporetto 1, 82 to Rialto, lines to Fondamenta Nuove. Designs made by the owner; especially appealing are the pins, earrings, and pendants in the form of small Venetian palaces.
Cartier, San Marco 606 (Campo San Zulian), 30124, tel 041 522 2071, vaporetto 1, 41, 42, 51, 52 to San Zaccaria. Diamonds, the famous "tank" watches, and superb gifts of gold and silver.
Ganesha, San Polo 1044 (Ruga Rialto) 30125, tel 041 522 5148, vaporetto 1 to San Silvestro. Amber, coral, and semiprecious stones (moonstone, garnet, aquamarine) set to modern designs, with a more youthful, even ethnic accent. Reproductions of ancient Mediterranean designs.
Missiaglia, Piazza San Marco 125, 30124, tel 041 522 4464, vaporetto 1, 41, 42, 51, 52 to San Zaccaria, 1 to Vallaresso, 8 to San Marco. Since 1846, this shop has offered the best classic and modern Italian designs.
Nardi, Piazza San Marco 69, 30124, tel 041 522 5733, vaporetto 1, 41, 42, 51, 52 to San Zaccaria, 1 to Vallaresso, 82 to San Marco. A lavish array of pieces in coral, diamonds, jade, and a variety of other stones, in designs that range from the simple to the fabulous.
Roberto Tiozzo, San Marco 740 (Marzaria San Zulian), 31024, tel 041 522 1217, vaporetto 1, 41, 42, 51, 52 to San Zaccaria. Despite its small size, this shop contains a wonderful selection of jewelry (gold Venetian charms a specialty, particularly the lion of

San Marco) as well as silver-framed icons and little silver forcolas. Will also make simple repairs.
Tiffany, San Marco 705 (Marzaria San Zulian), 30124, tel 041 520 0324, vaporetto 1, 41, 42, 51, 52 to San Zaccaria. Sold from a shop called La Bauta, the great American name is clearly at home here, offering diamonds, gold, and silver that are the equal of any Italian designer but with a noticeably sleek American style.
Vivici, San Marco 262 (Marzaria dell'Orologio), 30124, tel 041 522 5309, vaporetto 1, 41, 42, 51, 52 to San Zaccaria. Everything from silver gondolas to gold religious medals, as well as the little silver coins stamped "5"—a whimsical version of the Venetian mythical "mad money" (what they call *cinque schei di mona* or the fool's five cents).

LEATHER & OTHER ACCESSORIES

Florence is more famous for leather, but there's still plenty here to choose from.
Furla, San Marco 4833 (Marzaria San Salvador), 30124, tel 041 277 0460. Also San Marco 4954 (Marzaria del Capitello), 30124, tel 041 523 0611, vaporetto 1, 82 to Rialto. Very chic but not outrageously expensive purses, tote bags, and keychains. Chunky silver jewelry, and keychains with their trademark bear.
Hermès, Piazza San Marco 125, 30124, tel 041 521 0117, vaporetto 1, 41, 42, 51, 52 to San Zaccaria. The great French designer's bags and silk scarves translate very well into Italian.
Louis Vuitton, San Marco 1255-56 (Calle Larga dell'Ascensione), 30124, tel 041 522 4500, vaporetto 1, 82 to Vallaresso, 82 to San Marco. It is perfectly easy to know the real thing when you see it, and the selection here of luggage, hand-bags, and purses of all types is all you could wish for.

Mandarina Duck, San Marco 193 (Marzaria del'Orologio), 30124, tel 041 522 3325, vaporetto 1, 41, 42, 51, 52 to San Zaccaria. Luggage, handbags, and backpacks that are cooler than Coach, even if they are made of heavy-gauge nylon. The colors are striking.

Marforio, San Marco 5033 (San Salvador), 30124, tel 041 522 5734, vaporetto 1, 82 to Rialto. A Venetian tradition since 1875, Marforio has designer handbags, luggage, wallets, leather boxes, and umbrellas.

Vogini, San Marco 1292 (Calle Larga dell' Ascensione), 30124, tel 041 522 2573, vaporetto 1 to Vallaresso, 82 to San Marco. Vogini has top-of-the-line handbags, from classic styles to real works of art. Should you feel the urge for a purse shaped like a kitchen iron or a country house, this is the place.

PAINTINGS & ART

All the great artists in Venice aren't dead already. There are plenty working today, offering original works at a wide variety of prices.

Giovanni Aricò, San Marco 2630 (Fondamenta della Prefettura), 30124, tel 041 523 7814, vaporetto 1 to Santa Maria del Giglio. The sculptor of the bronze doors on the Teatro Goldoni makes statues and other decorative items such as lamps in bronze, marble, and other materials.

Itaca, Castello 5267/a (Calle delle Bande, Santa Maria Formosa), 30122, tel 041 520 3207, vaporetto 1, 41, 42, 51, 52 to San Zaccaria, 41, 42, 51, 52 to Ospedale. Monica Martin's enchanting little watercolors of Venice under starry skies endow the city with a more playful air than usual.

Loris Marazzi, Dorsoduro 2903 (Campo Santa Margherita), 30123, tel 041 523 9001, vaporetto 1 to Ca' Rezzonico. Whimsical wooden sculpture: wooden books and bow ties, briefcases, even a wooden bra

hanging on a clothesline. Larger, more ambitious pieces as well.

Maquette, Dorsoduro 2727/b (Calle Lunga San Barnaba), 30123, tel 041 523 8250, vaporetto 1 to Ca' Rezzonico. This cluttered little workshop in a former butcher shop (the metal hooks are still outside the door) offers an appealing assortment of paintings, prints, and drawings of Venetian scenes by a number of local artists. Some of the smaller, naive oil paintings have real charm and are very reasonably priced. Erratic hours; better to phone first.

Osvald Bohm, San Marco 1349-1350 (Salizzada San Moisè) 30124, tel 041 522 2255, vaporetto 1 to Vallaresso, 82 to San Marco. Wide variety of paintings, prints, and watercolors. Vintage black-and-white photographs of Venice are also available from the Naya Collection, some of which have been compiled into a book that is on sale here.

Roberto Ferruzzi, Dorsoduro 523 (opposite Guggenheim Collection gift shop), 30123, tel 041 520 5996, vaporetto 1, 82 to Accademia, 1 to Salute. "Bobo" Ferruzzi's distinctive paintings of Venice may not be everyone's taste; their powerful colors and muscular brushwork are almost the opposite of the sinuous pastel approach many painters prefer. Strange but true, though, there really are days in which the city looks like this, from the sunset behind the Redentore to San Giorgio at dawn to the summer sun blazing down on a deserted square in Malamocco.

ART SUPPLIES

All those artists have to get their materials somewhere.

Arcobaleno, San Marco 2968 (Calle delle Botteghe, Santo Stefano), 30124, tel 041 523 6818, vaporetto 82 to San Samuele. If you have any artistic leanings, a visit to this unprepossessing little hardware store will surprise you: Scores of jars of powdered colors ready

for you to custom-mix, as well as the glass *tesserae* for assembling your own mosaics.

Testolini, San Marco 1744-8 (Fondamenta Orseolo), 30124, tel 041 522 9265, vaporetto 1 to Vallaresso, 82 to San Marco. Sketchbooks, pencils, pastels, and a full range of other artist's and architect's supplies.

SHOES

The greatest Italian art form, some would say.

Bruno Magli, San Marco 1583-85 (Frezzeria), 30124, tel 041 522 3472, vaporetto 1 to Vallaresso, 82 to San Marco. Also San Marco 1302 (Calle Vallaresso), 30124, tel 041 522 7210, vaporetto 1 to Vallaresso, 82 to San Marco. Also San Marco 2288 (Calle Larga XXII Marzo), 30124, tel 041 520 8280, vaporetto 1 to Santa Maria del Giglio. One of the greatest names in luxury shoes, offering both classic and more adventurous designs.

Fratelli Rossetti, San Marco 1477 (Salizzada San Moisè), 30124, tel 041 522 0819, vaporetto 1 to Vallaresso, 82 to San Marco. Once you become a fan, you're loyal for life to this top-of-the-line shoemaker for men and women.

La Parigina, San Marco 727-28 (Marzaria San Zulian), 30124, tel 041 522 6743. Also San Marco 733-36 (Marzaria S. Zulian), 30124, tel 041 523 1555, vaporetto 1, 41, 42, 51, 52 to San Zaccaria. Wide selection of brands for men and women, notably the English classics, Clarks and Church's.

Rolando Segalin, San Marco 4365 (Calle dei Fuseri), 30124, tel 041 522 2115, vaporetto 1 to Vallaresso, 82 to San Marco, or 1, 82 to Rialto. The last artisan in Venice to make shoes by hand, though his backlog of orders makes it difficult to have a pair custom-made very quickly. The shop is filled with many excellent commercial shoes, and there are a number of his more fanciful, one-of-a-kind shoes for sale, if they happen to fit you. **Timberland**, San Marco 4336-4337 (Calle dei Fuseri), 30124, tel 041 523 1827. Before you say "seen that," take a look. There may well be some styles here made for the European market. **Zecchi**, San Marco 288-300 (Marzaria del'Orologio), 30124, tel 041 520 4453 or 041 523 2090, vaporetto 1, 41, 42, 51, 52 to San Zaccaria. Some of the most elegant designs you'll find anywhere in Venice, but don't be thinking of a bargain.

STATIONERY

Venetian books and printing were in the vanguard of European culture for centuries, and paper here is still plentiful and lovely.
Biblos, San Marco 739 (Marzaria San Zulian), 30124, tel 041 521 2908, vaporetto 41, 42, 51, 52 to San Zaccaria. Also: San Marco 2087 (Calle Larga XXII Marzo), 30124, tel 041 521 0714, vaporetto 1 to Santa Maria del Giglio. Also: San Marco 221 (Marzaria de l'Orologio), 30124, tel 041 241 8693. There is an extensive selection here of notebooks, boxes, frames, and other articles of paper, leather, and even glass (the Venetian glass "fountain" pen is unusual, and actually works).
Carta Marina, Castello 6376 (Calle Gallina, Sts. Giovanni e Paolo), 30122, tel 041 521 0019 or 041 610 591, vaporetto 41, 42, 51, 52 to Fondamenta Nuove. This is as much a workshop as it is a store, a tiny place is full of very unusual papers (some with little flowers embedded into them), photo albums, and a variety of gift items; in addition, Marina carries on the great Venetian craft of bookbinding.
Legatoria Polliero, San Polo 2995 (Campo dei Frari), 30125, tel 041 528 5130, vaporetto 1, 82 to San Tomà. Picture frames, trays, and notebooks of distinctive paper made by this family of craftsmen. Some items (frames, bookbindings,

trays) also in leather.
Il Papiro, San Marco 2764 (Calle del Piovan, San Maurizio), 30124, tel 041 522 3056, vaporetto 1 to Santa Maria del Giglio. Several rooms full of paper goods, bookmarks, and greeting cards with Venetian scenes, paper frames, tiny address books, and so on.
Il Prato, San Marco 3633 (Calle de la Mandola), 30124, tel 041 523 1459, vaporetto 1, 82 to Rialto, 82 to San Samuele. Good selection of notebooks, boxes, albums, and picture frames with beautifully printed paper.
Testolini, San Marco 1744-48 (Fondamenta Orseolo), 30124, tel 041 522 9265, vaporetto 1 to Vallaresso, 82 to San Marco. Writing paper, greeting cards, wrapping paper, pens, and general office and desk supplies.

MISCELLANEOUS

COSMETICS
Coin Beauty, San Marco 4558 (Campo San Luca), 30124, tel 041 523 8444, vaporetto 1, 82 to Rialto. Large cosmetics and perfume store for men and women, with most international brands, including Clinique.
Giada, Dorsoduro 3117 (Campo Santa Margherita), 30123, tel 041 241 0532, vaporetto 1 to Ca' Rezzonico. Half of this little shop is devoted to health foods, the other half to natural cosmetics. Charming little cakes of soap embossed with Venetian motifs: the Rialto Bridge, the Basilica of San Marco, and the Palazzo Ducale.
Lush, Cannaregio 3822 (Strada Nova) 30121, tel 041 241 1200, vaporetto 1 to Ca' d'Oro. Another English natural-cosmetics firm but with way more attitude than the Body Shop a few doors down. These products are high quality but made of everything imaginable, and often packaged to look like food (deli refrigerator cases heighten the effect). Soaps sold by the chunk, hacked off of huge cheese-like forms. Pricey, but irresistible.

COSTUMES
If you want a fantastic Venetian period outfit to go with your Carnival mask (or not), there are a number of theatrical costumers who rent and also sell their handiwork. Among the best are:
Pietro Longhi, San Polo 2604/b (Frari), 30125, tel 041 714 478, vaporetto 1, 82 to San Tomà. Gorgeous 18th-century-style brocade gowns and wigs, and the full lineup of outfits for men who may want to play Casanova or some other character.
Stefano Nicolau, Cannaregio 5565 (San Giovanni Crisostomo), 30121, tel 041 520 7051/9749, vaporetto 1, 82 to Rialto. This young Venetian has made his name designing for theater, opera, film, and television, and by now has amassed an extremely large number of costumes.

SILK
Color Casa, San Polo 1989-1991 (Campo San Polo), 30125, tel 041 523 6071, vaporetto 1, 82 to San Tomà. This store has a range of neckties, scarves, and tassels, as well as an assortment of unique bags made or trimmed with the remnants of the silk and velvet drapery fabrics.
Ethnos, San Marco 2958/a (Campo Santo Stefano), 30124, tel 041 528 9988, vaporetto 82 to San Samuele. Interesting array of elegant handmade silk evening bags, plus some pieces of modern jewelry with an ethnic aspect.
Venetia Studium, San Marco 2403-406 (Calle Larga XXII Marzo), 30124, tel 041 522 9281, vaporetto 1 to Santa Maria del Giglio. Also: San Polo 3006 (Campo dei Frari), 30125, tel 041 713 393, vaporetto 1, 82 to San Tomà. Also: San Marco 723 (Marzaria San Zulian), 30124, tel 041 522 9859, vaporetto 41, 42, 51, 52 to San Zaccaria. Even if you don't want to carry home one of their Fortuny silk lampshades, this shop has a wide range of evening bags, jewelry bags, scarves, and foulards in pleated silk and cut velvet, all in the most ravishing colors.

ENTERTAINMENT

Nighttime isn't really Venice's best time; the Venetian is a homebody at heart. This is not to say that there's nothing to do in the evenings, but you may also find that a day of walking the city has left you longing more for a deep sofa than nightlife.

Two very useful free publications offer up-to-date listings in English of the month's events. *Un Ospite di Venezia (A Guest of Venice)* is a fat little booklet usually available at your hotel's reception desk; it is published by the Golden Keys association of hotel concierges. The other is *Leo*, a magazine full of articles and suggestions that is published every three months by the Tourist Promotion Bureau, and is available at the APT office in the mouth of the Piazza San Marco.

Venice still disseminates a lot of information with posters on public billboards. It sounds very inefficient, but you'd be surprised how many events you find out about by coming across posters or smaller, photocopied notices.

If you feel very adventurous, consult Venice's daily newspaper, *Il Gazzettino* (only in Italian). The second section has listings of events for that day only; unfortunately, they rarely list ticket prices.

Your hotel will probably book tickets for you on request. Many travel agencies also offer tickets to concerts and other events. Tickets to La Fenice can be bought at their desk at the Cassa di Risparmio di Venezia (Venice Savings Bank) between Campo Manin and Campo San Luca (mornings only).

Summertime isn't the best for indoor activities; few places are air-conditioned, and everyone is either at the beach or in the mountains. The typical summer festivals are usually out beyond the historic center.

Concerts tend to start later than you may be accustomed to, at either 8:30 p.m. or even 9:00 p.m. Dinner is sacred.

If you see "By invitation" listed instead of ticket prices, don't give up. Invitations can be surprisingly easy to obtain. Ask at your hotel or phone.

BARS & NIGHT CLUBS

There are certainly places to hang out at night, but don't count on using a credit card. Irish pubs seem to have found their home away from home here as in countless towns and cities all across the globe.

Al Paradiso Perduto, Cannaregio 2540 (Fondamenta della Misericordia), 30121, tel 720 581, vaporetto 1, 82 to San Marcuola, 41, 42, 51, 52 to San Alvise or Guglie. Wildly eclectic range of music here at "Paradise Lost," and equally mixed clientele, largely students.

Da Codroma, Dorsoduro 2540 (Fondamenta Briati), 30123, tel 041 524 6789, vaporetto 1 to Piazzale Roma, 51, 52 to Zattere, 82 to San Basilio. Live music, from blues to jazz to ethnic, every week in an old-fashioned neighborhood bar that hasn't been fixed up too much.

Fiddler's Elbow Irish Pub, Cannaregio 3847 (Campiello Testori, Strada Nova), 30121, tel 041 523 9930, vaporetto 1 to Ca' d'Oro. Irish staff, Guinness, Irish music outside in summer.

Margaret Duchamp, Dorsoduro 3019 (Campo Santa Margherita), 30123, tel 041 528 6255. No live acts, but the latest cool recordings for the very cool clientele.

Il Nono Risorto, Santa Croce 2338 (Sotoportego di Siora Bettina), 30125, tel 041 524 1169. Blues, jazz, and whatever else sounds good.

CINEMA

Venice was once full of movie theaters, but the number has shrunk drastically. Movies, on TV and in the theater, are unabashedly dubbed into Italian, and always have been (there are entire generations of Italians who have no idea what John Wayne really sounds like). Note that the Italian title of an American film may not be an exact translation of the original.

Cinema Accademia, Dorsoduro 1019 (Accademia), 30123, tel 041 528 7706, vaporetto 1, 82 to Accademia. Relatively current films, with a special calendar of showings of movies in English.

Cinema Giorgione, Cannaregio 4612 (Rio Terrà dei Franceschi, Santi Apostoli), 30121, tel 041 522 6298, vaporetto 1, 82 to Rialto, 1 to Ca' d'Oro, 41, 42, 51, 52 to Fondamenta Nuove. Venice's only "foreign" film house, showing a cutting-edge variety of indie films in their original language, usually English or French. Films from other countries are subtitled in Italian.

Cinema Rossini, San Marco 3988 (Fondamenta Salizzada del Teatro) 30124, tel 041 523 0322. Standard Hollywood fare.

OPERA, DANCE, & CLASSICAL MUSIC

There's more to music in Venice than Vivaldi; though the choice isn't always large, it can range from a concert of Persian music to Gregorian chant to the Venice Gospel Ensemble. Watch for notices of free concerts by school choirs on tour from the U.S. and other countries.

The quality of musical performances is usually high, and if the concert hall is a church or scuola, as it often is, the setting will be a bonus.

Although Italy has a peerless history of great church music, it is hardly ever performed, at least not in the context of the services for which it was written. Easter morning at the Basilica of San Marco will be one of your few opportunities to hear some of the pieces that were written for this incomparable setting. Dance is relatively rare and almost always limited to visiting troupes.

BAROQUE MUSIC

There seem to be countless performances of Vivaldi's *Four Seasons* and similar works of the baroque era. The locations and groups may vary, but the standard is good, if nothing remarkable. Occasionally in costume, and/or by candlelight. Some of the choices are:

Associazione Richard Wagner, tel 041 523 2544. This cultural group occasionally organizes concerts of Wagner's music. Call for information.

Church of San Bartolomeo, Campo San Bartolomeo, tel 041 277 0561, vaporetto 1, 82 to Rialto. Interpreti Veneziani perform in this building, no longer used as a church.

Church of Santa Maria Formosa, Campo Santa Maria Formosa, 30122, tel 041 984 252, vaporetto 1, 41, 42, 51, 52 to San Zaccaria. Home to the Collegium Ducale orchestra.

Church of Santa Maria della Pietà ("the Vivaldi church"), Riva degli Schiavoni, 30122, tel 041 523 1096 vaporetto 1, 41, 42, 51, 52 to San Zaccaria. Tickets on sale in hotels, at Nalesso music shop (see p. 255) or at the box office. This church, small but high-ceilinged, is perfect for Vivaldi's music, and the joyous Tiepolo paintings seem to be in perfect harmony.

Fondazione Giorgio Cini, Isola di San Giorgio, tel 041 528 9900, vaporetto 82 to San Giorgio. The Cini Foundation frequently offers a post-Vivaldi repertoire, from Brahms to Boulez.

German-Italian Cultural Association, Cannaregio 4118, 30131, tel 041 523 2544. This group often schedules concerts of various German composers in the Palazzo Albrizzi.

Prigioni Art Circle, Ponte della Paglia, 30124, tel 041 984 252, vaporetto 1, 41, 42, 51, 52 to San Zaccaria. Interesting concerts held in the Old Prisons across from the Palazzo Ducale with programs that venture beyond the predictable.

Scuola Grande di San Giovanni Evangelista, San Polo 2454, 30125, tel 041 786 764 (Venetian Concert Society), vaporetto 1 to Riva di Biasio. The main hall is a splendid setting for recitals by performers such as pianist Andras Schiff.

Scuola Grande San Teodoro, Campo San Salvador, 30124, tel 041 521 0294. Venetian Rondo performs in the magnificent building that once belonged to one of Venice's confraternities.

OPERA

Ai Musicanti, San Marco 1092 (Campo San Gallo), 30124, tel 041 520 8922, vaporetto 1 to Vallaresso, 82 to San Marco. A fairly new place with two nightly performances of light opera arias and favorite Italian songs by young singers on their way up.

La Fenice, Palafenice, island of Tronchetto, tel 041 521 0161, vaporetto 82 to Tronchetto. Since fire destroyed its historic theater, this world-class opera company has soldiered on in a huge tent out in the back of beyond. Visiting dance companies also perform here.

Theater here is virtually always in Italian. Any occasional English-language performances would be listed in *Ospite* or *Leo*.

Fondamenta Nuove, Cannaregio 5013 (Fondamenta Nuove), 30121, tel 041 522 4498 or 041 523 1988. A small group with an avant-garde slant.

Puppet shows: During Christmas and Carnival, watch for notices announcing performances of *burattini* (puppets).

Teatro a l'Avogaria, Dorsoduro 1617 (Calle dell' Avogaria), 30123, tel 041 520 96130. A neighborhood company that puts on modest plays, including Goldoni.

Teatro Goldoni, San Marco 4650 (Calle Goldoni), 30124, tel 041 520 7683, vaporetto 1, 82 to Rialto. Venice's premier theater, offering Shakespeare, Greek tragedy, and, of course, Goldoni.

With all the walking that the average Venetian day entails, you may not feel the need for more exercise, but if you are keen on a particular activity, there are a number of options.

Golf The Lido boasts one of Italy's best courses, the Golf Club Lido, Via del Forte, Alberoni, tel 041 731 333.

Rowing is obviously the sport most suited to Venice. Many rowing clubs have kayaks (which they also call canoes) and shells, as well as Venetian-style rowing boats. You will be expected to demonstrate your competence or take a few lessons first. Temporary memberships are usually required by the club. Contact: Canottieri Diadora, via Sandro Gallo 136/b, Lido, tel 041 526 5742. Reale Società Canottieri Bucintoro, Dorsoduro 10, 15, 261, Zattere tel 041 522 2055/041 520 5630/041 523 7933. Società Canottieri Francesco Querini, Cannaregio 6576/e, Fondamenta Nuove, tel 041 522 2039.

Running is popular with Venetians, and the best places are along the Zattere, the Fondamenta Nuove, and the gardens of the Sant' Elena area of Castello.

Soccer The Venice team plays on intermittent Sunday afternoons in the Pierluigi Penzo stadium at Sant' Elena in Castello, tel 041 985 100. Tickets are on sale at the two Venice branches of the Banca Antoniana Popolare Veneta.

Swimming is possible in the ocean at the Lido or from beaches at the Alberoni, beyond Malamocco. The city has two indoor pools: the Piscina Comunale on the Giudecca at Sacco Fisola, 82, tel 041 528 5430, and at Sant' Alvise, Cannaregio 3161, tel 041 713 567. Both closed July and Aug.

Tennis can be played on the Lido at the Tennis Club Cai del Moro, Via Ferruccio Parri 6, tel 041 770 801, which also has a pool and a gymnasium.

LANGUAGE GUIDE

USEFUL WORDS & PHRASES

Yes *Si*
No *No*
Excuse me (in a crowd or asking for permission) *Permesso*
Excuse me (asking for attention) *Mi scusi*
Hello (before lunch) *Buon giorno*, (after lunch) *Buona sera*
Hi or Bye *Ciao*
Please *Per favore*
Thank you *Grazie*
You're welcome *Prego*
Have a good day! *Buona giornata!*
OK *Va bene*
Good-bye *Arrivederci*
Good night *Buona notte*
Sorry *Mi scusi* or *Mi dispiace*
here *qui*
there *lì*
today *oggi*
yesterday *ieri*
tomorrow *domani*
now *adesso/ora*
later *più tardi/dopo*
right away *subito*
this morning *stamattina*
this afternoon *questo pomeriggio*
this evening *stasera*
open *aperto*
closed *chiuso*
Do you have? *Avrebbe?*
Do you speak English? *Parla inglese?*
I'm American (man) *Sono americano*, (woman) *Sono americana*
I don't understand *Non capisco*
Please speak more slowly *Potrebbe parlare più lentamente?*
Where is…? *Dov'è…?*
I don't know *Non so*
No problem *Niente*
That's it *Ecco*
Here/there it is (masculine) *Eccolo*, (feminine) *Eccola*
What is your name? *Come si chiama?*
My name is… *Mi chiamo…*
Let's go *Andiamo*
At what time? *A che ora?*
When? *Quando?*
What time is it? *Che ora è?*
Can you help me? *Mi può aiutare?*
I'd like… *Vorrei…*
How much is it? *Quanto costa?*

MENU READER

breakfast *la (prima) colazione*
lunch *il pranzo*
dinner *la cena*
appetizer *l'antipasto*
first course *il primo*
main course *il secondo*
vegetable, side dish *il contorno*
dessert *il dessert/dolci*
wine list *la lista dei vini*
the bill *il conto*
I'd like to order *Vorrei ordinare*
Is service included? *Il servizio è incluso?*

ANTIPASTO

sarde in saor fried sardines with sweet-sour onions
capparossoli local small clams steamed with garlic
seppioline small local cuttlefish
peoci mussels
baccalà mantecato creamy spread of dried codfish

PASTA SAUCES

all'amatriciana tomato sauce with chili and bacon
bigoli in salsa mild anchovy and onion
alla carbonara with bacon, eggs, and pecorino cheese
alla busera shrimp and tomato
pasta e fagioli thick soup of pasta and beans
alle vongole white clam sauce
al ragù bolognese sauce
col nero di seppie cuttlefish ink

MEATS

anatra duck
capriolo mountain goat
fegato alla veneziana liver and onions
rosbif all'inglese roast beef
la bistecca beefsteak
ben cotta well-done
non troppo cotta medium
appena cotta rare
al sangue very rare
il filetto fillet steak
il carpaccio finely sliced raw beef
il coniglio rabbit
il maiale pork
il manzo beef
il pollo chicken
le polpette meatballs
la porchetta cold roast pork with herbs
il prosciutto ham, *crudo* raw, *cotto* cooked
il tacchino turkey
la trippa tripe
il vitello veal

FISH & SEAFOOD

l'alici/acciughe anchovies
l'aragosta/astice lobster
il calamaro squid
i gamberetti shrimp
il granchio crab
il polipo octopus
le sarde sardines
la sogliola sole
il tonno tuna
la trota trout
san pietro John Dory
branzino sea bass
orata gilthead
cefalu grey mullet
seppie cuttlefish
griglia mista mixed grilled fish
frittura mista mixed fried fish
baccala alla vicentina dried salt cod in tomato sauce
bisato or *anguilla* eel
coda di rospo monkfish tail

VEGETABLES

l'aglio garlic
gli asparagi asparagus
il carciofo artichoke
la carota carrot
il cavolfiore cauliflower
i fagiolini fresh green beans
l'insalata mista/verde mixed-green salad
la melanzane eggplant
le patate potatoes
i piselli peas
i pomodori tomatoes
gli spinaci spinach
il tartufo truffle
le zucchine zucchini
castraure small early artichokes
fondi di carciofo artichoke hearts
peperonata simmered peppers

FRUIT

l'albicocca apricot
l'arancia orange
le ciliegie cherries
le fragole strawberries
la mela apple
la pera pear
la pesca peach
la pescanoce nectarine
il pompelmo grapefruit
l'uva grapes

ILLUSTRATIONS CREDITS

Abbreviations for terms appearing below: (t) top; (b) bottom; (l) left; (r) right

Cover (tl), Gettyone/Stone. (tr), Gettyone/Stone. (br), Powestock/Zefa. (bl), AA Photo Library/Clive Sawyer. (spine), Gettyone/Stone

1, AA Photo Library/S. McBride. 2/3, Thad Samuel Abell II/National Geographic Society. 4, Robert Leon. 9, M. Barnett/Art Directors and Trip Photo Library. 11, Sylvain Grandadam/Franca Speranza Srl. 12/13, Joe Cornish. 14, Gino Russo/The Travel Library. 15, AA Photo Library/S. McBride. 16/17, Robert Holmes. 18/19, AA Photo Library/S. McBride. 20, Brian McGilloway/Robert Holmes. 21, N. Mackenzie/Gettyone/Stone. 23, Tessa Traeger. 24/25, Thad Samuel Abell II/National Geographic Society. 26/27, Mark Cator/Impact Photos. 28, Palazzo Ducale/Scala, Florence. 30, Museo Correr/Scala, Florence. 31, Leonardo Loredan (1463–1521) Doge of Venice from 1501–21, c. 1501 (oil on panel) by Giovanni Bellini (c. 1430–1516), National Gallery, London, UK/Bridgeman Art Library. 32/33, Museo Correr/Alinari – Fototeca. 35, Archivo Iconografico, S.A./Corbis UK Ltd. 36/37, Ca Rezzonico/Scala, Florence. 37, Museo del Risorgimento/Scala, Florence. 38, Archivio Naya/Bohm – Venezia. 39, Albert Moldvay/National Geographic Society. 41, M. Barlow/Art Directors and Trip Photo Library. 42/43, Scuola Grande di San Rocco/Scala, Florence. 44 Private Collection/Fine Art Photographic Library. 45, James Davis Worldwide. 46, Museo Bilbliografico Muscale, Bologna/Scala, Florence. 47, J. Morris/Axiom Photographic Agency. 48/49, Images Colour Library. 50, AA Photo Library/S. McBride. 52, AA Photo Library/S. McBride. 53, AA Photo Library/S. McBride. 54, John Heseltine Archive. 57, Siegfried Tauqueur/Franca Speranza Srl. 58, AA Photo Library/S. McBride. 59, AA Photo Library/S. McBride. 60, Mark E. Smith/Franca Speranza Srl. 61, John Heseltine Archive. 62, Inge Morath/Magnum Photos. 63, AA Photo Library/S. McBride. 64/65, Images Colour Library. 66, AA Photo Library/S. McBride. 67, AA Photo Library/S. McBride. 68, Farabolafoto. 69, D. Cilia/The Travel Library. 70, Sarah Quill/Venice Picture Library. 71, AA Photo Library/S. McBride. 75, AA Photo Library/S. McBride. 76, L. Barbazza/Marka. 77, Robert Leon. 78/79, The Travel Library. 81, G. Gilbert/Art Directors and Trip Photo Library. 82, J. Blackman/Art Directors and Trip Photo Library. 82/83, Simeone Huber/Gettyone/Stone. 84, S. Marco (museo)/Scala, Florence. 85t, S. Marco/Scala, Florence. 85b, S.

Marco/Scala, Florence. 86, P. Goycoolea/Hutchison Library. 87, T. Gervis/ Robert Harding Picture Library. 88/89, Robert Holmes. 89, John Heseltine Archive. 90, H. Rooney/Eye Ubiquitous. 92, Mark E. Smith/Franca Speranza Srl. 94, AA Photo Library/S. McBride. 95, AA Photo Library/S. McBride. 96, AA Photo Library/S. McBride. 97, Popperfoto. 98, J. Morris/Axiom Photographic Agency. 99, AA Photo Library/S. McBride. 102/103, AA Photo Library/S. McBride. 104, St. Vincent Ferrer Altarpiece, c. 1465 (polyptych) by Giovanni Bellini (c. 1430–1516), San Giovanni e Paolo, Venice, Italy/Bridgeman Art Library. 105, Alinari – Fototeca. 106/107, Sylvain Grandadam/Franca Speranza Srl. 107, AA Photo Library/S. McBride. 108/109, AA Photo Library/S. McBride. 109, Robert Holmes. 111, AA Photo Library/S. McBride. 112, Mimmo Jodice/Corbis UK Ltd. 113, Scuola di San Giorgio degli Schiavoni/Scala, Florence. 114, Sarah Quill/Venice Picture Library. 115, Madonna and Child by Antonio da Negroponte (15th century), San Francesco della Vigna, Venice, Italy/Bridgeman Art Library. 116/117, AA Photo Library/S. McBride. 117, AA Photo Library/S. McBride. 118/119, Museo Storico Navale, Venice/Scala, Florence. 119, Sarah Quill/Venice Picture Library. 120, Robert Leon. 121, Mark E. Smith/Franca Speranza Srl. 123, M. Winch/Axiom Photographic Agency. 124/125, AA Photo Library/S. McBride. 125, The Martyrdom of St Lawrence (altarpiece) by Titian (Tiziano Vecellio) (c. 1488–1576), Gesuiti, Venice, Italy/Bridgeman Art Library. 126, AA Photo Library/S. McBride. 127, AA Photo Library/S. McBride. 130, AA Photo Library/S. McBride. 131, The Presentation of the Virgin (oil on canvas) by Tintoretto (Jacopo Robusti) (1518–94), Madonna dell'Orto, Venice, Italy/Francesco Turio Bohm/Bridgeman Art Library. 132/133, The Nun's Visiting Day by Francesco Guardi (1712–93), Ca' Rezzonico, Museo del Settecento, Venice/Bridgeman Art Library. 133, Sarah Quill. 134/135, Robert Leon. 135, Sarah Quill/Venice Picture Library. 136, John Heseltine Archive. 137, AA Photo Library/S. McBride. 138/139, AA Photo Library/S. McBride. 139, AA Photo Library/S. McBride. 140, Robert Leon. 141, Carlos Freire/Hutchison Library. 143, AA Photo Library/S. McBride. 145, AA Photo Library/S. McBride. 146/147, AA Photo Library/S. McBride. 147, AKG, London. 148/149, AA Photo Library/S. McBride. 149, AA Photo Library/S. McBride. 150, Mark E. Smith/Franca Speranza Srl. 151, Venice, Galleria Int. d'arte moderne/Cameraphoto/AKG, London. 152, AA Photo Library/R. Walford. 153, Richard Philpott/Zooid

Pictures. 154, Scala, Florence. 155, AA Photo Library/S. McBride. 156, Sarah Quill/Venice Picture Library. 157, AA Photo Library/D. Miterdiri. 158, Self Portrait, engraved by William Holl (1807–71) pub. by William Mackenzie (engraving) by Titian (Tiziano Vecelli) (c. 1488–1576) (after) Private Collection/Bridgeman Art Library. 159, C. Rennie/Art Directors and Trip Photo Library. 160, AA Photo Library/S. McBride. 161, AA Photo Library/S. McBride. 162, John Heseltine Archive. 162/163, Alinari – Fototeca. 164/165, Vision of St. Augustine by Vittore Carpaccio (c. 1460/5–1523/6), Scuola di San Giorgio degli Schiavoni, Venice, Italy/Bridgeman Art Library. 166, AA Photo Library/S. McBride. 167, John Heseltine Archive. 168t, Sylvain Grandadam/Franca Speranza Srl. 168b, Self Portrait by Tintoretto (Jacopo Robusti) (1518–94), Philadelphia Museum of Art, Pennsylvania, PA, USA/ Bridgeman Art Library. 169, John Heseltine Archive. 170, AA Photo Library/S. McBride. 171, Robert Holmes. 173, AA Photo Library/S. McBride. 174/175, AA Photo Library/S. McBride. 176, Sarah Quill/Venice Picture Library. 176/177, Martyrdom of St. Sebastian, 1556 by Veronese (Paolo Caliari) (1528–88), San Sebastiano, Venice, Italy/Bridgeman Art Library. 180, AA Photo Library/S. McBride. 181, Galleria dell'Academia, Venice, AKG, London/Cameraphoto. 182, Fondazione Cini, Venice/Cameraphoto/AKG, London. 183, Accademia, Venice/Alinari – Fototeca. 185, Accademia, Venice/Scala, Florence. 186, Mark Henley/Impact Photos. 187, The Tempest by Giorgione (Giorgio da Castelfranco) (1476/8–1510), Galleria dell'Accademia, Venice, Italy/Bridgeman Art Library. 188, D. Cilia/The Travel Library. 189t, M. Cator/Impact Photos. 189c, D. Cilia/The Travel Library. 189b, AA Photo Library/D. Miterdiri. 190, John Heseltine Archive. 191, AA Photo Library/S McBride. 192, D. Donadoni/Marka. 193, Roberto Soncin Gerometta/Franca Speranza Srl. 194, Robert Leon. 195, M. Barlow/Art Directors and Trip Photo Library. 196, Christ in the Garden of Gethsemane by Palma Giovane (Jacopo Negretti) (1548–1628), Santa Maria della Visitazione Zitelle, Venice, Italy/Bridgeman Art Library. 196/197, Sarah Quill/Venice Picture Library. 198/199, Correr Museum, Venice/Alinari – Fototeca. 199, Valentina/Farabolafoto. 200/201, P. Enticknap/The Travel Library. 201, Rufus F. Folkks/Corbis UK Ltd. 202/203, M. Winch/Axiom Photographic Agency. 203, Robert Leon. 204, G. De Besanez/Marka. 204/205, M. Cristofori/Marka. 205, D. Donadoni/Marka. 206, Richard Philpott/Zooid Pictures. 207, John

The world's largest nonprofit scientific and educational organization, the National Geographic Society was founded in 1888 "for the increase and diffusion of geographic knowledge." Since then it has supported scientific exploration and spread information to its more than nine million members worldwide.

The National Geographic Society educates and inspires millions every day through magazines, books, television programs, videos, maps and atlases, research grants, the National Geography Bee, teacher workshops, and innovative classroom materials.

The Society is supported through membership dues, charitable gifts, and income from the sale of its educational products. Members receive NATIONAL GEOGRAPHIC magazine—the Society's official journal—discounts on Society products, and other benefits.

For more information about the National Geographic Society, its educational programs, publications, or how to support its work, call 1-800-NGS-LINE (647-5463), or write to: National Geographic Society, 1145 17th Street, N.W., Washington, D.C. 20036 U.S.A.

Printed in the U.S.A.

Published by the National Geographic Society
John M. Fahey, Jr., *President and Chief Executive Officer*
Gilbert M. Grosvenor, *Chairman of the Board*
Nina D. Hoffman, *Executive Vice President, President, Books and School Publishing*
Elizabeth L. Newhouse, *Director of Travel Publishing*
Barbara A. Noe, *Senior Editor and Project Manager*
Cinda Rose, *Art Director*
Carl Mehler, *Director of Maps*
Joseph F. Ochlak, *Map Coordinator*
Gary Colbert, *Production Director*
Richard S. Wain, *Production Project Manager*
Lise Sajewski, *Editorial Consultant*
Caroline Hickey, *Senior Researcher*
Lawrence Porges, *Editorial Coordinator*
Verena Phipps, *Contributor*

Edited and designed by AA Publishing (a trading name of Automobile Association Developments Limited, whose registered office is Norfolk House, Priestley Road, Basingstoke, Hampshire, England RG24 9NY. Registered number: 1878835).
Virginia Langer *Project Manager*
David Austin, *Senior Art Editor*
Allen Stidwill, *Editor*
Bob Johnson, Keith Russell, *Designer*
Inna Nogeste, *Senior Cartographic Editor*
Cartography by AA Cartographic Production
Richard Firth, *Production Director*
Steve Gilchrist, *Prepress Production Controller*
Picture Research by Zooid Pictures Ltd.
Drive maps drawn by Chris Orr Associates, Southampton, England
Cutaway illustrations drawn by Maltings Partnership, Derby, England
Coral reef illustration by Ann Winterbotham

ISSN 1536-8610

Printed and bound by R.R. Donnelley & Sons, Willard, Ohio. Color separations by Leo Reprographic Ltd., Hong Kong. Cover separations by L.C. Repro, Aldermaston, U.K. Cover printed by Miken Inc., Cheektowaga, New York.

Visit the society's Web site at http://www.nationalgeographic.com

The information in this book has been carefully checked and to the best of our knowledge is accurate. However, details are subject to change, and the National Geographic Society cannot be responsible for such changes, or for errors or omissions. Assessments of sites, hotels, and restaurants are based on the author's subjective opinions, which do not necessarily reflect the publisher's opinion. The publisher cannot be responsible for any consequences arising from the use of this book.

NATIONAL GEOGRAPHIC
TRAVELER

A Century of Travel Expertise in Every Guide

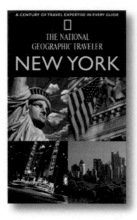
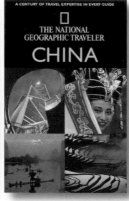
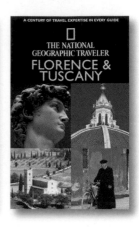